For Zion's Sake

The Judeo-Christian Tradition in American Culture

Fuad Sha'ban

Pluto Press
LONDON • ANN ARBOR, MI

First published 2005 by Pluto Press
345 Archway Road, London N6 5AA
and 839 Greene Street, Ann Arbor, MI 48106

www.plutobooks.com

British Library Cataloguing in Publication Data
A catalogue record for this book is available from the British Library

ISBN 0 7453 2237 9 hardback
ISBN 0 7453 2236 0 paperback

Library of Congress Cataloging in Publication Data applied for

10 9 8 7 6 5 4 3 2 1

Designed and produced for Pluto Press by
Chase Publishing Services Ltd, Fortescue, Sidmouth, EX10 9QG, England
Typeset from disk by Newgen Imaging Systems (P) Ltd, Chennai, India
Printed and bound in Canada by Transcontinental Printing

Dedicated to
My Wife
For inspiring confidence in times of despondence,
For bringing discipline to chaotic work habits,
And for valuable support and advice

Contents

Acknowledgements

During the years spent on this research, I accumulated debts to so many people. The Bibliography will serve as a partial acknowledgement to those who preceded me in dealing with some aspects of this subject.

Over a period of 40 years of teaching at the Universities of Damascus, King Saud, Duke, the UAE, and the University of Petra in Amman, Jordan, many colleagues and students have enriched my research and contributed with discussion and suggestions to the thinking that led to this work.

The initial stage of the work began in 1982–83 when I was Visiting Scholar at Duke University on sabbatical from Damascus University. At that time, James B. Duke Professor Ralph Braibanti, Director of Islamic and Arabian Studies at Duke, invited me to hold the position of Senior Research Fellow, also providing me with office space, secretarial assistance, and occasions to participate in the Outreach Lecture Program. I am grateful for this opportunity and the amenities. Most of all, I am grateful for Professor Braibanti's continued interest in my research and for the many hours of discussions with him which clarified a number of points and made this work a pleasure. Down through the years, my association with him has been an inspiration. Professor Braibanti also granted me permission to use the "Foreword" which he had written for my book *Islam and Arabs in Early American Thought: The Roots of Orientalism in America.*

While at Duke University, I had many stimulating discussion sessions with the late Professor Clarence Ghodes, Professors Louis Budd and Buford Jones. Their ideas and comments have been very helpful even when we disagreed on some points. I am very grateful to each of them. Professor Budd has read and commented on some of my works, and has continued to be a friend and supporter. He has also kindly granted me permission to use the "Introductory Essay" which he had written for my book *Islam and Arabs in Early American Thought: The Roots of Orientalism in America.*

The Perkins Library at Duke University is an ideal venue for serious research, not only by virtue of its large collections, but also for the helpful attitude of its staff. Many persons, especially those working in the Reference, Manuscripts, Rare Book, Documents, and

Interlibrary Loan Departments, cheerfully offered their expert assistance. I am grateful to the Manuscript Department for permission to quote from the "Bergh" and "Andrews" papers.

While working with original material on missionary activities, my search led me to the collections of the Office of History of the Presbyterian Study Center at Montreat, North Carolina. I am grateful to the Curator for allowing me to use their facilities and holdings.

I have also had the opportunity to be invited to take part in seminars, conferences and public lectures by many institutions, and gained some insight by the reactions and comments of the audience and participants. Of these institutions, mention should be made of Juma'a Al-Majed Cultural Center in Dubai, the UAE Cultural Center in Abu Dhabi, the Georgetown Center for Muslem-Christian Understanding, the Syrian National Library, the University of Petra, Eastern Mediterranean University, and the Association of Professors of English and Translation in Arab Universities (APETAU).

Professor Norton Mezvinski has been a most ardent supporter of my work on American Christian Zionism. He continues to confirm in his current research my conclusions on this subject. Professor Mezvinski's perceptive and profound treatment of Jewish Fundamentalism is matched by his work on Christian Zionism.

Dr. Clare Brandabur, an avid reader and exacting critic, has for years provided relevant material and critical comments which certainly enhanced my treatment of this subject.

Dr. Carol LaHurd has shown a continuous interest in my work and offered innumerable suggestions and texts without which the work would have suffered, especially regarding the position of mainline Christian churches.

Two persons who have made a most profound contribution to my research are Professors Tareq T. and Jacqueline S. Ismael. They have for over 15 years read and commented on my works, used my previous book on American Orientalism in their classes and invited me to read papers at many conferences. Above all, the Ismaels' friendship is a gift that every serious researcher would be fortunate to have.

At the University of Petra, I have received the support of former President Professor Mahmoud Al-Samra and current President Professor Amin Mahmoud. To each of these two friends I owe a debt of gratitude. At Petra also I especially wish to mention the keen interest and imput of Professors Khaled Al-Karki, Bilal Al-Jayousi and Nihal Amira. My friends at Petra, Mr. Muhammad Mazen Al-Ansari and Dr. Layla Na'em have been constant in supporting my work and offering solid criticism.

In Damascus, Syria, I have benefited from the suggestions and critical comments of Professor Muhammad Al-Imadi, Dr. Adnan Mardini and Mr. Muhammad Farouq Al-Zein. Their thoughts and works on Christian Zionism and American Orientalism are very insightful.

The management and editors of Pluto Press have been very gracious and helpful in bringing this work to fruition.

In December 2004 it was officially announced that the Arabic version of this book won the Zarqa University Award for the Most Outstanding Book on the Arab-Zionist Conflict (2004). I wish to express my gratitude to the Zarqa University (Zarqa, Jordan) Administration and the Award Committee for this honor.

My wife, Mary, has helped so much in my research and writings that any acknowledgement will fall short of expressing my gratitude. Her untiring help with typing, proofreading and comments has made a definite contribution to this work.

I should mention here that I have significantly revised and included in this book the material from the following chapters of my book *Islam and Arabs in Early American Thought: The Roots of Orientalism in America*: "A Place For My People", "The Star in the West", "The Vision of Zion" and "American Travellers in the Orient".

I have consistently used the spellings Muhammad, Al-Qur'an, and Muslem because they are closer to the Arabic pronunciation. I realize that "Muslem" is not the usual rendition, but it is, in my view, the correct one. I have, however, retained the original spelling of these words in quoted texts.

As a Muslem Arab, I find much of the material I have dealt with offensive and prejudiced. I hope, however, that I have not allowed my feelings to interfere with an objective treatment of the subject.

Foreword

This study by Professor Fuad Sha'ban is weighted with a special relevance and urgency by the congruence of several events occurring during the last few decades. One of these events, found in the United States, has antecedents which can be traced as far back as the founding of Plymouth Colony. I refer to contemporary millenarianism, which has become enmeshed in the web of a Christian quest for Zion, thereby contorting our perception of Islamic and Arab affairs. This phenomenon has been explored and popularized by the late Professor Edward Said's *Orientalism*. In the present work by Professor Sha'ban it is explored in greater depth by analysis of both literary and religious texts and behavior from our colonial beginnings to the present.

It is well known to anyone who has studied the diffusion of Islam and Arab civilization in the West that both confront a seemingly ineradicable antagonism. It is common to trace this feeling to the Crusades of the twelfth and thirteenth centuries which generated a paranoic repugnance toward Islam. This was reflected in Canto 28 of Dante's *Inferno* which consigns Muhammad and Ali to the ninth bolgia along with the most dangerous sowers of discord and disunity (*seminator di scadalo e di scisma*). Muhammad is regarded as the figure who promoted the greatest schism in the Christian world, and his punishment—being split from chin to crotch—is the cruelest described in the *Inferno*. Allegorical though it is, the *Inferno* was undoubtedly a reflection of medieval thought; the Crusades were in progress, though waning, during Dante's lifetime and were undoubtedly the single most momentous international event of the period. This attitude, more latent than explicit in recent times, was resuscitated by Salman Rushdie's *Satanic Verses* (1988) and the recent attacks on Islam and the Prophet Muhammad in Christian Right statements in the US, in which much of the metaphoric and allegorical vituperation of the Middle Ages was restored in contemporary literary, political and religious garb. This stunning reminder of an almost forgotten period of hatred accounts for much of the Muslim world's reaction today.

There are many reasons for this perception of Islam by Christendom and the West. A third Abrahamic monotheism, emerging after only eight centuries, incorporated some of the doctrine of its two predecessors and claimed to be the final and superior divine revelation. Unlike the older faiths of Hinduism, Buddhism, Judaism, and the secular faiths of Taoism and Confucianism, it was activated by a dynamic zeal for global propagation which directly confronted the same Christian impulse. Christian territoriality was threatened by the dynamism as Islam spread in Asia and Africa and to the very threshold of Vienna. It destroyed the possibility of a world coterminous with Christendom. It continues today to manifest a vigor and zeal which other major religions have lost.

The ancient antagonism between the Christian West and Islam continues to be evident in the contemporary world. It is well developed in a variety of sources and is traced through some strands of literature by Edward Said in his *Orientalism* and in politics and print and audiovisual media by such works as *Split Vision* edited by Edmund Ghareeb, *The TV Arab* by Jack Shaheen, Michael W. Suleiman's *The Arabs in the Mind of America,* Edward Said's *Covering Islam*, and Grace Halsell's *Prophesy and Politics.* Its nadir in the realm of political disinformation was reached when Amos Perlmutter, writing in the *Wall Street Journal* of October 4, 1984 ("The Containment Strategy for the Islamic Holy War"), characterized the bombing of the American Embassy in Beirut as being "under the banner of an Islamic *jihad.*" "It is," he continued, "a general Islamic war waged against the West, Christianity, modern capitalism, Zionism and Communism all at once." Even before the fall of Communism, Perlmutter emphatically suggested that American policy must "decide that our war against Moslem populism is of the utmost priority, not the longterm struggle against the Soviet Union." He thus raised the threat of holy war (*jihad*), a complex doctrine now loosely used by Muslem militant groups but the application of which is repudiated by most of the Muslem world. This assertion of the universal enmity of Islam is gross hypergenerality of the complex political positions of 46 avowedly Islamic nations and 1 billion Muslems scattered over the globe. Its defiance of history is suggested by a few events selected from many. Morocco was the first nation to recognize the sovereign independence of the United States and has remained a friendly nation ever since. Iran under the Shah was a close ally and a bulwark of American policy in the area. Pakistan has had close military and economic ties with the United States since 1953. Malaysia and Indonesia have had cordial relations; Bangladesh has had close economic aid-receiving ties. The Gulf States, especially Oman and Saudi

Arabia, have been important economic and strategic partners with the United States. Egypt and Lebanon have maintained postures of friendship. Syria in its revolt against French occupation in the 1940s took the American Constitution as its model. Jordan remains a constructive influence in the quest for peace in the Middle East. The Perlmutter assertion is the culmination of centuries of defamed imagery. Its echoes still resound in Christian Right quarters and some official statements.

Added to this seven-century-old legacy of suspicion, if not hostility, are several new contemporary factors. The first of these is the Arab–Israeli conflict, which results in massive campaigns of disinformation and vituperation damaging to Islam and to the Arab image. The second is the rise of Arab militancy and bellicosity, the consequence of frustration over Palestine, but seemingly supporting (however unfairly) misconceptions of terrorism, belligerence, and intransigence. Distortion of the concept of holy war (*jihad*) is symbolic of this. In its most profound sense, *jihad* is man's internal struggle between good and evil.

The third factor, dealt with so comprehensively by Professor Sha'ban, is peculiar to American culture. It is the phenomenal rise in the United States in visibility and political power of evangelical fundamentalist Protestant Christianity with its emphasis on the Old Testament and on "biblical inerrancy," i.e., the literal interpretation of Scripture perceived as the infallible word of God. This doctrine emphasizes the special status of Israelites and Zion and warns that divine retribution will be meted out to whoever disagrees. This is coupled by what might be called the Judaization of Christianity, in which the Judaic antecedents of Christian doctrine and Jewish genealogy of Christ and the Holy Family are given so much emphasis that the distinctions between the two religions are blurred, if not lost. The propagation of these ideas by highly effective television preachers, the foremost of whom has been the Reverend Jerry Falwell, powerfully reinforces earlier misconceptions by linking Judaism and Christianity and, at least by implication, isolating Islam as the enemy of both. Since these ideas touch the very essence of the Arab–Israeli dispute, namely, the status of Palestine and Jerusalem, they are hardly conducive to increasing an empathy for Islam or for Arabs. O. Kelly Ingram has analyzed this phenomenon as Christian Zionism (*The Link*, Vol. 16, November 1983).

This Old Testament literalism has been advocated by a growing portion of American Protestant evangelicals found mostly in the

South and Southwest. The statements of policy adopted unanimously by the National Council of Churches since 1980 is quite different from the fundamentalists' views and is very similar to the
Vatican's position. Both the Roman Catholic and the Orthodox
churches show a greater appreciation of Islam and an affinity with
Arab culture. The existence of the Pontifical Institute of Arabic
Studies and the policies enunciated by the Second Vatican Council,
as well as the Twenty-Four Declarations issued by the Vatican–
Muslem Conference in Libya in 1976, make this clear. The Roman
church embraces within its fold a variety of Eastern Orthodox rites,
in some of which Arabic is the liturgical language. Ironically, the
Crusader legacy and the conquest of Spain, both occurring in the
context of an undivided Christendom, have not resulted in a theological or institutional antagonism towards Islam in the Catholic
Church. That feeling now resides in the evangelical fundamentalist
realm. Telling evidence of this can be seen in the official Vatican
stand on Palestinian rights, Jerusalem and Vatican pronouncements
on Islam. A comprehensive review of the Vatican's position was
given by Archbishop Renato R. Martino, Permanent Observer of the
Holy See to the United Nations, "The Holy See and the Middle East"
at a Fordham University Colloquium, April 10, 1989. The Vatican's
stand is in stark contrast with fundamentalist views on these issues.
This view is shared totally by Greek Orthodoxy and, to a lesser
extent, by the Episcopal and Presbyterian churches.

The vision of Zion portrayed in the present work of Professor
Sha'ban shows the depth of these beliefs which have now come to
the fore in the context of the Arab–Israeli question. It reveals a
dimension which has heretofore been eclipsed, or at least isolated,
from the political context of our times. He shows us incontrovert-
ibly that fundamentalist views of Zion are not new, but are deeply
rooted in American nineteenth-century literary and religious
sources. They are strengthened by antecedent views of the Crusades
against the "infidel" allegorized in the *Inferno* and are given new
meaning and strength by contemporary events which plunge them
into the maelstrom of global politics. The consequence is that the
emotional circumstances sustaining a Western alienation with Islam
and Arabs are given new meaning. American attitudes towards Islam
and Arabs are not the consequence of Palestinian desperation over
the 1948 establishment of Israel. It is the millenarian attitude,
embedded in Old Testament prophesy linked with the quest for a
New World Zion—fantasized in such place names as Salem, Sinai,

Nazareth, Providence, New Jerusalem, Bethel, Mount Olive, New Bethlehem, Zion, and similar New World communities—that distorts our perceptions. The appeal is dangerously subliminal. The New Jerusalem of fantasy is materialized in the recreation of the Old Jerusalem. Since 1948 much Christian doctrine, prayers, and hymns have been modified to eliminate suggestions of Jewish blame for the crucifixion of Christ. A comparable expurgation of the myth of Zion and its equation with contemporary Israel is needed before Islam can be placed in its proper historical and theological relationship with Judaism and Christianity.

But the identification and classification of sources of thought and the construct of their patterns of relationship is a critical step in correcting false imagery. Professor Sha'ban has gone beyond the "Orientalist" exposition in revealing the profundity of this attitude and the web of relationships in literature and religion. For those interested in widening the appreciation of Islamic and Arab culture, this is not a revelation which can be greeted with joy or with equanimity, even though its masterful and objective exposition must be regarded with respect and admiration.

Ralph Braibanti
James B. Duke Professor of Political Science
Duke University
King Faisal Distinguished International Lecturer
American-Arab Affairs Council

Introductory Essay

In 1878 a now forgotten humorist caught the public's fancy with "A Threnody," which began:

> What, what, what
> What's the news from Swat?
> Sad news,
> Bad news
> Cometh by the cable led
> Through the Indian Ocean's bed,
> Through the Persian Gulf, the Red
> Sea and the Med-
> Iterranean—he's dead—
> The Akhoond is dead!

The third of its four irregular stanzas best typifies its condescension:

> Mourn, city of Swat,
> Your great Akhoond is not,
> But laid 'mid worms to rot—
> His mortal part alone, his soul was caught
> (Because he was a good Akhoond!)
> Up to the bosom of Mahound.
> Though earthly walls his frame surround
> (Forever hallowed be the ground!)
> And skeptics mock the lowly mound
> And say He's now of no Akhoond!
> His soul is in the skies—
> The azure skies that bend above his loved
> metropolis of Swat.
> He sees, with larger, other eyes,
> Athwart all early mysteries—
> He knows what's Swat.

"A Threnody" came from George T. Lanigan (1845–1886), a "literary comedian" who, as one way of earning his keep, wrote poems for the Sunday edition of the *New York World*.[1] Other newspapers across the country applauded it; an anthologist reprinted it later in the same year (and it still appears in several collections of light verse). Eugene Field, a well-remembered newspaper poet and humorist, would complain during the presidential election of 1884:

> When the writer has written with all of his might
> Of Blaine and of Cleveland a column or more,
> And the editor happens along in the night
> (As he generally does betwixt midnight and four)
> And kills all the stuff that that writer has writ,
> And calls for more copy at once, on the spot—
> There is none for the writer to turn on and hit
> But that distant old party, the Akhoond of Swat.

"A Threnody" carried the epigraph: "The Akhoond of Swat is dead—London Papers of January 22, 1878." Very few readers knew or would care to learn more about him. It was enough that a tiny, faraway, presumably benighted territory had regarded him as a potentate. Two or three years later when Mark Twain, projecting the anthology that became his *Library of Humor*, planned to include material by Lanigan, he fumbled for the title of the poem on "that Eastern savage that died."[2] He would also plan to quote "A Threnody" in *Following the Equator*, although the book as printed would simply list the Akhoond of Swat among the "sumptuous" names of India.

That adjective underlines the important clue. Americans had reacted, from a haze of ignorance, to an unusual name. In spite of their ethnic mixture, they were quick to find comedy, more playful than malevolent, in a proper name outside their official tradition. If they had heard that the Akhoond—the spelling wavers according to the system of transliteration—had been named Abdul Ghafur they might have guessed a Muslim origin before laughing again, but only a rare expert could have pinpointed Swat more closely than Twain. If scolded for ethnocentrism, they would have protested that they saw no harm in the fun. When Lanigan elsewhere defined a "Musselman" as a "man of strength" he intended neither harm nor compliment.

Professor Fuad Sha'ban's *Islam and Arabs in Early American Thought: The Genesis of Orientalism in America*, by mapping the contours of nineteenth-century attitudes, presents the serious setting for the literary comedians (as scholars have agreed to call them), who once lightened the columns of metropolitan as well as small-town news-papers with verse, anecdotes, sketches, and jokes. For the image of the Muslem they were both a result and a cause. Hungry for subjects because of a revolving deadline, they were driven to exploit any motif that might amuse readers. Petroleum Vesuvius Nasby (born David R. Locke), best known for his grassroots political humor, var-ied his repertoire with *The Morals of Abou Ben Adhem*, which hid a Yankee in a white turban and flowing black robe; the "imposture was a very safe one, for his auditors knew as little of Persia as he did."[3] Nasby also meant no harm. His con man did give sound, if florid, crackerbarrel advice free of charge.

Alert to every saleable technique and idea, the literary comedians honed parody into one of their slickest genres, and they inevitably used it upon the vogue of Orientalism among British authors. Abou Ben Adhem, every constant reader knew, borrowed his name from a famous, kindly poem by Leigh Hunt. As the literary comedians came to depend on a breezy irreverence of tone, the "Dream of Baghdad" made an especially inviting target, familiar to all. To prove the pop-ularity that the Arabian Nights cycle enjoyed during the nineteenth century would be to labor the obvious; any skeptic needs only to scan the Union Catalogue from the Library of Congress for the myriad editions in English for various levels of readership. Though exotic fantasy is always vulnerable, its shapes spun out of Orientalism raised expectations so high that the honest traveler or stay-at-home realist would also feel driven to deflate them.

But the literary comedians were as much cause as effect, since they encouraged the currency of stereotypes. During the Crimean War they could poke fun at all sides.[4] Muslems, however, presented an attractive victim in the United States because they had few advo-cates to protest the distortion inherent in comedy. Furthermore, they allowed surefire laughs based on Western pride in a technology that made other cultures look backward, if not stupid. Beneath the guffaws, darker attitudes operated. The obligatory joking about the cruelty reported of Ottoman rulers may do credit to American humane-ness, or may merely open another path for gallows humor—still, a reader today can also suspect a vicarious sadism. More certainly, the frequent joking about slave maidens, dancing houris, and harems appealed to prurient appetites that gentility kept hidden at home. (Few American males discussed the Mormons without an inner tingle about polygamy.) The Middle Eastern travel books of George W. Curtis and Bayard Taylor likewise titillated Victorian repression by sketching scenes forbidden to their own pallid novels.

Insularity is still stronger and broader than humor as a barrier to objective insights. Even those minds stretched across a nearby national boundary by the social sciences can relapse into fatigue as if they were to explore outer space. I know too little about other cultures to judge whether the United States is egregiously insular (and not merely by its tendency to monopolize the word "American"), but every country or tribe resists adjusting to the variety of humankind around the globe. Perhaps just because peoples do vary so wondrously, we keep retreating to stereotypes, to rigid images of "the others"—to use Professor Sha'ban's phrase.[5]

Not everyone in the United States has as yet managed to accept the distinctiveness of Western Europe or, closer to home, South and Central America; and Canada attracts tepid interest on the few campuses where it is studied by its close neighbor. Nevertheless, ignorance about the Muslim is astonishing for its tenacity among Americans. How many of them today would feel embarrassed by George William Curtis' once popular *Nile Notes of a Howadji* (1851)? It claimed hegemony for the West because the "Egyptians and Easterns" were "imbeciles"—"picturesque and handsome" but too torpid to copy the "clean, and comely, and comfortable" society he hailed from. "That the East will never regenerate itself, contemporary history shows."[6] Curtis, an active progressive at home, ignored contemporary Egyptian politics and religion. His reveries focused on its deepest layers of antiquity so soulfully that its descendants looked all the more degenerate.

His own descendants can judge him forgivingly because his blindness had several causes. New World democracy welcomed any opportunity to cheer onward the struggles for national liberation elsewhere, such as from the Austro-Hungarian Empire and, still more avidly, from the decaying Ottoman Empire. Specifically, the British and American literati grew bitterly anti-Turkish on behalf of Greek independence. In general, the dominant voices of the New World preached Protestantism as a beneficent cultural force. This article of faith justified elevating Jesus Christ far above Muhammad as a model for conduct. It also encouraged what a recent analyst calls "the Protestant Passion"—the "driving force of American history"—which created an "insatiable desire to redeem mankind from sin and error."[7] Though emphasizing the missionary impulse,

Professor Sha'ban does not exaggerate its many-tiered influence, from intellectuals like Curtis on down to the barely literate millions whose only important book was the Bible—perhaps absorbed mostly through sermons and Sunday School lessons. The mental and emotional expropriation of Palestine for Christianity was made explicit. Implicitly, the Bible was interpreted to glorify the social and economic values of the middle class. That synthesis of religion and the Western work-ethic was echoed in the McGuffey Readers for all grades of the elementary schools.[8] Islam posed a further, active, and urgent challenge to the millennialists who preached that the Kingdom of God would not return to earth until all the heathen had been converted.

Historians of ideas can offer false comfort by diagramming a previous cast of mind. Since we can identify its mistakes, we have presumably overcome them. But the nineteenth-century blindness toward the Muslim persists. A black historian of ideas may give the soundest explanation by adding the factor of racism. After forbidding any official dogma, the polity of the United States developed a "civil religion," which he labels "Americanity." It has worked out a "mutually accommodative relationship" with Christianity and Judaism to establish a "semi-secular" creed that "grants to civil power the support and respectability of religion." Americanity includes faith in the altruism of its Manifest Destiny within global politics, where it carries the old white man's burden.[9] I add that Americanity has grown dangerously ahistorical. While regularly invoking a lofty past and promising a noble future, it learns little from the actual course of history.

Discussions of the mass mind tend to shift blame away from the intelligentsia. However, Professor Sha'ban treats the figures of the literary canon only briefly because he wants to reflect the spread of constituencies. Moreover, critics too easily take the presently canonical authors as representative or influential for their time. Herman Melville's *Clarel*, ignored in 1876, is now given great cultural significance. On the other hand, Washington Irving, whose prestige at one time could scarcely be exaggerated, has shrunk to a story or two in college anthologies and only a few specialists know about *Mahomet and His Successors*. Overall, the situation can oblige either the sanguine or gloomy observer. Many canonical authors enter briefly into Professor Sha'ban's pages because they did perceive a world beyond the Anglo-Saxon, European horizon. Yet they seldom wrote directly, much less empathetically, about the Muslim countries. As for the belletristic travelers to the Middle East, like Curtis or Taylor or Charles D. Warner, they misled or blinded the public more than they enlightened it.

Mark Twain offers the richest example among today's standard authors. Now mediating between high and low culture, he had aimed at a mass audience, and he remains so popular as to command interest for any subject. Yet the academicians discuss him more seriously each year, willing to forgive his ties to the literary comedians. He makes a fine reflector in both senses of the metaphor. He picked up mass attitudes accurately and quickly, and in turn he emitted and certainly affected them. While epitomizing misperceptions of the Muslem, in his final years he approached and perhaps contributed to a sounder insight.

Samuel L. Clemens began his climb toward Mark Twain in newspaper offices, which trained him as a spokesman to, if not for, Americanity. Along with politics, his reminiscences of boyhood include Bible tracts, which were often enlivened by drawings to arouse a child's imagination, and *The Innocents Abroad* casually remembers "that picture of the Queen of Sheba visiting Solomon." Furthermore, young Sam Clemens swallowed his doses of the McGuffey Readers dominated by solemn moralizing, but spiced with selections like "The Arab and His Horse." He had many other chances of encountering such tales, including those used by newspapers as a filler, for example. His autobiography remarks about a friend's son that "being seven years old, he was of course acquainted with the Arabian Nights," and *Following the Equator* (ch. 39) recalled those lively visions "when you were a boy and steeped your spirit in the tales of the East." Risen to a practicing journalist, Twain now and then drew on the "Dream of Baghdad" for a familiar example or comparison. In 1867, exclaiming over the first girlie musical in New York City, he built up to the "whole tableau resplendent with columns, scrolls, and a vast ornamental work, wrought in gold, silver and brilliant colors—all lit up with gorgeous theatrical fires, and witnessed through a great gauzy curtain that counterfeits a soft silver mist! It is the wonders of the Arabian nights realized."[10]

His first acclaimed book, *The Innocents Abroad* (1869), vibrated with his tension between fantasy (more exotic than pious in his case) and the disillusionment that struck many a Christian pilgrim to the Middle East. Though Twain brought along images from his Sunday School classes, his latent agnosticism soon let him toy with them sardonically. But ethnic stereotypes, themselves overlapping, intersected confusingly with religious groupings. In the 1860s Twain was still mindlessly anti-Semitic, that is, Anti-Judaic. While in Palestine he did wonder, however, if the Israelites of the Old Testament had not been Arabs on every other count.[11] Fortunately, for the total results anyway, perplexity seldom blocked him from producing the copy he needed to make a living.

Muslems perplexed Twain enough on their own. Ashore in Morocco on the voyage out, he exulted about finding the "true spirit" of the Arabian Nights. Such romanticizing could not last, and his more recent travels in the Sandwich Islands should have inoculated him against it. He soon reported that the ruler of Morocco was a "soulless despot," as was Abdul Aziz, the Sultan of the Ottoman Empire. Because Syria was suffering under "inhuman tyranny" ("I wish Europe would let Russia annihilate Turkey a little"), he decided that its "people are naturally good-hearted and intelligent, and with education and liberty, would be a happy and contented race" (ch. 42). Nevertheless, other Arabs were inherently "savages," and Muslems were mired in "paganism." Whether from genetic or religious inferiority, the Middle East wallowed in dirt and foul odors that clouded any romance. There is no need to pile up examples of his jovially harsh humor, such as claiming that his towel and cake of soap "would inspire respect in the Arabs, who would take me for a king in disguise." Inevitably, he hinted at the prurient side of exoticism, most notably in his "Slave Girl Market Report" from Constantinople. His praise of the legendary Crusaders, intended tactically to soften his sarcasms about Protestant smugness, sounded fervent when set next to his slurs about the Arabs he saw.

Twain's little-known O'Shah letters in 1873 partly deserve their obscurity, but it may also result from later lack of interest in their subject. Because he was already in England, the *New York Herald*, which prided itself on its foreign coverage, hired him to write up the state visit of Nasr-Ed-Din of Persia. More than Twain let on here, he realized that the European powers were maneuvering for spheres of influence or, more crassly, for economic penetration of the Middle East. But in joking about British efforts to "impress" the Shah, he essentially ignored imperialism. By then a professional humorist, he met the expectations of the *Herald*, which puffed each of his five O'Shah ("O, pshaw?") letters with jaunty editorials about a "passionate child of the East" and his "pampered despotism."[12]

Twain dutifully condescended from democratic heights. Emphasizing Oriental ignorance and cruelty rather than glamor, he featured a "splendid barbarian, who is lord over a few deserts and a modest ten million of ragamuffins." For instance, the Shah "never sees any impropriety in chopping a subject's head off for the mere misdemeanor of calling him too early for breakfast." Wryly if not confusingly, after declaring "our religion is the right one, and has fewer odd and striking features than any other," Twain did concede that, remembering how "our ancestors used to roast Catholics and warm their hands by the fire," the Persians "are really our brothers after all." In a better apology, he equivocated later that the humor in the letters "was not his but was added by a Herald employee without authorization."

The critics who revere *The Adventures of Huckleberry Finn* are startled to learn that while Twain was finally finishing his masterpiece during the summer of 1883 he also put major effort into "1,002d Arabian Night." Having completed over 20,000 words and 131 drawings, he wanted to publish it, perhaps anonymously, "right after Huck." But everybody who read the manuscript discouraged him, surely because its parody of Scherezade's longwindedness is self-destructing. Nobody since then has perceived literary or comic merit in "1,002d Arabian Night."[13] Nor do its raucously cheerful yet superior tones lead to a sounder acceptance of Islam; curiously, its reader finds no reason to suspect that the author had ever visited the Middle East. Soon, however, Twain's comedy did call for much more serious thinking, although he left no glaring clue as to why, in the early 1890s he would already turn skeptical about Western imperialism or would apply to Islam his gift for soaring beyond nativist and even anthropocentric vision.

Tom Sawyer Abroad (1894) has never rated as a major novel. Therefore only children and scholars know that its first chapter ridicules the Crusaders by making Tom fail to convince Huck and Jim that Christianity should "go and take the land away from the people who own it." That sympathy for the rights and customs of the living inhabitants colored the trio's adventures in North Africa and Egypt. Also, when drawing on five tales from the Arabian Nights, *Tom Sawyer Abroad* leaned toward friendly irony and workaday problems rather than romanticism.[14] Therefore *Following the Equator* (1897) may backslide when its India chapters invoke the Arabian Nights for atmosphere. Still, while primarily conscious of Hinduism, it now and then notices the Muslim culture and Mughal tradition much more respectfully than readers of *The Innocents Abroad* could anticipate. Twain was slowly becoming a shrewd cosmopolitan. The "Conclusion" of *Following the Equator* presented as its epigraph: "I have traveled more than anyone else, and I have noticed that even the angels speak English with an accent."

Twain was growing away not only from Protestant insularity, but also its optimism. In 1898 he wrote 45 somber quatrains modeled on Edward Fitzgerald's *Rubaiyat*, without parody.[15] About the same time he began struggling with his dark, relativistic manuscripts centered on a "Mysterious Stranger." After 1900 he boldly confronted the expansionism of the industrialized powers. The title of his most effective essay, "To the Person Sitting in Darkness," was made savagely ironical. During the final ten years of his life he accused Western missionaries as the sometimes naive, sometimes willing agents of greed that destroyed alien cultures in the name of progress. Still, Twain's admirers must always pull up short of hagiolatry on any score. For instance, in order to attack Mary Baker Eddy as a new religious despot he would argue that "Christian Science, like Mohammedanism, is restricted to the unintelligent, the people who do not think."[16]

The ultimate, dangerous reality is that someone so capable of elemental human warmth (as well as venom) and so venturesome as Twain could not reach an adequate, stable objectivity toward the Muslim. Though he learned to reject the missionarying animus, he kept honoring the Manifest Destiny of the United States as the embodiment of progress for supposedly benighted societies. Though his experiences on the silver and gold frontier, and then in Hawaii, should have awakened him, the "Dream of Baghdad" was so bewitching that he could never clear his eyes or even stop resenting the mundane people and places he found instead. Or, sometimes hungry for applause instead of just royalties, he sagged into a literary comedian again. Like Lanigan and other hacks, he could not resist exploiting the stereotypes the public liked to see. In the overall accounting for Twain's career, his flexibility of heart and mind helps to explain why he has lasted up into our times, beyond a horde of competitors, and how he did move toward a genuine empathy with "the others." Nevertheless, Americans at best moved toward such a perception so erratically that Professor Sha'ban would perceive the need for this study.

He combines objectivity with empathy because his Middle Eastern origins are balanced by education in the United States and close personal bonds. Fully aware of British and European Orientalism, he does not indict Americans as being particularly misled. Rather, he strikes an engaging tone; avoiding sardonic irony or even scolding, he allows readers to form their own verdict. While comprehending the pressures that pit nations against each other, he concentrates on the operative attitudes within the United States, not its rivalries. But his Introduction outlines his demonstrable insights so capably that no Foreword needs to anticipate them. It needs only to regret that he had to be heroically selective about a subject radiating in many rich directions.

Surely Professor Sha'ban, while examining the United States, has made Oriental culture clearer to the West. His book warns once more that the world is round, that intellectual sins will orbit back to punish their source. The conscience of nineteenth-century Westerners must have suffered, at some level, for excluding the Muslim from shared humanity. Their descendants can do for themselves not the penance but the boon of learning better, because reality is more satisfying and safer than ignorance or fantasy. Professor Sha'ban will help them meet the Muslim with sound curiosity, openness, and pleasure.

Louis J. Budd
James B. Duke Professor of English
May 1990   Duke University

Introduction

The profundity, as well as the breadth, of the American emotional and intellectual attachment to an Oriental perspective during the four centuries of the European presence in North America, is greater than commonly supposed. This attachment, which is still the basis for America's involvement in the Orient, was in the making from the founding of the colony at Plymouth; it became a mature constituency by the end of the Civil War. And although the establishment of the American Oriental Society in 1842 marked the beginning of a more active stage in the development of American's involvement in the affairs of the Arab World, there had been a number of related activities throughout the history of the American people.

When the early Puritan colonies were founded, the immigrants based their conduct in life on the firm belief that they occupied a special position in a Providential plan. They, as the "chosen," were heirs to a covenantal promise and were entrusted with the task of rebuilding the Kingdom of God, the "little American Israel." This Kingdom became the symbol of their spiritual and temporal labors in the New World. The Puritans strove, collectively, to bring about the New Jerusalem, the ultimate city of Protestant Christianity.

When America became an independent political state, its citizens continued to use the same symbol to refer to their ideal community. To make their argument more poignant, they added comparisons with the "decadent" state of Europe and with "corruption" in the "Romish" church. The combination and interaction of these factors in American thinking, together with later developments on the American scene during the nineteenth and twentieth centuries, gave a new direction to the energy of the American people towards the Orient, the Holy Land in particular. During that period, Islam was introduced to the American nation both as a rival force and as an alien religion. Furthermore, America witnessed a surge of religious enthusiasm marked by the ascendancy of adventist and millenarian churches and expectations. The missionary movement also gained momentum, and American men and women went out to "spread the word of God" throughout the world, especially in the Levant.

During the nineteenth century also, the American nation was operating within the continent on the principle of Manifest Destiny, which in practical geo-political terms meant expansion to the West and annexation of territories. It was then that the symbolic Kingdom of God was transferred into a concrete endeavor in the Holy Land, and thus the Orient became for many Americans the field of action for both the political and religious sides of Manifest Destiny.

Many Americans strove to reach this sacred goal in obedience to the will of God. They included missionaries, colonizers, diplomats, travelers, researchers, scholars, and many others. Some Americans, enchanted by the world of the Arabian Nights, tried to realize the dream of Baghdad, or, more often, bemoaned the passing away of that world. In either case, the Orient was a field of labor open to Americans. Back home, hundreds of books and articles were written on the Orient and on Islam and the Prophet Muhammad, a definite sign of continued interest in the affairs of the region. This is the essence of the American Orientalist discourse which was so alive in the nineteenth century, and which continues to be a major American concern today.

Americans have maintained a continuing involvement with the Holy Land, often amounting to personal identification with the region and an assertion of ownership. And their argument, their claim to the region, was in part seen as an order from God that they should "stand as sure in Asia as in America." This was the divine order which the missionary Eli Smith and many religious as well as lay Americans obeyed. It was the missionary expression of Manifest Destiny.

The Orientalist political claim was just as well-documented as that of the missionary and the laborer in the cause of Zion. David Porter and Dabney Carr, Consuls in the Ottoman domains, William Lynch, leader of an official expedition to the Holy Land, Richard Haight, traveler in the Orient, and scores of other Americans based their claim to proselytize and incite "revolt" on the American Constitution which guaranteed the right of free expression, political and religious, for every American. The American flag was to be a beacon of light in a land engulfed in darkness, and American naval forces were to aid in spreading that light, if need be. The call to "stand on the Heights of Calvary and proclaim to the followers of the Pseudo-Prophet" was as much a political expression as it was missionary.

Indeed, there was a constant overlapping of religious, political, and purely humanitarian idiom in the Orientalist discourse. The land was "sitting in darkness," "benighted," under despotic rulers; the people were "degraded," "enslaved," "backward" ("primitive" in more sympathetic statements). "We," said the American benefactors, will "possess," "occupy," and "reclaim" the land; "we" will teach "them" the principles of American education and politics. To decide the future of the Arab World and the fate of its peoples was not only a privilege, but an obligation both for the missionary, the politician and the layman. No national boundaries, no international treaties, and no principles of self-determination were relevant in the case of the Arab World and its people. The Orient was an object to be dealt with; the Oriental a passive, mute recipient of the treatment. The benign death sentence by Moncure Conway—"the East has given its message to the world and must retire"—and the mournful nostalgic death announcement by George William Curtis are expressions of this American Orientalist discourse. But there were other statements, less sympathetic and more authoritarian. The practice of "carving up" the Arab World, restructuring and dividing it among the European powers, was not an uncommon exercise. These efforts to civilize and enlighten are in their contexts the precursors of the modern exercises in "nation-building" and "reform."

The right to "possess" and "carve up" the Arab World has been demonstrated in modern times in actions such as the Sikes-Picault secret agreement, the Balfour Declaration, the series of decisions by both Houses of the United States Congress regarding Jerusalem and Israeli settlements in the West Bank. Recently, it appeared in the "pragmatic" argument voiced by President Bush that it is not realistic to respect the Palestinians' rights to return to their homeland and that it is not realistic to expect the Israeli settlements in the West Bank to be dismantled. The continuity and the persistence of the Western habit of deciding the fate of the Arab World is also evident in the absence of the slightest hint as to the Arab World's role in deciding its fate.

There were overtones of racial superiority and prejudice in many of the statements made by Americans. Jessup and Lynch provide two obvious examples, but they were representative of the general attitude of many Americans. To "Anglo-Saxonize" and to "Americanize" the Orient meant to raise it from a state of abject "ignorance" and "heathenism"; in present-day language, "reconstructing," and "democratizing." Americans were also to decide whether Arabs were capable of being converted, or, better still, were to be "removed," and a better race to be "gathered in the land."

American involvement in the Orient has developed in the past century into a full-grown independent idiom and practice whose relations with its European counterparts are not those of a satellite. Its activities now take many directions: intellectual, academic, political, religious, and others. The Middle East Studies Association of America is the umbrella organization of many academic institutions which have made great strides in the various fields of Orientalist studies. These modern academic interests in the Orient were preceded on a limited scale by works published as early as the beginning of the nineteenth century in the *Transactions of the American Philosophical Society*, the *Journal of the American Oriental Society*, the *Proceedings of the American Numismatic Society*, the *North American Review*, the *Methodist Review*, and other learned journals. There were also other individual efforts such as those by William Thomson, Edward Robinson, and William Lynch, to name only a few. Many popular journals and periodicals published (almost on a daily basis) articles of Orientalist concern in order to satisfy an increasing public interest in the subject.

It is evident that the American political and religious involvement in the affairs of the Arab World is still part of the Orientalist discourse and has increased tremendously during the last 50 years. However, the basic notions and beliefs which prompted the earlier involvement are to varying degrees in play today. This work attempts to demonstrate the continuity of the factors in American culture which today play an important role in shaping America's dealings with the Arab World, and the Holy Land in particular.

Chief among these factors is the Judeo-Christian tradition which has been a part of American religious beliefs from the beginning. In fact, although the term itself is rather new, this "Judeo-Christian tradition" has been maintained in the Western World by the tremendous influence of the Bible on the daily lives of Christians, at least since the Protestant Reformation. One of the complaints Luther raised against the Church of Rome was the monopoly it held on reading and interpreting the Scriptures. With the Reformation came the translation of the Bible, both Old and New Testaments, into the vernacular languages of Europe. In time, the holy texts of Christianity became available to the reading public, and the Old Testament, which formed the larger bulk, with its stories of the Israelites, entered into the cultural heritage of Christians. The language of the Bible also became a source of people's daily discourse.

The formative influence of the Old Testament mythology and metaphor was recognized by, among others, T.S. Eliot in his celebrated essay "Notes Toward the Definition of Culture" (1937). Eliot advanced the notion that the cultural unity of the Western World derives from "its heritage of the civilizations of Greece, Rome and Israel."[1] In emphasizing the historical depth and cumulative nature of this heritage and its peculiar "Westernness," Eliot argued that even "if Asia were converted to Christianity tomorrow, it would not thereby become part of Europe."[2] In a simple statement, Eliot propounded two important points: first, that one of the three major sources of Western culture was "Israel," i.e., the myths perpetrated by the Old Testament; and, secondly, that Christianity has been appropriated by the West, and that Asia, including the Arab Orient is non-Western, i.e., non-Christian. In fact, Eliot goes as far as to say that the common tradition of Christianity is what made the West what it is today.

This formative power of biblical language is taken a step further by another prominent American critic. Northrop Frye (*The Great Code: The Bible in Literature*, 1982; *Words With Power*, 1990) stated that the Bible with its language, myths, metaphors, and typology; this "huge, sprawling tactless book [sits] inscrutably in the middle of our culture."[3] The Bible, Frye said, is the framework and context of all thinking; it "is the mythology of the Western World." In the course of the history of a group of people, the repetition of their myths and metaphors gradually creates an "order of words" and an "order of things" which constantly grow and expand through their use by writers and others even as they continue to use the essential archetypes of their mythology.

The myth of the Promised Land, whether it operates on the conceptual, ritualistic or practical level, is a perfect example of Northrop Frye's two "orders" of words and things. These orders had already existed in American culture before Americans went to the Holy Land and wrote about it; their public was aware of the signifiers in their idiom and symbols and of the signified. The Biblical literature which was read by every child attending Sunday School or church service gave an air of familiarity and a claim of ownership to the names of places and characters of the Holy Land. Willa Cather recognized this in 1936:

The Bible countries along the Mediterranean shore were very familiar to most of us in our childhood. Whether we were born in New Hampshire or

Virginia or California, Palestine lay behind us. We took it unconsciously and unthinkingly perhaps, but we could not escape it. It was all about us, in pictures on the wall, in the songs we sang in Sunday School, in the "opening exercise" at day school, in the talk of old people, wherever we lived. And it was in our language—fixedly, indelibly.[4]

The biblical heritage—in the last 50 years popularized in the States as "Judeo-Christian"—has exercised more influence on Americans simply because it was the basic, perhaps only, religious component in the lives of the early English immigrants to the New World.

Palestine and the Promise—the order of things—were a fixed, indelible order in the discourse of the nation. It is the same language which informed the writings of the Puritan settlers, Barlow and Dwight, American travelers to the Arab Orient, and, more importantly for the modern world, Bush, Pat Robertson and hundreds of influential figures.

The propelling to an American presidential race in 1988 of an Evangelical preacher who has openly supported Israel was significant since it came at a crucial time in the Arab–Israeli dilemma. The support given to Israel by the American evangelical churches (Jerry Falwell's is an obvious example) and by many political figures are reminders of American zeal in the cause of Zion in the nineteenth century. Central to this, of course, is the application of fundamentalist thinking which equates the language of scriptural prophecies with modern political developments.

Another instance of the existence of this American quest for Zion is the unwavering support by successive American administrations of Israeli violations of international conventions on human rights and of international law. The constant use of the veto in the Security Council to block any censure of Israeli atrocities, including crushing the bones of young Arabs, demolishing homes, and displacing the Arab population, all show a persistence of Zionist dominance in the American Oriental discourse as well as callousness toward the plight of the Arab victims. In effect, the efforts of the nineteenth-century American political planner and religious enthusiast to "remove" the inhabitants—"occupiers"—from the land and replace them with a "better race" are still at work today. The overwhelming American public support of Israeli policy and practices, and heartless disregard of the plight of millions of Palestinian Arabs, fly in the face of traditional American concern for human rights and sense of justice. The stereotyping and stigmatizing of the Arab and Muslim in the media, in school textbooks, and in popular literature have their precedents in nineteenth-century America. References of this type to other religions or ethnic groups, even if less sinister, would have been a *casus belli* and would have called forth claims of anti-Semitism or racism.

The author of "Orientalism" in the June 1853 edition of *Knickerbocker* summed up the many variations of the American attitude by describing the romantic world of the Arabian Nights, the "heathenism of the Mahometan imposture," the rebuilding of New Jerusalem, and the plan to elevate the Orient to a civilized state. "God," he said,

> gives the intelligent and civilized power, not to prey upon the weaknesses of his creatures, but to elevate them in the scale of being, to rescue from eternal anarchy, stagnation, and despotism, the magnificent domains of the East. By the same right, Americans may unfurl the stripes and stars in the harbor of Jeddo, and open Japan to the world. By the same right, western powers may divide the Mohametan world, displace sterility with cultivation, ignorance with refinement, and rapine with protection, but not the converse.[5]

The destiny of the Orient was perceived to be firmly locked to that of America, and the part to be played by the United States was drawn by the hand of God. The Holy Land, like the American West, seemed "to have been reserved by Providence to be the meeting-place of the Anglo Saxon on his eastern and western path of empire." As for the argument for annexation, here again there was no need for justification. Annexation, with the seal of prophecy, is its own justification. "Our nation has increased six millions since the last census, and has annexed within a few years a territory nine times the size of France ... and no power but the Almighty [could] conceivably prevent the Democratic element of America from making its impress upon the Orient." And how could the Almighty conceivably prevent such a destiny when everything tended to point to the fact that "the prophecy of Isaiah is approaching fulfillment in the East."[6]

This is American Orientalism of mid-nineteenth century. It remains active today. It is a fabric, a mosaic, of many threads and pieces, with an intense involvement in the Orient as the principal motif. It includes religious zeal to fulfill the vision of Zion, nostalgic yearning for the dream of Baghdad, continued official interest in the internal affairs of the Orient, the increasing popularity of travel in the Orient, missionary concern for the "lost" Muslim souls, and the urgency of the task of spreading the benefits of the American experience. These, and more, are given added poignancy, and made peculiarly

American, by the Puritan rhetoric of the Jeremiad which distinguished the American experience from the beginning and continues today to influence public and official attitudes.

It must be recognized here that a considerable number of Christian churches, groups and individuals have consistently and publicly opposed the policies and statements of the Christian and Political Right regarding Islam, Arabs, and the Palestinian question.

Fuad Sha'ban
Amman, December 2004

Part I
In the Beginning

I
Christopher Columbus and the Quest for Zion

Christopher Columbus, "Admiral of the Ocean Sea," has been traditionally portrayed—especially in popular works—as an adventurer who sought by exploring undiscovered regions of the world to obtain power, fortune and fame. Like his contemporaries, Columbus believed that there was in the Orient a "Great Khan" whose country held the prospect of inexhaustible gold and riches for whoever arrived there first.

He insisted that if he sailed west across the Atlantic, he would eventually reach the Orient by circumnavigating the earth. Columbus spent several years trying, without success, to convince the kings and princes of Europe of the possibility of his scheme, and to get the necessary material and political support for his "Enterprise of the Indies." Eventually, his proposal found favor at the court of Spain, his adopted country.

King Ferdinand and Queen Isabella agreed to support and finance his voyage, and, in return, Columbus promised the Spanish monarchs sovereignty over the lands and peoples he would discover. His reward, Columbus stipulated, would be stewardship for him and his offspring over these newly discovered territories. The four voyages made by Columbus, his discoveries and his subsequent life story have all been amply described and documented in hundreds of books and papers. What had not been as well studied and documented until recently are the deep religious beliefs and motives which prompted Columbus to venture on his "Enterprise of the Indies." And it is these beliefs and motives that concern us here because of their relevance to the "quest for Zion" in Western culture.

In his letters and journal entries, Columbus expressed pride and satisfaction in his maritime adventures and voyages which, he said, took him to all corners of the known world. He also prided himself on his skills as "Admiral of the Ocean Sea" and on his extensive knowledge of geography and astronomy and all the sciences which were necessary for arduous voyages.

Yet all of these skills and all the maps and aids he took with him were secondary to the most useful guide on which Columbus depended throughout his life: the Bible and the prophecies of the sacred text, and the firm belief that God had chosen him as an instrument to fulfill these prophecies. He said once: "God made me the messenger of the new heaven and the new earth of which he spoke in the Apocalypse of St. John [Rev.21:1] after having spoken of it through the mouth of Isaiah; and he showed me the spot where to find it."[1]

The principal factor which governed Columbus's life and motivated his activities was—as he put it in a letter to the Spanish monarchs—to spread the light of the Gospel throughout the world and to enlist the newly converted peoples in the life-and-death war with the empire of Muhammad.[2] His ultimate goals included the "recovery" of the Holy Land, especially Jerusalum, in preparation for the Kingdom of God.[3] In fact, it was his deep religious convictions in prophecy which, according to *The New Millennial Manual*, enabled him to convince Ferdinand and Isabella to finance his "Enterprise of the Indies."[4] And the "Enterprise" was to be the first stage in a new Crusade which would enable the Spanish monarchs to "recapture" the Holy Land and restore the Christian faith there. Throughout his life, Columbus insisted that Providence was always guiding his steps and directing his efforts.

In fact, at the end of his first voyage, and in a letter to the Spanish court dated February 15, 1492, Columbus said that the Bible was his lifetime roadmap for the fulfillment of divine prophecies and the rebuilding of Zion. This letter was subsequently printed and translated into many European languages. In it, Columbus summed up his global program "to conquer the world, spread the Christian faith, and regain the Holy Land and the Temple Mount."[5]

During the last voyage (1502–04), Columbus recorded in his journals that he heard voices and saw visions of God urging him on to carry out His mission. This belief in a Providential mission is what motivated Columbus to so relentlessly pursue his project of the "Enterprise of the Indies." He wrote:

Who would doubt that this light, which urged me on with a great haste continuously, without a moment's pause, came to you in a most deep manner, as it did to me? In this my voyage to the Indies, Our Lord wished to perform [a] very evident miracle in order to console me and others in the matter of this other voyage to the Holy Sepulchre [Jerusalem].[6]

To realize the originality as well as the significance of Columbus's missionary efforts and zeal to fulfill the "prophecies," one should remember that his campaign preceded the Protestant Reformation and the resulting emphasis on Old Testament prophecies and missionary drive. This zeal and the literal interpretation of sacred text prophecies led Delno West to describe Columbus as "the first American hero with all the rights and privileges, myths and legends, and criticisms the title carries."[7]

In his obsession with the rebuilding of Zion and the preparation for the Coming Kingdom, Columbus anticipated the early Puritan settlers in the New World, the nineteenth-century end-times churches and missionary establishment, and the present-day American grand plans for the world. In essence, Columbus's program is a roadmap for the modern campaign of the Christian Right in America today. Indeed, his plans have been recognized by successive generations of Americans, from Samuel Sewall's suggestion in 1697 that the immigrants' new home be called "Columbia" instead of America, to the song "Columbia, Columbia, To Glory Arise" chanted by American troops in the Revolutionary War, to President Reagan's description of Columbus as the "inventor of the American dream" on October 3, 1988 when the President signed the "Columbus Day Proclamation."

Columbus's contemporaries recognized the religious factors which motivated his efforts and maritime adventures. His son Ferdinand, for example, recognized his extreme obsession with the fulfillment of sacred prophecies, describing him as "so strict in matters of religion that ... he might be taken for a member of a religious order."[8] One of his contemporaries, Bishop Bartolomé de las Casas, spoke admiringly of his deep faith and frequent prayers and confessions. He also recorded Columbus's claims to a divine mission to fulfill the sacred prophecies. Commenting approvingly on Columbus's Providential mission, Bishop de las Casas said: "But since it is obvious that at that time God gave this man the keys to the awesome seas, he and no other unlocked the darkness, to him and to no other is owed forever and ever all that exists beyond those doors."[9]

Recent studies of Columbus's life and career have recognized these aspects of his faith. Samuel Eliot Morrison, for example, wrote that "this belief that God destined him to be the instrument to spread the light of Christianity was much stronger than his quest for fame and riches."[10] Kay Brigham also stated the belief that he knew what

God had predestined him to do within His plan for the world.[11] Following his last voyage, Columbus wrote in a letter to the Spanish monarchs suggesting that he would be the best guide to lead a "fifth Crusade," adding that

> Jerusalem and Mount Zion are to be rebuilt by the hands of Christians as God has declared by the mouth of His prophet in the fourteenth Psalm [vv. 7–8]. The Abbé Joaquim said that he who should do this was to come from Spain; Saint Jerome showed the holy woman the way to accomplish it; and the Emperor of China has, some time since, sent for wise men to instruct him in the faith of Christ. Who will offer himself for this work? Should anyone do so, I pledge myself, in the name of God, to convey him safely thither, provided the Lord permits me to return to Spain.[12]

The divine mission to which Columbus alluded in his letters and journals came to him through visions of the Holy Ghost telling him that "God will make your name known through the world, and shall give you the oceans which were closed to others."[13] To support these claims, Columbus often cited Psalm 2:6–8:

> Yet have I set my King upon my holy hill of Zion.
> I will declare the decree: the Lord hath said unto me,
> Thou art my Son; this day have I begotten thee.
> Ask of me, and I shall give thee the heathen for thine inheritance, and the uttermost parts of the earth for thy possession.

During Columbus's lifetime Europe was witnessing many great events, the most important of which was the European conquest of the Iberian Peninsula and the expulsion of Muslims and Jews from it. According to Columbus, 1491 was truly a "Wonderful Year," simply because these events were indications of the fulfillment of biblical prophecies. These were "signs of the times," and Columbus and many of his contemporaries saw in them the hand of God working out the events of history within His overall plan for the world.

Columbus also saw the hand of God working in the accession to the Spanish throne of the truly faithful Ferdinand and Isabella. For, had not the Abbé Joachim of Fiory predicted that the restoration of the Holy Land would happen at the hand of a Spaniard? If the Spanish monarchs were willing to take up the task, Columbus proposed, he would be willing to equip an army of 1,000 horsemen and 50,000 soldiers. "Victory will be yours if you are believers," he told them.

Columbus drew an analogy between himself and King David; just as David left Solomon great treasures to build the Temple, he, Columbus, wanted to finance and guide a final Crusade to liberate Jerusalem and rebuild the Temple. From the Temple, said Columbus, the Messiah would rule the Kingdom, and thus "the New World will save the Old City, the City of David."[14]

Columbus was so certain of his role in God's plan that he wrote to the Spanish monarchs in his later years about the success of his first voyage:

> I spent six years here at your royal court, disputing the case with so many people of greatest authority, learned in all the arts. And finally they concluded that it was all in vain, and they lost interest. In spite of that it later came to pass as Jesus Christ our Savior had predicted and as he had previously announced through the mouth of His holy prophet ... I have already said that reason, mathematics, and maps of the world were of no use to me in the execution of the enterprise of the Indies. What Isaiah said was completely fulfilled.[15]

Columbus wrote in detail about his beliefs and his sacred mission in his only (incomplete) book which he gave the significant title: *Libro de las Profecías* (*The Book of Prophecies*). Adopting the title of the last book of the New Testament which was mainly prophetic in nature, Columbus compiled in this work many texts from scripture to support his claim to a Providential mission. When Columbus sent this book to the Spanish monarchs, he wrote them a letter asking them to ponder the prophecies which he cited, especially those concerning the conversion of heathens and regaining the Holy Land.

According to Delno West,

> Christopher Columbus' attraction to prophetic interpretation of events set the stage for New World eschatology ... He came to the conclusion that his discoveries were providential and part of a broader scheme which would lead to a final series of historical events including the recapture of Jerusalem, the rebuilding of the temple, and the salvation of all Jews, infidels and pagans.[16]

These firm beliefs in a Providential plan and Columbus's role in it are the antecedents of one of the strongest formative factors of American culture, the Judeo-Christian tradition and the quest for Zion. This mission is summed up in a passage from a letter

Columbus wrote to the tutor of Prince John of Spain explaining the significance of October 12, 1492, the day on which his crew spotted land on his first voyage: "God made me the messenger of the New Heaven and the New Earth of which he spoke in the 'Apocalypse' by St. John, after having told of it by the mouth of Isaiah; and He showed me where to find it."[17]

The zeal shown by Christopher Columbus to discover a Western route to the Orient may have been partly motivated by material considerations. Nevertheless, contemporary accounts as well as Columbus's numerous statements prove that his overriding purpose was to play a principal role in regaining possession of the Holy Land and prepare for the millennial reign of Christ.

In this, Columbus can be considered the beacon which he inadvertently placed in the New World and which generations of Americans have used as a model for their endeavors to fulfill the same goal.

Part II
Zion in America

2

A Place for My People: The Pilgrims in the New World

> I will appoint a place for my people Israell, and I will plant them, that they may dwell in a place of their owne, and move no more. (Second Samuel; 7:10)
>
> John Cotton, "God's Promise to his Plantation," 1619

Puritan beliefs and the Puritan way of life have had a continuous and lasting influence on prevailing American religious, as well as secular, tendencies and in the shaping of American history. This influence can be seen in the evolution of the American governmental system, in social behavior and habits, in the various religious movements such as the Great Awakenings and the Revivals, in the missionary tendencies of the American nation, and in the sociopolitical attitudes of Americans toward the "others,"—Muslems and Arabs in particular. The influence of Puritanism on the development of American thinking is best described by the modern American religious historian Sidney E. Ahlstrom, who says that "the architects of the 'Puritan way' [were] … in a very real sense the founders of the American nation," and that "Puritanism, for weal or woe, provided the theological foundation and molded the prevailing religious spirit in virtually all the commonwealths which declared their independence in 1776. With lasting effects and hardly less directness it conditioned the people's social and political ideals."[1]

It is indeed in the Puritan beginnings of the American nation that we should look for the formative factors which shaped America's image of itself, its self-awareness and analysis, and, by contrast, its awareness of and attitude towards the Arab World, its land and people.

It is unnecessary for the present study to relate the story of the settlement of the New World and the subsequent religious, political and social developments of the American people. The story is well-known and has been documented many times over by able historians.[2] However, it is important to examine a number of ideas and themes in order to explore the way in which they contributed to the shaping of the American concept of Arabs, Muslems, and their part of the world. This selection is not the result of a random process, neither is it inclusive; only a few of the most influential and popular ideas will be treated. The aim of this analysis is to show how these ideas have influenced, in varying degrees, the basic attitude of Americans toward the Arabs and Muslems, and how this attitude shaped their behavior on coming in contact with them.

Briefly, the selection includes the following ideas:

(1) The existence of an overall Providential plan within which the Puritans and Pilgrims saw their immigration to the New World and the role which was assigned them by God.
(2) The conviction that those Protestants who emigrated from Europe (especially from England), and settled in the New World were God's people, chosen by divine ordinance to escape the corruption and iniquities of the Old World.
(3) The settlers in America enjoyed a covenantal relation with the Creator and were thus partners in a divine mission.
(4) As covenanted people, Americans saw their religious community as the Church of Visible Saints and considered the members of that community to be citizens in the Kingdom of God.
(5) Partnership in the covenant implied the awesome duty of enlightening and saving the rest of the world.

Although these ideas are by their very nature visionary and idealistic, they continue to shape the behavior and attitude of American private individuals and public figures. Furthermore, in spite of an idealistic and visionary nature—perhaps one should say because of it—these ideas have frequently resulted in encouraging a superior, sometimes racist, attitude towards the rest of mankind.

THE PILGRIM FATHERS AND THE PROVIDENTIAL PLAN

The principle of a Providential plan is a central concept in Puritan theology and behavior. Puritans saw every detail in their daily life, indeed in life generally, as the unfolding of a Providential plan which existed from the beginning of time. That is to say, the hand of Providence governs their actions and their destiny, as well as the shape and existence of things in the universe. Nothing happens in vain; everything leads to a preconceived goal. In Puritan diaries and journals—Samuel Sewall's *Diary* is a good example—it can be seen to what extent the belief in Providence influenced the thinking of the Puritans and their way of life. It was within the framework of this Providential plan that the Pilgrims saw their journey to the New World. As agents of God's will, the Pilgrim Fathers considered the founding of their communities in the New World as a sign of manifest, divine election and favor.[3]

The literature shows that from the selection of a particular group of people to emigrate to the New World to the choice of a special place for them—and the roles assigned them in the new life—all was considered to be part of the will of God. When John Cotton wrote his essay on "God's Promise to His Plantation," he quoted on the title page this passage from the Scriptures: "Moreover I will appoint a place for my people Israell, and I will plant them, that they may dwell in a place of their owne, and move no more (2 Sam. 7. 10.)."[4] Cotton presented the concept clearly when he told the settlers that "the appointment of a place for them ... is the first blessing," and every single step from their selection to "the placing of a people in this or that country is from the appointment of the Lord."[5]

The first ecclesiastical historian of the new nation, Cotton Mather, deemed it necessary, later in the seventeenth century, to keep these thoughts alive in the memory of "the posterity of those that were the undertakers, lest they come at length to forget and neglect the true interest of New England." Mather's "reminder" elucidated this point:

> Briefly, the God of Heaven served as it were a summons upon the spirits of his people in the English nation; stirring up the spirits of thousands which never saw the faces of each other, with a most unanimous inclination to leave all the pleasant accommodations of their native country, and go over a terrible ocean, into a more terrible desert, for the pure enjoyment of all his ordinances.[6]

The immigrants settling in the New World, like the Protestants of Europe, believed in a Providential plan. But what gave the concept added poignancy is that the immigrants, as well as their descendants, firmly believed that they held a special position in this plan. They were, as it were, hand-picked, chosen by God for the fulfillment of his will. Thus it is that the Pilgrims and subsequent generations of Americans were constantly applying to their situation the religious analogy of the "chosen people." The leader of one of the earliest groups of settlers, John Winthrop, saw the analogy even in God's punishment inflicted on his followers. "It may be by this means," he said, that God will induce them to repent of their former sins, and through that punishment save them from the

> desease, which sends many amongst us untimelie to their graves and others to hell, soe he carried the Israelits into the wildernesse and made them forgett the flesh potts of Egypt, which was sorie pinch to them att first but he disposed to them good in th'end. Deut. 30.3.16.[7]

In the early religious dissenting movements and controversies, contending parties used these scriptural analogies to lend strength and credibility to their respective arguments. In the Letters of Roger Williams to Winthrop, for example, Williams saw the situation of his party and their case in the light of the persecuted "people of God, wheresoever scattered about Babel's banks, either in Rome or in England, etc." But to Winthrop, Williams said,

> Your case is the worst by far, because while others of God's Israel tenderly respect such as desire to fear the Lord, your very judgement and conscience leads you to smite and beat your fellow servants, expel them from your coasts, etc., and therefore, though I know the elect shall never finally be forsaken, yet Sodom's, Egypt's, Amalek's, Babel's judgements ought to drive us out, to make our calling out of this world to Christ, and our election sure in him.[8]

In a different context, the case of the Christian settlers as God's chosen was used by Increase Mather to explain the intervention of divine power on the side of the settlers in their fights with the Indians. It was cause for prayer and rejoicing, he said, to realize "how often have we prayed that God would do for us as in the Days of Midian, by causing the Heathen to destroy one another, and that the Egyptians might be set against the Egyptians. The Lord hath answered that Request also." The Indian heathens were, in answer to the prayer of the settlers, killing each other,

> yea not only such Indians as do pretend Friendship to the English ... but also some of those that were once in Hostility against us, did help to destroy their own Nation, Friends and Kindred, that so they might do Service for us.[9]

If the settlers in the New World conceived of themselves as the chosen people of Scripture, it was only natural that their leaders should be portrayed as the Prophets and personalities of the Old and New Testaments. Many analogies of this kind can be seen in the writings of Americans down through the centuries. One interesting case is the eulogy by Increase Mather for the Governor of New England where the latter is described on his deathbed "like Jacob, [he] first left his council and blessing with the children gathered about his bed-side; and, like David, 'served his generation by the will of God.' " For the Governor's epitaph, Mather saw fit that "the words of Josephus about Nehemiah, the governor of Israel, we will now use upon this governour of New-England, as his Epitaph."[10]

This concept of Americans as God's people remained a constant factor in the thinking of American religious as well as lay leaders, although at times it took on certain variations and colorings to fit particular situations. Even George Washington, a man not known to mix religion with politics, in his "Address to the Hebrews of Savannah," compared the situation of the Israelites with that of the European emigrants to America. Washington expressed his hope that just as God had delivered the Israelites from oppression in Egypt,

> and planted them in the promised land, whose providential agency has lately been conspicuous in establishing these United States as an independent nation, still continue to water them with the dews of heaven, and to make the inhabitants of every denomination participate in the temporal and spiritual blessings of that people whose God is Jehovah.[11]

The analogy of the "Chosen People" was to play an important part in the tremendously popular missionary enterprise of the nineteenth century. A modern historian of American thought, Perry Miller, sums up the concept in the following words: "For many decades the Puritan colonies had been geographically set apart; the people had been thoroughly accustomed to conceiving of themselves as a chosen race, entered into specific covenant with God."[12]

THE COVENANT WITH GOD'S CHOSEN PEOPLE

The idea of a people "entered into specific covenant with God" had a strong hold on the minds and imaginations of Americans of successive generations. As a general rule, Protestant theology assumed that those who believed in the true Church of Christ had a special relationship with the Creator, referred to as the Covenant of Grace. The Covenant implied not only God's favor by election, but also, and just as importantly, that momentous duties were enjoined upon the believers as a result of that election. For American Puritanism the Covenant and its conditions were binding upon Americans, not simply as regards religious affairs and devotions, but their daily life itself was expected to be governed by the Covenant. Throughout the history of the American nation, there have been frequent statements which confirm this belief. Thus the Covenant has to be taken seriously if one is to understand the shape given by the Puritans to their religious as well as social and political institutions, leading to and including the American Declaration of Independence, the Constitution and the system of government.

The importance of this special relationship with the church and with God has been rightly emphasized by many historians of American religion. Sidney Ahlstrom, speaking of the Puritans, said that

> the clue to their understanding of regeneration, as well as to their theories for ordering the church and society, is the covenant. It was around this point that the particular dogmatic interests of the English and later the New England Puritan theologians were oriented. Theirs was a covenant theology.[13]

Ahlstrom quoted a contemporary Puritan, John Preston, who preached the principle that the Covenant "is the ground of all you hope for, it is that that every man is built upon, you have no other ground but this, God hath made a Covenant with you, and you are in covenant with him."[14]

If this seems to suggest that the settlers had no choice but to be partners in the Covenant, it is because it was so intended. Nor would they have had it any other way. The choice had been made for them by divine authority, and they willingly entered into the Covenant. Early expressions of this covenantal relationship with God are found in the constitutions (sometimes called "compacts") of the earliest Puritan colonies in the New World. When he wrote the history of these communities, Cotton Mather spoke with total conviction of "the covenant whereto these Christians engaged themselves." As an example which should be emulated by other Christian communities, Mather "lay before all the Churches of God" the text of the Covenant of the Salem community "as it was then expressed and enforced."[15]

The text of the Salem Covenant,[16] as cited by Mather, illustrates the application of the concept of the Covenant to every aspect of life. It calls upon its members and followers to consider themselves to be the People of God, to renounce all ways of life contrary to the teaching of Jesus Christ, to act towards one another as He instructed, to comport themselves decorously and in a brotherly fashion in church and society, to advance the Gospel but not to offend others (including Indians), to obey their superiors and governors in church or state, to work and live as the stewards of the Lord and to bring up their children and influence their servants to acknowledge their relationship to God and the Covenant.

This, then, is the true covenant to which the first waves of settlers bound themselves. The conditions named therein were to regulate their relations with one another, with "those that are within or without," and with God. They were also to serve as the constitution for church and state, and, as we will see later, they were to figure in the subsequent framing of the political thinking and behavior of an independent America, beginning with the Founding Fathers. More important for the present study, this covenantal relation with God and the duties assumed by the people of the Covenant, one of which was "to spread the light," were very instrumental in shaping the American attitude to, and perception of, other people—whether native Indians, Arabs, Muslims, or still others who stood outside the Covenant.

Although they saw themselves as latter-day Israelites, the Puritans of New England did not rest their title to the chosen people simply on the similarity of their respective situations. They took the original promise made by God to Abraham as the basis of all subsequent covenantal partnerships. They thought of themselves as the "seed of Abraham" and beneficiaries to the promise given to him. They were also the faithful members of the true church of God; for a member of the community to qualify for the Covenant and promise, membership in the church was a precondition.

A significant example of this connection between church membership and the Covenant comes from one of the earliest records of the settlement of New England. Cotton Mather related how the new settlers at Salem, on their arrival in 1629 "resolved, like their father Abraham, to begin their plantation with 'calling on the name of the Lord' ". Although they had been advised to reach an agreement on the form of church government before they left for New England, all the immigrants could agree upon was the "general principle, that the reformation of the church was to be endeavoured according to the written word of God." Accordingly, they sought the advice of their "brethren at Plymouth" who gladly instructed them on how they could find a lesson "in the laws of our Lord Jesus Christ, for every particular in their Church-order." Finally, and after obtaining the approval of the messengers of the church of Plymouth,

> they set apart the sixth day of August, after their arrival, for fasting and prayer, for the settling of a Church State among them, and for their making a Confession of their Faith, and entering into an holy Covenant, whereby that Church State was formed.

The "Covenant of the Church State" was an establishment into which the whole community entered, once the general principles were agreed upon. It was, in a way, a communal baptism into the Church of Christ. But that was not enough. Every member of the community had to be admitted into the church through an individual profession of faith. "Some were admitted by expressing their consent unto their confession and covenant," some after submitting to oral (and some to written) examinations by giving answers to questions about religion "as might give satisfaction unto the people of God concerning them." Two points are paramount in this process: first, that the community was basically considered the "people of God" through an acceptance of the covenant of Abraham and "the children of the faithful were Church-members, with their parents; and that their baptism was a seal of their being so." Secondly, that every individual, before being admitted to a particular church, "should publickly and personally own the covenant; so they were to be received unto the table of the Lord."[17]

This early American formula of the Covenant placed the American community, particularly confirmed church members, in a special position in the world, a position of which they were quite conscious. With this special position firmly established, the association of the Covenant, through descent from Abraham, gained in importance as Americans directed their efforts to proselytizing the rest of the world. To be qualified for the task, and to be a nation which partakes of divine favor and divine mission, devout Americans often identified themselves with biblical missionary characters and situations. But the most convincing connection used persistently was the succession from Abraham. In the context of nineteenth-century zeal for evangelizing the nations, Samuel Worcester presented this same argument in "Two Discourses" in 1805 (especially relevant because Worcester's "Discourses" were written in connection with missionary efforts). Briefly, his argument goes like this: God treated all mankind in the way of the covenant, first through Adam, then Noah, then Abraham. "He made a covenant with Abraham" which he fulfilled by conferring His blessings on Abraham and all his posterity, and ultimately He bestowed this blessing on all humankind. "And in this way," said Worcester, "he continues to treat with mankind. All the blessings, which from generation to generation, he bestows upon the church and upon the world, are bestowed in pursuance of some existing covenant."[18] Since God said to Abraham "In thee all the nations shall be blessed," the blessings will eventually reach the whole world. There were conditions, however. A person had to be "of the faith" and to be baptized in the church through Christ. Baptism took the place of circumcision, a substitution deemed necessary to disprove the limitation of the promise to the Jews; and faith in the true church was a condition which gave Americans precedence over "nominal" Christians, Papists in particular. Worcester's conclusion drives the point home:

> For as many of you as have been baptized into Christ, have put on Christ. There is neither Jew nor Greek, there is neither bond nor free, there is neither male nor female; for ye are all one in Christ Jesus. And if ye be Christ's, then ye are Abraham's seed, and heirs according to the promise. If ye be Christ's, then are ye brought into a covenant relation to Abraham.[19]

The Covenant is thus said to be in existence to the end of time and it includes all mankind—but those who accept Christ, and are of faith, are the children of Abraham; theirs is the responsibility of extending God's blessings to the rest of the world. Worcester therefore called on the American missionaries who were about to embark on their evangelical journey to the Holy Land to

> Go, and from the heights of Calvary and of Zion proclaim to the long lost tribes of Israel, to the followers of the Pseudo-prophet, to the bewildered people of different lands, tongues, and religions, the fountains there opened, for the cleansing of all nations—the banner there displayed, for the gathering of all people.[20]

THE JOURNEY AS PILGRIMAGE TO THE KINGDOM OF GOD

For the religious-minded settlers in America and for prospective immigrants, journeys, pilgrimages and evangelical sojourning were not activities undertaken primarily for pleasure or even to satisfy intellectual curiosity. In fact, in the tradition of Protestant Christianity, the life of a Christian was considered a spiritual journey, a pilgrim's progress, aspiring to reach God's kingdom. Often this theme of the spiritual journey through life led to a symbolic Holy Land, as one can see from the titles *A Brief Account of my Soul's Travel Toward the Holy Land* (Isaac Penington, 1681) and *A Declaration to the World, of my Travel and Journey out of Egypt into Canaan through the Wilderness, through the Red Sea, from Under Pharoah* (Thomas Greene, 1659).[21] For the immigrants to the New World, the similarity which they saw between their conditions and those of the Israelites was not limited to the dangers faced in a new hostile environment; it actually became an extended spiritual metaphor in which biblical geography blended with real-life experiences and included the story of the flight from Egypt, crossing the desert and sea, and facing a vast inhospitable wilderness. On the eve of their departure to the New World, John Winthrop's followers listened to a sermon by John Cotton who, using biblical association and idiom, assured them that "when God wrappes us in his ordinances and warns us with the life and power of them as with wings, there is the land of Promise."[22] And when William Bradford reflected on the miserable state of the Pilgrims after their voyage across the ocean, his language was reminiscent of scriptural experiences: Bradford recalled that

> it is recorded in scripture as a mercie to the apostle and his shipwraked company, that the barbarians shewed them no small kindness in refreshing them, but these savage barbarians, when they mette with them (as after will appeare) were readier to fill their sides full of arrows then otherwise.[23]

In conclusion to this section of his "History," Bradford asked: "what could now sustaine them but the spirite of God and his grace?" Should not the descendants of these settlers, asked Bradford, remember that their fathers "were Englishmen which came over this great ocean, and were ready to perish in the wilderness ... Yea, let them which have been redeamed of the Lord, shew how he hath delivered them from the hand of the oppressour."[24]

The blend of realistic description of the Pilgrims' plight with biblical idiom does not take anything away from Bradford's sincere religious sentiments and temporal concerns.

The same blend of sincere feelings, realism and biblical allusions informs Cotton Mather's description of the voyage and experience of the immigrants who arrived in New England in 1623, among whom

> were diverse worthy and useful men, who were come to seek the welfare of this little Israel; though at their coming they were so diversely affected as the rebuilders of the Temple of Jerusalem: some were grieved when they saw how bad the circumstances of the friends were, and others were glad that they were no worse.[25]

But the Pilgrims were not daunted by the difficult circumstances which they faced; they were men of vision, and their aim was to "rebuild the Temple of Jerusalem." In the words of Vernon Parrington, "it was to set up a kingdom of God on earth that the Puritan leaders came to America."[26] This overriding concept of the Kingdom of God within which the Puritans saw themselves as partners and co-workers with God is quite important for a proper understanding of American attitudes toward others who did not belong to the kingdom. It is also important because of the Puritan representation of the kingdom as a stage leading to more momentous events. The idea was recognized by William Bradford who, writing of the Pilgrims, said that

> A great hope and inward zeal they had, of laying some good foundation, or at least to make some way thereunto, for the propagating and advancing the gospell of the kingdom of Christ in those remote parts of the world; yea, though they should be but even as stepping stones unto others for the performing of so great a work.[27]

The idea of establishing the Kingdom of God, or God's American Israel as it was often called, was a dominant American religious vision throughout American history. In his excellent study, *The Kingdom of God in America*, H. Richard Niebuhr described the forms taken by this idea in American thought. "In the early period of American life," Niebuhr said,

> when the foundations were laid on which we have all had to build, "kingdom of God" meant "sovereignty of God"; in the creative period of awakening and revival it meant "reign of Christ"; and only in the most recent period had it come to mean "kingdom on earth."[28]

In all of these stages, however, Americans considered themselves citizens of this kingdom, favored by the Governor and partners in a great enterprise; John Winthrop recognized this when he said that God may have "some great worke in hand whiche he hath revealed to his prophets among us."[29] American citizenship in this kingdom was never seriously challenged, and, consequently, as we shall see later, during the periods of Awakening, Independence and Revivals, and up to the present time, Americans felt impelled by the sense of divine mission which comes with this citizenship to spread the light among other, less fortunate nations.

Even while the first waves of Puritan settlers were busy establishing their new homes under very adverse conditions, they were constantly reminded of a sense of responsibility toward the "others," stemming from that special position which they assumed in the Providential plan. To be partners in the Covenant and members of a chosen band in the Church of Grace brought certain privileges, but also heavier duties than those carried by ordinary men. The Covenant was an essential condition for election and grace, but, once attained, this election puts the elect in a peculiar position vis-à-vis the rest of the world.

True Christians, and this is how the New England settlers saw themselves, are "the light of the world."[30] This is the way they were addressed in Scriptures: "Ye are the light of the world" (Math., v, 14). And the true Christian Church, the home of the Kingdom of God in the New World, is, to use Stephen Olin's phrase, the "depositary and sole agent" of the Gospel.[31] This principle was essential for the Puritan settlers from the first day they set foot in the New World. John Winthrop's "Conclusions" advanced practical, indeed very mundane, economic grounds for settling a "plantation in new England." The first justification, however, according to Winthrop, is "the propagation of the gospell to the Indians. Wherein first the importance of the worke tending to the inlargment of the Kingdome of Jesus Christ and winning them out of the snare of the Divell and converting others of them by their meanes."[32] Although other material grounds were advanced, spreading the light of the Gospel remained a top priority. This early missionary spirit is a forerunner to the zeal with which nineteenth-century American evangelists set out to convert the rest of the world. The missionary spirit, according to a nineteenth-century devout American scholar, is "a vital element in Christian character [and] a fundamental principle of our holy religion. By an eternal law, whoever believes in Christ must proclaim him to others. Whoever embraces Christianity, must diffuse it." Finally, which is especially the lot of Americans, "whoever is converted to God, and through faith made a partaker of Christ's love, is by that very fact set apart to the work of saving others. He has a mission to fulfill in regard to the spread of religion."[33] This is how the settlers looked at their situation and at the rest of the world, and this is how many Americans, religious and secularist, have felt ever since.

Just as the Pilgrims conceived of themselves as agents in God's plan to establish "His Kingdom," they and their descendants also assumed the inevitability of their mission to the rest of the world. Their church was the bearer of the true light and it was their duty to compete with the false missionaries of the "Antichrist" in the New World, as their Protestant partners in the church were doing in the Old World. To be sure, one of the motives which prompted Winthrop and his company to establish a plantation in New England was "the Dilligence of the Papists in propagating their religion and superstition and enlarginge the kingdome of Antichrist thereby with all the manifest hazards of their persons and depe endangerments of their estates."[34] The same conviction that theirs was the "true light" led nineteenth-century American missionaries to clash with the Roman Church and Islam in the Levant and in other parts of the world. They held to the belief that the Christian church, the church to which they belonged, "is the true light, in distinction from all other systems, whether of religious or moral ... [which] were for the most part positively and universally mischievous in their entire action and tendencies. They led to evil, and that continually."[35]

Prominent in this attitude are two characteristics which remained the hallmark of the American missionary enterprise and also distinguished the political attitudes of the newly independent nation in the nineteenth century. There is, for one thing, a sense of urgency and tremendous importance attached to this unique (perhaps even monopolistic) position of American Protestantism. Secondly, the missionary impulse, despite the dangers and pitfalls it involved, was optimistic of reaching fulfillment of its goals.

There was no doubt in the minds of the devout that God had elected this nation to be His agent in spreading the light. This was reflected time and again in the writings and sermons of American divines. "A sense of mission to redeem the Old World," says Frederick Merk, possessed the Pilgrim Fathers and their descendants which "appeared thereafter in successive generations of Americans" and remains unaltered.[36] One of these generations of mission-driven

Americans was the mid-nineteenth-century generation; and looking in retrospect at the roots of the American nation, a nineteenth-century writer saw with conviction that the "character of our population shows us eminently that God has appointed us to be a missionary people"; he drew a picture of America as a missionary nation, called by destiny to use the blessings of its geography, its freedom and security, to civilize "so motley a group of heathen and Mohammedan, Buddhist and Papist, white, colored and mixed, bond and free."[37]

A sense of urgency and importance, then, was the direct result of the appointment by God and of the worldwide application of that missionary commission. The New England Puritans and their American descendants considered the world in dire need of their help and believed that they were delegated by God to answer that need. American missionaries and evangelists today use the same language, and although politicians and statesmen shy away from naming God as the Commissioner, they site the "call of history" and similar terms to indicate essentially the same concept.

3

The Star in the West: The United States as the Light of the World

Twice twenty years have roll'd away.
Since on this memorable day,
Was Independence born;
The child of heav'n—of earth the joy,
Whom no base Herod could destroy.
Though feeble and forlorn.
May all other nations, in time, too rejoice
To have, for their rulers, the men of their choice—
The King of all kings, but no other obey,
And blest Independence the Universe sway.
William Ray, "Independence: An Ode," 1816

The vision of the Puritan ideologues did not end with the establishment of the independent political state. In fact, in spite of the political atmosphere which characterized the polemics of the Revolution and Independence, many of the basic premises of the early American religious communities continued to inform the idiom and thinking of these two periods. The most obvious among these early premises are: the belief in the unfolding of divine will in the establishment of the United States of America; the covenantal nature of the new American system and the blend of religious and sociopolitical principles in this "ideal state"; and the compelling sense of mission felt by American nationalists toward the rest of the world. These premises, moreover, were all operating within the framework of an active awareness by Americans of the unique nature of their experiment in the history of man.

To begin with this last idea, there was a general agreement that the new American situation was a unique experiment—never witnessed before in the annals of mankind. This point was emphasized by Americans from many walks of life who were overjoyed by the novelty of their experiment and the opportunities it held for them, for their nation's posterity and for the rest of the world. During the first few decades of Independence, intellectual visionaries such as the Connecticut Wits, as well as practical politicians, expressed this notion in no uncertain terms. "For our situation," Joel Barlow maintained, "is in many respects not only new to us, but also to the world." Realizing that the opportunities opened up to the new system would render it "as novel as it is important," Barlow reminded his generation that it was their duty to make full use of the opportunity; for, he said:

> There has been no nation either ancient or modern that could have presented human nature in the same character as ours does and will present it; because there has existed no nation whose government has resembled ours. A representative democracy on a large scale, with a fixt constitution, had never before been attempted, and has no where else succeeded. A federal government on democratic principles is equally unprecedented, and exhibits a still greater innovation on all received ideas of statesmen and lawgivers.[1]

This was the time for the "powerless potentates of reason," said Barlow, to watch the new developments and learn a lesson in political science and the principles of democratic government. The enthusiasm generated in the hearts of Americans was not limited to one group or class. Intellectuals, politicians, and religious extremists alike saw the unique nature of their experiment, each in their own frame of reference.

GOD'S AMERICAN ISRAEL

But this new nation, which evolved into what was considered the perfect state, was not only the fruit of the efforts of its founders. Although this country, "freedom's sacred temple," was "built by immortal patriots' hands,"[2] its patriots were only carrying out the will of God. The United States of America, to quote Timothy Dwight, was a happy state,

> by HEAVEN design'd
> To reign, protect, employ, and bless mankind;[3]

While recognizing their happy situation and their own part in bringing it about, these Americans were visibly conscious of the part played by the hand of Providence. They had no doubt whatsoever that a superior power had brought this new nation to such a perfect state; they were also quite certain that the same power had prepared them for a tremendous task.

The establishment of this ideal American state, moreover, was not seen only as the unfolding of a superior Providential plan. Prophecies revered by Christians were read into this momentous event. "God's American Israel," said another American intellectual, was the fulfillment of the vision of Noah and the realization of Deuteronomy (26:19) "to make thee high above all nations which he hath made, in praise, and in name, and in honor; and that thou mayst be an holy people unto the Lord thy God."[4]

Throughout the period of the Revolution and Independence there were frequent references by preachers, educators and politicians to the unfolding of a manifest divine plan in these auspicious events. According to this plan, America had been there from the beginning of creation, and was now opportunely thrust upon the world scene. The new nation, God's peculiar people, "after having been concealed for so many years from the rest of the world, was probably discovered in the maturity of time, to become the theatre for displaying the illustrious designs of Providence, in its dispensations to the human race."[5] The new state also inherited from its Puritan ancestors the firm conviction that its citizens were favored and selected by God to establish His Kingdom in this newly independent territory and to extend that Kingdom to the rest of the world.

On other continents, they believed, revolutions had been the outcome of accident—especially in Europe where sound judgment and human rights were preyed upon by caprice and tyranny. Empires were established on foundations of ignorance and self-interest. Not so on the "Western continent."[6] This new experiment, unknown to human legislators anywhere else, "was imposed upon the fathers of the American Empire" by the Divine law-maker. A "beneficent providence, the God of order and justice," according to Barlow, brought to perfection the United States of America and provided it with the necessary qualifications to lead the rest of humanity from darkness to the new light.[7] The concept of light figures prominently in these qualifications and, without being ambivalent, takes on both secular and religious meanings in the writings of Americans. In a poem by William Ray, the figure of light is clearly within the Christian tradition, but it also speaks of Independent America as a phenomenon emerging from Jehovah's throne—"a star arising in the west."[8] Such was the secularized, indeed the nationalized, Kingdom of God as

Americans conceived of it when they achieved their independence. America was qualified to assume the role of that Kingdom, and foremost among her qualifications was a system of governance which valued the ideals of the Enlightenment while still adhering to the age-old principles of obedience to God and church. Thus the authors of the Constitution found it natural that to be free and independent meant also to maintain "firm reliance on the Protection of Divine Providence."[9] The new system was to be a covenantal form of state; a covenant was drawn by the people to govern their experiment in statehood, but it was to be drawn before God, and in obedience to His will. The state of peace and happiness which was achieved by Americans, as seen by Joel Barlow, was a condition predicted in Scripture, where it was referred to as the millennial period. It was the "sun of glory [which illumined] JEHOVAH's throne."[10]

The ecclesiastical and sociopolitical covenant of the Puritans was dressed in the new garb of an eighteenth-century system of rational thought. A modern American historian described the American nation at every stage of its early development as "the result of the consecutive unfolding of God's covenant with mankind, now come to a climax on this continent; for Americans the exercise of liberty becomes simply the one true obedience to God."[11] Obedience to God implied respect for the law and enjoyment of political and civil liberties. In spite of the insistence of the Founding Fathers on the separation of church and state and on the sanctity of individual religious freedom, there was then, and still is at present, a persistent association between the ideals of the American political system and those of American Christianity.

The first advocates of separation of church and state and toleration of religious freedom regarded Protestant Christianity as an essential ingredient for the success of the new experiment. Daniel Webster's well-known statement that Christianity "must ever be regarded among us as the foundation of civil society"[12] summed up the prevailing sentiment among his contemporaries and was echoed later by such statements as that made by President Eisenhower that "without God there could be no American form of Government, nor an American way of life." Eisenhower went on to call on the American people to pray to Almighty God

> each day ... to set and keep His protecting hand over us so that we may pass on to those who come after us the heritage of a free people, secure in their God-given rights and in full control of a government dedicated to the preservation of those rights.[13]

It was this underlying belief in the essential role of religion in the American experiment—a heritage of the first American political systems, called "compacts" or "covenants"—which prompted political as well as religious missionaries to combine and treat with equal importance the two components of religion and politics in their efforts to convert the rest of the world. Founders of the American Bible Society were conscious of this dichotomy in the American role when, in the Society's Constitution, they addressed "the People of the United States of America," urging them to recognize the "great political event" as a sign of God's favor and of the coming of the millennium.[14]

Citizens of the young state were often reminded of this happy blend of religion and politics in their national experiment and of the serious duties they shouldered. On the Fourth of July, 1812, Enoch Lincoln delivered an Independence Day Oration in Worcester, Massachusetts, in which he said: "Fellow citizens! while we cling to our natural and social rights, let us be faithful to our civil duties. So shall our country rise unrivalled in wisdom; its population be numberless as the rays of the firmament and Heaven above exceed our felicity."[15] To emphasize the importance of American religious-political conduct for the achievement of America's mission, Lincoln called on his fellow citizens to "be tolerant to opinion," and to make freedom of expression and belief a means of attracting others to the new system. "The politician is a slave until Religion also be free," he said, and concluded that diversity of opinion could only lead to a unity of belief. It can easily be recognized that in this early period of Independence the foundations were laid for the political religious system which in the second half of the twentieth century came to be known as "civil religion."

After Independence, and throughout the first half of the nineteenth century, many Americans were convinced that theirs was the ideal political state and the most likely setting for the Kingdom of God. Obviously, covenantal thinking was a dominant factor in these American religious and political beliefs. In fact, Sidney Ahlstrom's statement that "as night follows day, 'covenant thinking' carried over into the Puritans' ecclesiastical and social thinking"[16] can very well be applied to American patriotic feelings after Independence. The Puritan settlers' belief that they had been delivered from the iniquities and corruption of Europe to the Land of Promise was strengthened by the establishment of an independent state, and earlier American expressions of optimism and enthusiasm were echoed in the period which followed Independence. Lyman Beecher showed the typical national sentiment of his countrymen when he said that it was time for the American experiment to be made available to the rest of the world in order for it "to be emancipated and rendered happy."[17] Failing this, Beecher warned, "the whole creation shall groan and travail together in pain." In statements like this, the religious missionary idiom blends completely with the language of the enlightened social and political reformers.

THE UNIQUE NATURE OF THE AMERICAN EXPERIMENT

Advocates of the uniqueness of the American experiment did not have to look very far for proof that they were blessed by heaven with every qualification necessary for spreading the new system to the rest of the world. Geography, for one thing, provided what seemed to be convincing signs to prove the point. The continent of America, according to one writer, was so centrally situated that it made it possible for Americans to reach every part of the world with the light of the Gospel and of the American system. The author of an article in the *American Theological Review* (1859) expounded on the advantages of the geographical position of the United States, which, he said, being

> placed nearly between Africa and Europe on the east and Asia on the west, it attracts thither the adventurer and the oppressed from those lands, while it is so far removed from them all, as easily to keep aloof from their contentions. South America, too, is quite accessible. Indeed, radii drawn from our eastern, western, and southern shores, reach almost all Pagan, Mohammedan, and Papal lands, or rather most of them can be reached by nearly direct water communication.[18]

This happy geographical situation—the center of the world—would, according to the *American Theological Review*, enable Americans to extend "civilization and Christianity among degraded and benighted nations."[19]

This same central position, conversely, had the further advantage of insularity, one which protected the United States from invasion and from the corrupting influences of other, less civilized nations. The Founding Fathers realized this advantage even as they deliberated over the text of the Declaration of Independence. Addressing the Continental Congress which was drafting the Declaration, one of the delegates (Gouverneur Morris) spoke of "the great gulph which rolls its waves between Europe and America," and which forms a line of "full and lasting defence"[20] to protect the newly independent country. And at the meeting which endorsed the Constitution, Hamilton recognized the advantages of the geographical position of his country.[21] Insularity, then, worked for the dual purpose of reaching out to others with the light of civilization and protecting the country against outside dangers.

The variety of climatic conditions, terrain, and natural resources was also an advantage which attracted immigrants from all corners of the world to the United States. Immigrants "from every region where oppression reigns or poverty blights" would flock to the United States where, the *American Theological Review* said, "our great rivers, with our fast extending railroads, enable them to penetrate into fertile regions, where industry insures them a competence, and their rights are secure." They would also find the variety of climate adapted to their constitutions, whether they came from the northern or southern regions. It also would prepare Americans to go anywhere, "to carry thither and teach the principles of learning, liberty, and religion."[22] As for the great wealth in natural resources, the United States could accommodate more than "five hundred millions of people."[23]

In mineral wealth, the land had unexhaustible deposits of iron, lead, copper, and gold. With happy satisfaction, the writer exclaimed: "Half a million of years would be required to exhaust our fossil fuel, and the supply will surely be fully adequate to meet the largest wants of three hundred millions that may in a few centuries be congregated here."[24]

As early as 1809, Joel Barlow saw what came to be known half a century later as "Manifest Destiny," when he envisioned "the vast extent of continent that is or must be comprised within our limits, containing not less than sixteen hundred millions of acres, and susceptible of a population of two hundred millions of human beings."[25]

All of this wealth, and the fortunate geographical and political situation enjoyed by the newly created nation, were viewed as planned by Providence for the benefit of mankind.

AMERICAN CONCERN FOR THE REST OF MANKIND

One of the most enduring characteristics of nineteenth-century American nationalism was its outward look and missionary nature.

Founders and visionaries of the new American state (variously called "kingdom" and "empire") looked out to the rest of the world even as the groundwork of the new system was being laid. Only eleven years after Independence, Joel Barlow addressed the Connecticut Society of Cincinnati on the Fourth of July, describing the great results expected of the "Federal Convention now sitting at Philadelphia." There was immense confidence in that body of legislators, he said, owing to their past services to the nation, but much more was expected:

> If ever there was a time, in any age or nation, when the fate of millions depended on the voice of one, it is the present period in these states. Every free citizen of the American Empire ought now to consider himself as the legislator of half mankind.

And if every American citizen would only view the opportunities open to him, he would rejoice at the results to be achieved by "one rational political system upon the general happiness of mankind."[26]

In political and religious, as well as in literary statements, it was firmly asserted that the happiness of America meant, by logical extension, the happiness of the rest of the world. This was expressed by another enthusiastic patriot in a versified, though not more poetic, form:

> Yet there, even there, Columbia's bliss shall spring,
> Rous'd from dull sleep, astonish'd Europe sing,
> O'er Asia burst the renovating morn,
> And startled Afric in a day be born;[27]

Both the American sacred Kingdom of God and American political democracy were brought together by nationalist visionaries as a model for the Old World and for uncivilized nations. This model was to beam the light of the Gospel and of freedom to the world. The blend has been fully described by H. Richard Niebuhr in his celebrated work, *The Kingdom of God in America*. "The institutionalization of the kingdom of Christ was naturally accompanied by its nationalization," Niebuhr said, and, he continued,

> The old idea of American Christians as a chosen people who had been called to a special task was turned into the notion of a chosen nation especially favored. In Lyman Beecher, as in Cotton Mather before him, we have seen how this tendency came to expression. As the nineteenth century

went on, the note of divine favoritism was increasingly sounded. Christianity, democracy, Americanism, the English language and culture, the growth of industry and science, American institutions—these are all confounded and confused. The contemplation of their own righteousness filled Americans with such lofty and enthusiastic sentiments that they readily identified it with the righteousness of God ... It is in particular the Kingdom of the Anglo-Saxon race, which is destined to bring light to the gentiles by means of lamps manufactured in America.[28]

In retrospect, Niebuhr saw a "confusion of church and world," and a confounding of Christianity, democracy, Americanism, and all other American institutions.

There was little doubt in the minds of patriotic Americans that this new experiment was to be extended to the rest of the world. The *American Theological Review* writer of 1859 put special emphasis on this aspect of America's mission to the nations. He said that "now that Providence has shown how applicable this system is to the whole human family, the descendants of the Pilgrims should be satisfied with nothing short of its universal extension."[29] And, as if to explain that by the "system" were meant considerations other than religious, the writer went on to say that "our free political institutions furnish another evidence of our adaptedness and consequent duty to become a missionary nation."[30] America shared in the natural human "love of unbridled liberty," but, the writer continued, "in this country, however, hitherto we have been able to subject liberty to law."[31] Furthermore, social equality, a progressive educational system, and many other advantages convinced many Americans they were qualified to extend the experiment to all of mankind. Expressions such as these show how the sociopolitical developments in America became part of the religious belief that the new nation was directed by the hand of Providence.

Extension of the American system was to be for the good of mankind. That was the ideal of the missionary establishment and of the patriotic men who believed that theirs was a Revolution for the betterment of the human condition. Some propagators of the westward expansion of the United States also considered their efforts part of this reaching-out to the rest of mankind and not simply as acquisition of territory. In October, 1847, the editor of the *Philadelphia Public Ledger*, William Swain, put forth this idea very clearly:

We are believers in the superintendence of a directing Providence, and when we contemplate the rise and amazing progress of the United States,

> the nature of our government, the character of our people, and the occurrence of unforeseen events, all tending to one great accomplishment, we are impressed with a conviction that the decree is made and in the process of execution, that this continent is to be but one nation, under one system of free institutions. This is said in no spirit of prophecy, but in the conclusion of reason ... and the natural tendency of the moral and physical elements at work.[32]

In one bold and concise statement, Swain expressed the prevailing enthusiasm of his contemporaries—enthusiasm, however, that was warranted not only by prophecy, i.e. religion, but also by rational judgment.

AMERICA'S MANIFEST DESTINY

The belief in the United States as the new ideal state—the religious as well as the secular Utopia—played a significant role in the movement known as Manifest Destiny. This concept meant, among other things, the extension of the benefits of the American experience to the neighboring areas. In fact, not all people could qualify to emulate the American system. Manifest Destiny also meant that others were in need of the American helping hand, and the aim was not simply territorial expansion.

The intervention of Providence was at work in American efforts to "explode" old habits and establish new standards of morality and political conduct. This was to be achieved through spreading the light of the Gospel and of American revolutionary ideas. In this sense the American Revolution did not belong only to America; it was rather the property of mankind. Ezra Stiles described the new system in 1783 as a "recent political phenomenon of a new sovereignty arising among the sovereign powers of the earth ... [which] should be attended to and contemplated by all nations."[33] At about the same time, Joel Barlow enthusiastically described the great prospects which awaited the American nation. In a perfect blend of religious and sociopolitical missionary expression, Barlow called on all mankind to emulate the American model of government:

> But now no more the patriotic mind,
> To narrow views and local laws confined,
> Gainst neighboring lands directs the public rage,
> Plods for a clan or counsels for an age;

> But soars to loftier thoughts and reaches far
> Beyond the power, beyond the wish of war;
> For realms and ages forms the general aim,
> Makes patriot views and moral views the same
> Works with enlighten'd zeal, to see combined
> The strength and happiness of humankind.[34]

The "cause of political liberty," according to Niebuhr, was part of the whole humanitarian enterprise which characterized the American enlightenment of the nineteenth century.[35] Americans sincerely sought to bring their brand of enlightenment to the other peoples of the earth, especially to those who were "oppressed" and who sat "in darkness." The theme of light beaming from America to the four corners of the world was a favorite topic with Americans through the centuries. Ray's poem, "Spreading the Gospel: Star in the West," was prefaced with Revelation, "And I will give him the Morning Star," but the substance of that light derived also from a patriotic stand when the poet wrote, predictably, that "a star is rising in the West!" The lamp, as another poem by Ray illustrates, was an instrument of the American enlightenment. Although "Virtue, Vice, Liberty and Oppression, are beloved and detested by the good and bad of all countries and nations," it was America who had

> ....
> caught the flame
> O may it burn eternal!
> ....
> Where freedom's sacred temple stands,
> Built by immortal patriots' hands.[36]

Liberty became synonymous with the American system itself—basically a system of government and life identified with God's Covenant. This is the system of political and civil liberties which Ahlstrom saw as "simply the one true obedience to God."[37]

Yet it was not only the exercise of liberty which was considered by Americans to be the true obedience to God; the exercise had to be complemented with the spreading of liberty throughout the world. Timothy Dwight, Joel Barlow, William Ray, and countless other Americans joined in the exercise, which was also shared by such diverse nineteenth-century American travelers to the Orient as David Dorr, an American slave from Tennessee; Richard Haight, a gentleman from New York; and William Lynch, a US Naval officer. In the account of his journey "around the world," David Dorr said that

> the author of this book, though a colored man, hopes to die believing that this federal government is destined to be the noblest fabric ever germinated in the brain of men or the tides of time. Though a colored man, he believes that he has the right to say that, in his opinion, the American people are to be the Medes and Persians of the nineteenth century.[38]

William Lynch also exhibited a blend of American religious and national pride when, on the Sea of Galilee, he was able to lower the two boats carried there by his party. With the help of a group of Arabs, the boats were finally launched on the water and the Arabs cheered and shouted. But the Americans were silent:

> From Christian lips it would have sounded like profanation. A look upon that consecrated lake ever brought to remembrance the words, "Peace! be still!"—which not only repressed all noisy exhibition, but soothed for a time all worldly care.
>
> Buoyantly floated the two "Fannies," [the two boats brought by the American expedition from the States] bearing the stars and stripes, the noblest flag of freedom now waving in the world. Since the time of Josephus and the Romans, no vessel of any size has sailed upon this sea, and for many, many years, but a solitary keel has furrowed its surface.[39]

And when the American flag was flown atop Lynch's camp on his insistence, he remarked that "for the first time, perhaps, without the consular precincts, the American flag has been raised in Palestine. May it be the harbinger of regeneration to a now hapless people!"[40]

It became apparent that by virtue of this new experience, America was deemed more qualified for the task of spreading the light than any other nation, including the Christian nations of Europe. Americans enjoyed, in addition to their immense natural resources, a fortunate geographical location and an ever-increasing population, a freshness of outlook and innocence which distinguished them from the nations of the Old World. There were frequent comparisons of the American nation with European as well as Eastern countries. Europe was too steeped in her old ways, corrupt in morals, politics, and religion; her institutions were "to be suspected ... scrutinized, and brought to the test ... of the general principles of our institutions, and the habits and maxims, that arise of them."[41] But whereas Barlow was willing to put European institutions to the test, Dwight's rejection of these institutions and everything European was total and uncompromising. Set against the American "Hesperian climes" and the "happy isles, and garden'd realms" which "display Th'advancing splendours of prophetic day," Europe, and the rest of the world for that matter, presented a sorry spectacle indeed.

Europe's energy was spent and her innocence lost; America was pure and in the prime of youth. Europe's social and political institutions were despotic and old-fashioned; the American nation had devised a system which was to be a model for men everywhere. On the eve of the Revolution, an English immigrant (and a citizen of the world) announced the magnitude of America's undertaking and its effects on the future of mankind:

> The sun never shined on a cause of greater worth. 'Tis not the affair of a city, a county, a province, or a kingdom; but of a continent—of at least one-eighth part of the habitable globe. 'Tis not the concern of a day, a year or an age; posterity are virtually involved in the contest, and will be more or less affected even to the end of time by the proceedings now. ...
>
> Small islands not capable of protecting themselves are the proper objects for government to take under their care; but there is something absurd in supposing a continent to be perpetually governed by an island. In no instance hath nature made the satellite larger than its primary planet; and as England and America, with respect to each other, reverse the common order of nature, it is evident that they belong to different systems. England to Europe: America to itself.[42]

Joel Barlow voiced a similar sentiment when he stated that "on the western continent the scene was entirely different from that of the eastern continent where the foundations of empires were laid in ignorance." The new task, he said, was unknown to legislators of other nations, and "was imposed upon the fathers of the American Empire."[43] Dwight's eloquent burst of pride in America is magnified by the subsequent picture he presented of Europe:

> Profusely scatter's o'er these regions, lo!
> What scenes of grandeur, and of beauty, glow.
> It's noblest wonders here Creation spreads
> Hills, where skies rest, and Danubes pour cascades;
> Forests, that stretch from Cancer, to the Pole;
> Lakes, where seas lie, and rivers, where they roll;

> Landscapes, where Edens gild anew the ball,
> And plains, and meads, where suns arise, and fall.[44]

As for the Old World, Dwight said:

> Thrice wretched lands where, thousands slave to one,
> Sires know no child, beside the eldest son;
> And kings no pleasure, but from subjects' woe.[45]

In conclusion, Americans saw in their new nation a true hope for humanity, and recognized their responsibilities to the whole world in secular as well as in religious terms. This feeling was very instrumental in shaping America's attitude toward other nations.

4

The Great Seal of the United States of America

The National Seal of the United States of America—together with the American Constitution, the Declaration of Independence and the Bill of Rights—has occupied a prominent place in American official as well as public thinking. The National Seal is especially important for the present study because it is one of the earliest expressions of national pride and because of the symbols that it derives from the Judeo-Christian heritage. The Great Seal, as adopted by an Act of Congress on June 20, 1782, features on its two sides the following:

> That the Device for an Armorial Achievement and Reverse of the Great Seal of the United States in Congress assembled is as follows:
> **Arms**–On the breast of the American eagle is a shield with thirteen vertical white and red stripes beneath a blue chief. In the eagle's right talon is an olive branch, and in his left a bundle of thirteen arrows. In his beak is a scroll inscribed with the motto "E pluribus unum."
> **For the Crest**–Over the head of the eagle, a golden glory is breaking through a cloud, and surrounds a constellation of thirteen silver stars on a blue field.
> **Reverse**–In the zenith of an unfinished pyramid is an eye in a triangle surrounded with a golden glory. Over the eye are the words "Annuit Coeptis." On the base of the pyramid the numerical letters MDCCLXXVI, and underneath the motto "novus ordo seclorum."[1]

The official document on the Web which describes the Great Seal calls it "the fascinating story of America's most eloquent symbol and the heritage and hope it reflects."

The official document presenting the Great Seal states further:

> An essential founding document, the Great Seal was carefully created to represent the United States to the world and to the future. Consider it America's symbolic mission statement. Part roadmap, part time capsule, this remarkable message from the people who gave us our freedom is still the

best reflection of their vision for the nation they founded. When given the attention it deserves, the Great Seal of the United States can clarify our history and brighten our future.

These and many other statements by public and private individuals show the reverence with which the Great Seal is viewed. And what gives this Seal great significance is the fact that it was the first symbolic statement that the Federal Congress thought of—even before Independence—to carry the great principles and values which were the foundations of American cultural and political thought. Consequently, the story of the process and the design of the Great Seal and of the persons involved in it becomes very important here for a proper understanding of the Judeo-Christian factor in American culture. This process is an early example of the development of this factor not simply as a European heritage, but as a basic component of American thought.

While the Revolution was still in progress the Federal Congress wanted to devise a national seal which would reflect the ideals of the struggle for freedom and the values and principles which the new nation stood for. The Great Seal was a statement of principles announcing America's mission to the world. The following is a summary of this process.

On July 4, 1776, the Federal Congress appointed a committee to design and present to it a national seal. The Committee members were Thomas Jefferson, John Adams and Benjamin Franklin, two future presidents of the United States and one of the most prominent leaders of the nation. On August 3, the committee met and reviewed three proposals for the seal. Benjamin Franklin's proposed design, kept in his handwriting in the Department of States archives, reads as follows:

> Moses standing on the Shore, and extending his Hand over the Sea, thereby causing the same to overwhelm Pharaoh who is sitting in an open Chariot, a Crown on his Head and a Sword in his Hand. Rays from a Pillar of Fire in the Clouds reaching to Moses, to express that he acts by Command of the Deity.

Jefferson's suggested design also derives its symbolism from the same source. It reads: "Jefferson also suggested allegorical scenes. For the front of the seal: children of Israel in the wilderness, led by a cloud by day and a pillar of fire by night."

After some deliberation over the three suggestions, the committee submitted the following proposal:

> Pharaoh sitting in an open Chariot, a Crown on his head and a Sword in his hand passing through the divided Waters of the Red Sea in Pursuit of the Israelites: Rays from a Pillar of Fire in the Cloud, expressive of the divine Presence and Command, beaming on Moses who stands on the shore and extending his hand over the Sea causes it to overwhelm Pharaoh. Motto: Rebellion to Tyrants is Obedience to God.

The Congress subsequently formed two more committees for the same purpose, and, on June 20, 1782, the design suggested by the third committee was adopted as the official Seal of the United States. The Seal carries on side one the bald eagle with a constellation of 13 stars, randomly arranged, representing the states which formed the newly independent country.

The final design notwithstanding, it is quite significant that three members of the Continental Congress of the status of Adams, Jefferson and Franklin chose the story of the "flight from Egypt" as symbol of the birth of the nation. Nor was this symbol absent from the minds of the legislators when they adopted the final design of the Seal. Immediately after Independence one Congress member, Samuel Sherwood, gave an election campaign speech with the significant title *The Church's Flight into the Wilderness* where he quoted Exodus 19:4–6:

> Ye have seen what I did unto the Egyptians, and how I bare you on eagles' wings, and brought you unto myself. Now therefore, if ye will obey my voice indeed, and keep my covenant, then ye shall be a peculiar treasure unto me above all people: for all the earth is mine: And ye shall be unto me a kingdom of priests, and an holy nation. These are the words which thou shalt speak unto the children of Israel.

Following similar quotations from Exodus and Isaiah, Sherwood went on to explain the significance of the eagle in the National Seal: "God has, in this American quarter of the globe, provided for the woman and her seed ... leading them to the good land of Canaan, which he gave them for an everlasting inheritance."[2]

Another early statement with the same import was made by the religious leader David Austin who said in 1794: "If any should be disposed to ask what has become of the eagle, on whose wings the persecuted woman was borne in to the American wilderness, may it not be answered, that she hath taken her station upon the Civil Seal of the United States?"[3]

Another curious matter related to the Judeo-Christian tradition appeared later in the final version of the Seal. According to the 1782 decision by the Federal Congress, the 13 stars were scattered in a random constellation. However, on June 20, 1782 when Congress approved the final colors of the Seal, the stars appeared in the shape of the Star of David. The official statements by Congress and by contemporary sources do not provide an explanation for the change.

The Judeo-Christian tradition has remained until now a basic and constant part of the American cultural scene. The Founding Fathers, who insisted on the principle of separation of church and state, did not see any violation of this principle in their use of these religious stories and symbols for the most important national affairs.

5
The Vision of Zion: The American Myth
of the City on a Hill

> With sacred lore, this traveller beguiles
> His weary way, while o'er him Fancy smiles
> Whether he kneels in venerable groves,
> Or through the wide and green savanna roves,
> His heart leaps lightly on each breaze, that bears
> The faintest cadence of Idumea's airs.
>> John Pierpont, "Airs of Palestine," 1816

John Pierpont recounts in his long poem, "Airs of Palestine," a dreamlike epic journey in the style of classical poetry. But instead of looking to Parnassus or Olympus for inspiration, the poet invokes a different muse:

> No, no—a lonelier, lovelier path be mine:
> Greece and her charms I leave, for Palestine.
> …
> I love to walk on Jordan's banks of palm;
> I love to wet my foot in Hermon's dews;
> I love the promptings of Isaiah's muse:
> In Carmel's holy grots, I'll court repose,
> And deck my mossy couch, with Sharon's deathless rose.[1]

Pierpont's progress takes him on an imaginary pilgrimage to the Holy Land where he, "Religion's child," revels in the countless sacred associations, especially those connected with the woes of Zion. These verses, however, represent only one of the early American poetic attempts at articulating its first and most lasting myth: that of a vision of America as the city on a hill.[2]

THE PILGRIM FATHERS AND ZION HILL

Pierpont's poetic memory unfolds the nation's cultural "childhood"— one nourished by a vision of Zion in America. Dreamlike, and difficult to grasp at first, the vision remained nonetheless an aspiration which teased the imagination of its spokesmen. The pervasiveness of this myth is revealed in what R.W.B. Lewis calls "peculiar and distinctive dialogues."[3] Ralph Waldo Emerson, the spokesman for an America which should let go "the apron strings" of Europe, gives a lecture on the vices of slavery in which he invokes a biblical analogy of his nation as "a last effort of the Divine Providence in behalf of the human race."[4] This, however, should be placed in the context of the theme of America as "the Israel of our time" for a full understanding of its past and future implications. Herman Melville, the American novelist, and another prophet of American destiny, states the same theme in no ambiguous words. For him, just as Israel escaped the corrupt ways of the Egyptians and was given special dispensations, so

> we Americans are the peculiar, chosen people—the Israel of our time; we bear the ark of the liberties of the world. Seventy years ago we escaped from thrall; and, besides our first birthright—embracing one continent of earth—God has given to us, for a future inheritance, the broad domains of the political pagans, that shall yet come and lie down under the shade of our ark, without bloody hands being lifted. God has predestinated, mankind expects, great things from our race; and great things we feel in our souls. The rest of the nations must soon be in our rear. We are the pioneers of the world; the advance guard, sent on through the wilderness of untried things to break a new path in the New World that is ours.[5]

In this statement Melville recognizes America's attachment to its past and its future commitment, both seen in the framework of Scripture. In the idiom of the cultural discourse of Melville's generation terms such as "the peculiar, chosen people," the "first birthright," the "future inheritance," the "shade of our ark" were all too familiar, and they reached back to the source and origin of his nation's cultural heritage. Similarly, in the enthusiastic, optimistic language of the "great things we feel in our souls" and "the pioneers of the world," Melville gives utterance to the prospect of establishing the ideal state, which very often was the sociopolitical form of the Kingdom of God.

In a different medium of cultural discourse, but within the context of the same mythology, Pierpont's memory, "fancy's smile," takes him back and forth between the banks of the Ohio and those of the Jordan. The first river had been part of the poet's experience with geographical reality; the second he had inherited, along with the rest of his countrymen, as part of the national mythology. And this same poetic vision which sends Pierpont walking "on Jordan's banks of palm" had fired the Pilgrims' imagination to seek what Vernon Parrington so aptly describes as "the Canaan of their hopes";[6] it is also the same vision evoked by Timothy Dwight, Joel Barlow and their fellow Connecticut Wits for expressions of the heroic exploits of the "American Joshua's and David's." Still alluring in the nineteenth century, it sent thousands of Americans to the real "banks of Palm."

There were various expressions of this first American mythology to embrace Zion. What follows will be an attempt to reconstruct the pattern and development of the myth as it grew from a vision of America as a symbolic city on a hill, to a national commitment to rebuild the New Jerusalem, i.e., *the* City on a Hill. It will be seen that this externalizing of the myth was often a determining factor which influenced the attitude and behavior of Americans through the various stages of their national development.

As early as 1636, when John Cotton searched the pages of the Scriptures for a model constitution to be adopted by one of the new American commonwealths, he finally came up with what he described as a "Model of Moses his judicials." The process is related by a contemporary American historian:

It was then requested of Mr. Cotton that he would, from the laws wherewith God governed his ancient people, form an abstract of such as were of a moral and a lasting equity; which he performed as acceptably as judiciously. But inasmuch as very much of an Athenian democracy was in the mould of the government, by the royal charter ... Mr. Cotton effectually recommended it unto them that none should be electors, nor elected therein, except such as were visible subjects of our Lord Jesus Christ, personally confederated in our churches. In these, and many other ways, he propounded unto them an endeavour after a theocracy, as near as might be, to that which was the glory of Israel, the "peculiar people."[7]

Cotton, according to Mather, preferred the theocracy of God's "peculiar people" to "Athenian democracy," thus providing a precedent in political science for Pierpont and Dwight's rejection of the Parnassus Seven in favor of Isaiah's muse.[8]

Citizens of the New World considered themselves subjects of Jehovah, governed by principles of the Mosaic Law. And the Puritan immigrants to the New World had been prepared for this shift of emphasis in their everyday life by what Parrington describes as a "conscious discipline in ascetic Hebraism which was to change the Jacobean gentleman into a militant Puritan."[9] There are many examples of this process of change, but the one which stands out is the case of John Winthrop who, to use Parrington's words, "had gone to school to the English Bible, and the noble Hebrew poetry stirred the poetic imagination that was his Elizabethan birthright. Like so many of his fellow Puritans he delighted in the Book of Canticles."[10]

Winthrop, as well as his fellow immigrants, was aware of the special task placed in their hands and of the unique Providential relations they had with God. When Winthrop left his country of birth—the kingdom of Laud—for his adopted new home, the Kingdom of God, he bade a friend a pilgrim's farewell, saying with absolute faith:

> I know not how to leave you, yet since I must, I will put my beloved into his arms, who loves him best, and is a faithful keeper of all that is committed to him. Now, thou, the hope of Israel, and the sure help of all that come to thee, knit the hearts of thy servants to thyself in faith and purity.[11]

True to his Puritan heritage, Winthrop saw signs of God's approval of his decision, so he proceeded to sell his property and to prepare for the move to the land of promise. He also saw portents in what he considered God's hand in the plague which consumed the natives.[12] The chosen remnant in Israel knew what they were about to accomplish, and set about their task with conviction. God had provided them with a haven and it was their duty and privilege to respond to His election and move westwards to establish His kingdom. To create a Zion in the wilderness, an extraordinary faith and a firm belief in divine commission were needed. This faith was often expressed in statements like the one made by Winthrop, describing his understanding of God's commission:

> wee shall finde that the God of Israell is among us, when tenn of us shall be able to resist a thousand of our enemies, when hee shall make us a prayse and glory, that men shall say of succeeding plantacions: the Lord make it like that of New England: for wee must Consider that wee shall be as a City upon a Hill, the eies of all people are uppon us.[13]

In addition to his education in the school of the English Bible and in the "noble Hebrew poetry" of the Book of Canticles, Winthrop's imagination was fired by the tremendously gruelling experience he and his fellow immigrants had gone through in the process of removing to the New World. This personal experience lent a visual metaphor to their daily speech. Their everyday behavior was, according to Charles Feidelson, "neither a historical event nor an allegorical fancy but an experience that united the objectivity of history with the meaningfulness of Scripture."[14] They were in the habit of applying biblical metaphors with a sharpness which resulted from an unwavering belief in their assured place in the Scriptures among the prophets and sacred men of old. "The symbolization process," says Feidelson, "was constantly at work in their minds. For them, the word 'wilderness' inherently united the forty years of the ancient Hebrews with the trials of the New England forest."[15] For the Puritans, there was a kind of superimposition of the Scriptural story on their own experience. In their minds, as well as in the infinite mind of God, they believed the two were one and the same. The symbolic "wilderness" was invoked not only to represent the New England of the immigrants, but the Atlantic Ocean also presented the image of the wilderness of Sinai and the crossing of the Red Sea.

Well into the nineteenth century Americans were listening to political and religious sermons, reminding them of their Hebraic Scriptural identity. Within this visionary framework, Edward Johnson's advice to the Puritans to "pray continually with that valliant worthy Joshua that the Sun may stand still in Gibeon, and the Moone in the vally of Aijalon,"[16] thus fitting the timeless Scriptural metaphor into their daily existence. Within this framework also, election sermons throughout the seventeenth, eighteenth and nineteenth centuries were given the familiar titles: "The Way of Israel's Welfare" (John Whiting, Boston, 1688), "Moses and Aaron" (Thomas Buckingham, New London, 1729), and "The Prospect of the City of Jerusalem" (Isaac Stiles, New London, 1742).[17]

During the early period of the establishment of the settlements in America, the Puritan immigrants acted according to a firm assumption that they were the chosen few, the remnant in Israel who had defied the corrupt majority and sought refuge in the Canaan of their hopes. And, from the realm of spiritual geography, some visionaries among them sought to localize Scriptural places in their new home. Cotton Mather sincerely believed that Mexico City would be the New Jerusalem, the City on a Hill. This epic myth, as enacted in the daily lives of the American people, continued and became intensified in Revolutionary and Independent America.[18]

THE UNITED STATES AND THE KINGDOM OF GOD

When in 1771 Timothy Dwight thought of writing an epic to celebrate America's struggle for Independence, he modeled his poem on
Milton's *Paradise Lost*. The Book of Joshua supplied Dwight with the
bulk of the material for *The Conquest of Canaan*, where he treats the
War of Independence in the allegorical context of the wars between
the Israelites on the one hand and the peoples of Ai and Gibeon on
the other. The most dramatic part of the epic is the victory of the
Israelites led by Joshua—America's George Washington—over the
Canaanites. The opening of Book One sets the scene of the epic:

> The Chief, whose arm to Israel's chosen band
> Gave the fair empire of the promis'd land,
> Ordained by Heaven to hold the sacred sway,
> Demands my voice and animates the lay.
> … When now from western hills the sun was driven,
> And night expanding fill'd the bounds of heaven,
> O'er Israel's camp ten thousand fires appear'd
> And solemn cries from distant guards were heard,
> Her tribes, escap'd from Ai's unhappy plain,
> With shame and anguish mourn'd their heroes slain.[19]

A footnote to the first line of the epic explains that "wherever
Chief, Hero, Leader, etc., with a capital, respect the Israelitish army,
Joshua is intended."[20] Dwight dedicated *The Conquest of Canaan* "to
his Excellency, George Washington, Esquire, Commander in Chief
of the American Armies, The Saviour of his Country, the Supporter
of Freedom, And the Benefactor of Mankind."[21]

Even more significant is the letter which Dwight had sent earlier to
the American Revolutionary leader asking for permission to dedicate
the epic to him. The letter refers to the title of the intended epic as "The
Conquest of Canaan by Joshua." The character of Joshua as presented
in the "Argument" to Book One could easily be identified with that of
Washington, and especially relevant is the argument of Hanniel, who
attempts to prove the impossibility of fulfilling the Israelites' design to
return to the land of Canaan, "because of the strength, skill, and
numerous allies of their enemies." Hanniel informs the Israelites

that, if they should conquer Canaan, they will be ruined, during the war, by
the necessary neglect of arts and agriculture, difficulty of dividing the land,

of settling a form of government, and of avoiding tyranny; and concludes with a new exhortation to return to Egypt. Applause. Joshua replies, and beginning to explain the dispensations of providence, is interrupted by Hanniel, who first obliquely, and then openly accuses him of aiming at the usurpation of kingly authority; and asserts the return to be easy. Joshua vindicates his innocence with severity upon Hanniel; and allowing they can return, paints to them the miseries they will experience from the Egyptian king, lords, people, and manners, and from Providential dispensations terminating in their ruin.[22]

The biblical story of the Israelites and their journey to Palestine across the Sinai desert and the Red Sea was used by another poet of Dwight's generation, Joel Barlow. *The Vision of Columbus* (1787) is an epic which celebrates the history of the American nation from its very beginning to the end of time, seen by the great explorer in a vision through which the angel leads him. Book One of *The Vision of Columbus* describes the trip to the New World in a comparison with that of the Israelites to the Promised Land:

> As that great Seer, whose animating rod
> Taught Israel's sons the wonder-working God,
> Who led, thro' dreary wastes, the murmuring band
> To the fair confines of the promised land,
> Oppress'd with years, from Pisgah's beauteous height,
> O'er boundless regions cast the captured sight;
> The joys of unborn nations warm'd his breast,
> Repaid his toils and sooth'd his soul to rest ...[23]

Barlow's preoccupation with this vision of Zion was strong and deep-seated. In 1785 when the General Association of the Congregational Churches of Connecticut decided to undertake a revision of Dr. Watt's version of the *Book of Psalmody*, they entrusted the job of its revision to him. Barlow applied himself to the task with a good deal of enthusiasm, adding to his version the translation of some Psalms which had not been included by Dr. Watts. One of these additional Psalms, number 137, according to Barlow's biographer, Charles B. Todd, "has never been equalled, not even by Halleck, who attempted it in 1821."[24] Barlow's version clearly shows a personal involvement and feeling for the theme of the Psalm:

> The rivers on of Babilon
> There where we did sit down,

> Yea, even there we mourned when
> We remembered Sion.
> Our harp we did hang it amid
> Upon the willow tree,
> Because there them that us away
> Led in captivitee, etc.[25]

And the following is Barlow's version of the same:

> Along the banks where Babel's current flows
> Our captive bands in deep despondence strayed,
> While Zion's fall in sad remembrance rose,
> Her friends, her children, mingled with the dead.
> The tuneless harp that once with joy we strung,
> When praise employed, and mirth inspired the lay,
> In mournful silence on the willows hung,
> And growing grief prolonged the tedious day …[26]

The persistence of this vision in American thought appears in contradictory applications to completely different situations. One example is Timothy Dwight's identification of America not only as the chosen nation in his patriotic optimistic poems, but also in moments of pessimism and disillusionment—in his predictions of its apocalyptic death: "It is the day of the Lord's vengeance; the year of recompenses for the Controversies of Zion. The Earth is utterly broken down, the earth is clean dissolved; the earth is moved exceedingly."[27] The same vision informed both the hopeful and the hopeless situations. In the enthusiasm of the Revolution and Independence, Americans were compared to the chosen people fighting against the Egyptians and Canaanites. But when war against Britain was announced in 1812 and preparations for that battle were underway, David Osgood chided the war party from his church pulpit, quoting the Scriptures, "O children of Israel, fight ye not against the Lord God of your fathers; for ye shall not prosper."[28]

Finally, the situation of the American Indians presents another curious example of the progress of the vision of Zion in American history and thought. During the precarious establishment of the first few continental settlements, the Puritan immigrants (God's Chosen) saw in the Indians the enemies of Israel: they were analogous to the Egyptians and Canaanites, as we have seen in Chapter 2. During the nineteenth century, however, perhaps as a result of the intensity of millennial thinking, there was an inclination in some American circles to read into the history of the Indians of North America the story of the lost tribes of Israel. Serious scholarly investigations of this subject can be seen in *The Lost Tribes of Israel: Or the First of the Red Men* (Charles Evans? 1861) and *A View of the American Indians: Showing them to Be the Descendants of the Ten Tribes of Israel* (Israel Worsley, 1828).[29]

The argument must have been convincing enough for some of the Indians themselves to believe it; evidence exists in the following account. In 1818 Levi Parsons was appointed as a missionary and began preparing for his trip to the Holy Land. But, as a nineteenth-century historian of the missionary enterprise informs us, "Mr. Parsons had a strong desire to do something more, before leaving the country, for the spiritual interests of the people of Vermont." So Parsons performed the duties of a local missionary, until in September, 1818, the Prudential Committee of the American Board of Commissioners for Foreign Missions "thought proper to detain him awhile as an agent" to tour the State of New York. He proceeded to visit many towns and give sermons and talks on the missionary enterprise, thus

giving a fresh impulse to the missionary cause. One of the most interesting circumstances that occurred in connection with his mission, was his meeting with the Stockbridge Indians, then under the care of the missionary, John Sergeant. He preached to them when he was in a state of great weariness and exhaustion ... being inspired by the thought that possibly his audience might be the descendants of Abraham. When the sermon was over, the Indian chief, a fine, princely-looking fellow, delivered an address to Mr. Parsons, in the best style of Indian oratory. He thanked God that He had sent his servant among them, and had commissioned him to deliver to them "a great and important talk." He thanked the preacher also for his excellent counsels, and expressed the wish that they might answer the purpose for which they were designed. He then proceeded to read a "talk" in Indian and English, which he desired Mr. Parsons to deliver to "the Jews, their forefathers, in Jerusalem," ...[30]

During the first quarter of the nineteenth century, the timeless vision of America as the city on a hill was transferred to a definite geographical location of the Kingdom of God in the Holy Land of Scripture. There were many expressions, often very emotional, by pilgrims, tourists and missionaries bemoaning the present state of Palestine and longing for the day when the land would be peopled by its "rightful inheritors." Ellen Clare Miller looked at the vast area of the Levant in 1871 and said:

> Of these lands of the East are some of the most sublime words of prophecy written; and to the missionary there it may be given to advance even the literal fulfilment of the glorious promise made through the prophet Isaiah,— a promise spiritually fulfilled in peace, joy, and blessing, wherever souls are truly converted to God ...[31]

Miller then turned her thoughts to the promise "They Shall see eye to eye, when the Lord shall bring again Zion," and looked forward to its fulfillment:

> When the veil shall be uplifted
> From before all nations' eyes,
> When the light shall chase the darkness,
> And the lifeless bones arise;
> When each kindred, tongue, and people
> Shall go forth to seek the Lord,
> When they ask for the way to Zion,
> With their faces thitherward;[32]

Many reasons can be advanced to explain this shift of the American myth of God's Israel from the New World to the Holy Land. One important factor is that during the latter part of the eighteenth and the beginning of the nineteenth century, Americans were introduced to the Orient commercially, diplomatically and militarily, and in that process they rediscovered the Holy Land. During the same period the United States was experiencing a special religious fervor, as seen first in the Great Awakening and subsequent Revivalist movements. With this surge of religious interest came the two related phenomena of the missionary enterprise and the millennial tendency. Both of these latter movements were instrumental in exciting interest in the Holy Land and in creating a sense of urgency for the rebuilding of Jerusalem.

MILLENARIAN TENDENCIES AND AMERICAN INTEREST IN THE ORIENT

The concept of the millennium was present in American thinking all along, although the nineteenth century witnessed an intensification of its expectancy. Indeed, there are in American writings many references to the "signs of the times." One of these is relevant to the expectation of the Kingdom and came from the pen of Increase Mather. He said: "How often have we prayed that the Lord would divide, infatuate and frustrate the Councils of the Heathen that sought our Ruine. As sometimes David when pursued by Absalom prayed ..."[33]

Mather's editor recognized that the "end-of-the-world excitement" was not uncommon at the time. He explained that "for its Reproduction in that singular 'Corner of the World,' we can only account by Presumption that a millennial Excitement then prevailed there ... Hence it appears that 'End-of-the-world' Excitements are no new things, and are in a Manner periodical."[34] In fact, the signs-of-the-times excitement can be seen in the title of one of Mather's sermons: "A Sermon shewing, that the present Dispensation of Providence declare that wonderful Revolutions in the World are near at Hand; with an Appendix, shewing some Scripture Grounds to hope, that within a few Years, glorious Prophecies and Promises will be fulfilled" (1713).

Reading "special Providence" in current events continued to be a feature of American religious thought in the nineteenth century. "It is remarkable," Niebuhr said, "how under the influence of the Great Awakening the millennial expectation flourished in America."[35] The leading figure in the Great Awakening in America, Jonathan Edwards, said that

> is it unlikely that this work of God's Spirit, so extraordinary and wonderful, is the dawning, or at least a prelude of that glorious work of God, so often foretold in Scripture, which, in the progress and issue of it, shall renew the world of mankind ... We cannot reasonably think otherwise, than that the beginning of this great work of God must be near. And there are many things that make it probable that this work will begin in America.[36]

Edwards described the Great Awakening as "a great and wonderful event, a strange revolution, an unexpected surprising overturning of things, suddenly brought to pass." His observation of current events led him to conclude that this indeed was the time of redemption, "the great end of all the other works of God, and of which the work of creation was but a shadow." Edwards, together with his generation, was witnessing the real "work of creation which is infinitely more glorious than the old." He reached the important conclusion that "the New Jerusalem in this respect has begun to come down from heaven, and perhaps never were more of the prelibations of heaven's glory given upon earth."[37]

Clearly, the millennial tendency in this sense was peculiarly American, and millennial expectations are still at work at the beginning of the twenty-first century. A survey of the types of religious movements and denominations which flourished during the nineteenth century in America will show to what extent millennialism affected people's thinking. One such group was the Adventists, whom the contemporary *Hand-Book of All Religions* described as those who "regard the time and purpose of Christ's reappearance in the light of certain prophecies, which they interpret as predictions of his personal reign upon earth."[38]

A prominent religious leader was William Miller who was born in 1781 in Pittsfield, Massachusetts, and who started a millennial movement, announcing that the date of the Second Coming of Christ was to be the year 1843. His followers, known as the Millerites, grew into a sect of many thousands, and believed in the literal interpretation of the prophecy of the Second Kingdom. When the Rev. George Bush, the Prophet Muhammad's American biographer, edited Buck's *Theological Dictionary* for a revised American edition in 1854, he added an appendix on the "Advent Believers, or Adventists." He described this group as "a class of Christians connected with nearly all the evangelical denominations in the United States, who derive their name from the peculiar faith in the speedy coming of Jesus Christ, the second time, without sin unto salvation, to them that look for him."[39] Although Bush identified the religious beliefs of all Adventists with those of "the various sects with which they stand connected," he added that their peculiar principles were "originally propagated by Mr. William Miller of the Regular Baptist Church in Low Hampton, Washington Co., N. Y."[40]

The special contribution of most of these millennial sects to the American attitude to the Orient, and the Holy Land in particular, is the peculiar position they accorded to the Jewish people. According to the basic tenets of millennialism, the Jews were the foundations of this Second Kingdom, and their ingathering was a prerequisite for this great event. The *Hand-Book* described the principles which were held by most millenarians:

> By some writers the notion of Millennium is considered as nothing more than a retention in Christianity of the Judaic idea of an early kingdom, the eventual restoration of the Jerusalem that now is. The Jews hoped for a

temporal deliverer, and their hope centered itself in a temporal reign. The anticipation of an earthly reign involves to some extent a restoration of the Jews. Such anticipations, widened to include the Gentiles in the benefits, might be taken as the foundation of a certain class of Millennial expectations. Wherever the doctrine is confused with merely temporal ideas it may be regarded as unorthodox.[41]

Many of the leading clergymen of these sects felt that the time was ripe for the Coming of Christ but some, like William Miller, were more specific and set dates for the event. Miller came to the conclusion that the Second Coming would happen between March 21, 1843 and March 21, 1844.[42] Although that time passed without fulfillment of the prophecy in April 1844, his followers nonetheless remained

steadfast in their faith as to the correctness of their principles and mode of computing time, and their general dates for commencing the periods, but conclude there is some slight discrepancy in chronology. But are still in constant expectation of seeing their coming Lord ...[43]

In missionary literature, sermons, orations and reports there were constant references to the signs of the times and the millennium. The *Constitution of the American Bible Society* announced that "every person of observation has remarked that the times are pregnant with great events. The political world has undergone changes stupendous, unexpected, and calculated to inspire thoughtful men with the most boding anticipations." The Society realized especially that "an excitement, as extraordinary as it is powerful, has roused the nations to the importance of spreading the knowledge of the one living and true God, as revealed in his Son."[44] The *Constitution* concluded that there was no spectacle "which can be so illustrious ... as a nation pouring forth its devotion, its talent, and its treasures, for that Kingdom of the Savior, which is righteousness and peace."[45]

SIGNS OF THE TIMES AND THE MUSLIM WORLD

Many signs of the times were seen in current natural phenomena and in political international events—especially those which had to do with events in the Islamic World. The contemporary situation of the Ottoman Empire was often cited by millennialists as relevant to the Second Coming. Speaking of the approximate date of the great event in light of biblical prophecy, Bush said that

> the five months, and hour, day, month, and year, or 541 years and 15 days of Rev. ix., are believed to have commenced with the first entrance of Othman, the founder of the Ottoman empire, into Nicomedia, a Greek province, to commence his war, July 27th, 1299. And then the period ended Aug. 11th, 1840 the day the ultimatum of the allied powers of Europe was submitted to Mehemet Ali, and the fate of the empire was sealed.[46]

By far the most comprehensive view of the history of Islam and its current situation in light of biblical prophecy was that expressed by Henry Jessup, the influential, lifelong missionary who spent 53 years in the Arab World "spreading the light," and whose experience was recorded in his book *Fifty-Three Years in Syria (1850–1903).* Jessup's universal view of the world presented everything in the context of a preconceived plan which extends from the beginning of creation to the end of time—when the Church of Christ will rule the whole earth. All the "revolutions and convulsions[,] the wars and upturnings of the past 2,000 years," he said in an 1884 sermon, have "proved mighty auxiliaries to the advancing kingdom of our God."[47] Although there were those who were hesitant and skeptical of the value of missionary efforts, for Jessup "the triumphal chariot of His Kingly Majesty will move onward ... For the kingdom of God is a growth, an advance, a progress from lower to higher, from foundation to topstone, from seed to fruit, from type to antitype, from promise and prophecy to glorious fulfillment."[48]

The progressive nature of this advancing kingdom takes in all the events of history, including the entire progress of Islam. In fact, the rise and fall of Islam, to its final extinction, is an important factor in the fulfillment of the Divine plan. This thesis is obvious in the title of one of Jessup's "labours of love," *The Setting of the Crescent and the Rising of the Cross: or Kamil Abdul Massiah* (1898), and in a more detailed form in the entire treatment of *The Muhammadan Missionary Problem* (1879). According to Jessup, the hand of Providence can be seen in the concurrence of two momentous events which took place in the seventh century and which "were providentially related in the most intimate manner, as bearing upon the welfare of the race and the future development of Christ's kingdom in the world."[49] These two events are the rise of Islam and "the Christianization of the Saxon race in Britain."[50] Other events in the history of Islam also coincided with momentous events in the history of the Christian West. One such event is the overthrow of the Islamic army by Ferdinand in Granada in 1492, which led to the extinction or expulsion of the entire Muslem population of Andalusia. The year 1492, said Jessup, was "the very year in which Columbus discovered America, and thus opened a new field for the growth and development of that Christianized Anglo-Saxon race."[51]

In the more recent history of Islam there were events, wars, and revolutions which, though outwardly harmful to the Christian world, were considered to be designed by the hand of Providence to lead to the Coming of Christ's Kingdom. The Crimean War, for example, "which for a season convulsed the whole Turkish Empire, exciting latent Mohammedan fanaticism and threatening to roll backward the rising tide of light and liberty, resulted in guaranteeing protection and a civil autonomy to the evangelical communities in Turkey ... [and] gave England the right to insist upon" her prerogative to exercise that protection.[52] The sectarian strife in the whole of Syria, which also threatened the Christian communities there, resulted (according to Jessup) in more liberties and rights for these communities. The same thing happened as a result of the Bulgarian War of 1877 and, more important as an example of the working of the Providential plan toward the Kingdom of God is the Arabi Revolt in Egypt in 1882, when

> the wild spirit of Mohammedan bigotry broke out once more, and the streets of Alexandria ran with Christian blood ... The interposition of England, the defeat of Arabi, the check upon rising Moslem frenzy, and the shattering of the Pan Islamic league which had become a menace to progress and civilization in the East, all revealed again the working of that hand which makes no mistakes, and that wise and glorious Providence of God, which overrules all things for His own glory.[53]

There were other religious movements whose ideology stemmed from the central notion of the Second Coming. One of the most important is that of the Mormons, or the Church of Jesus Christ of Latter-Day Saints. Their main theology is the belief in "the literal ingathering of Israel, the restoration of the Ten Tribes, the personal reign of Christ on earth for a thousand years of Millennial glory, when the saints will reign with him and judge the Gentiles or unbelievers."[54] The notion of the Second Kingdom and of the rebuilding of Jerusalem was paramount, although in a different geographical perspective. The Mormons' final settlement in Salt Lake City came after years of hardship, and the building of the Mormon Temple was in preparation for the Advent of Christ and his Second Kingdom. The structure was so picturesque, according to a contemporary visitor, "especially when seen in the first glory of spring, that the stranger almost pardons the enthusiasm with which the inhabitants compare it to the New Jerusalem, as the seer of the Apocalypse beheld it."[55]

To the ranks of those movements we should add the Shakers, a sect which also believed in some kind of spiritual adventism. Although their concept of the "human tabernacle" was never clearly defined, they believed that the millennium was close at hand and that the believers had to prepare themselves to enter the heavenly Kingdom.

By the second half of the nineteenth century, the Adventist movements had become quite sizable in America—hundreds of books, sermons, articles and periodicals were written to advocate or refute the notion of the millennium.[56] According to George Bush, there were

> four or five millions of books and papers circulated during the last three years in the United States, British provinces, and foreign countries, wherever the English language is read. There have also been some of the writings translated into the French and German languages, and widely circulated. There are five weekly papers now published in the United States, devoted to the dissemination of this doctrine; and two in Canada.
>
> There are large congregations of Adventists in nearly all the Eastern, Northern, and Middle States.[57]

Whereas some of these movements believed in a literal interpretation of Scriptural prophecies regarding the Second Kingdom, some insisted on the figurative interpretation. Of the literalists, some considered the Holy Land—Zion Hill overlooking Jerusalem in particular—to be the geographical location of the Advent; others settled for American localities. In any case, the myth of America as God's Israel was given a more material vestige, and ultimately the spiritual metaphor of the city on a hill was transferred to a geographical location to be fulfilled in the Promised Land. The venture, however, was still to be an American one: many of the faithful persisted in the belief that they were partners in the Covenant and an important part of the Providential plan to rebuild the Kingdom of God. Americans were ready to help bring the great moment to fruition. So they looked to the "banks of Palm" and the Rose of Sharon as goals to be attained in reality.

THE MISSIONARIES AND THE REBUILDING OF JERUSALEM

In many religious quarters, especially in the missionary establishment, attempts were made to find in the American experience the fulfillment of prophecy regarding the rebuilding of Jerusalem. A sermon entitled "The Promised Land," delivered by Hyman Humphrey at Goshen, Connecticut, on September 29, 1819, tried to establish the analogy. Humphrey introduced the sermon with Joshua xiii, 1: "And there remaineth yet very much land to be possessed." The connection between "possessing the land" and the Biblical promise and prophecy was very clear to Humphrey, although his reference to the Promised Land was at first not presented literally. In fact, the church in his analogy becomes the nation of Israel. His opening statement reveals the obsession with the vision of Zion and the "conquest of Canaan," and shows the identity of the missionary establishment as the bearer of the responsibility:

> God, as the supreme Ruler and absolute Proprietor of the world, thought fit to give all the land of Canaan to Abraham and his posterity for an everlasting inheritance. This grant was again and again renewed and confirmed to Isaac and Jacob, as heirs of the promise. But they were not to take immediate possession. While the Canaanites were filling up the measure of their iniquities, the children of Israel sojourned and were oppressed in Egypt; and it was not till the time of Moses, that they were delivered from that terrible bondage ... upon the top of a mountain, which overlooked the fertile plain of Jordan, Moses yielded up at once his commission and his life—not, however, till he had, by divine authority, invested Joshua with the supreme command ...

The chronicler continues to tell the story of Joshua, his bravery, his dedication to the conquest of Canaan, and his determination to claim the "promised heritage." With age upon him, Joshua, by dividing the remaining land by lots, still called upon his people to drive out "the heathen." Humphrey's sermon concludes that there is still much land to be claimed and

> that immense regions of the earth, which belong to the church, are still unsubdued;
> that the ultimate conquest and possession of all these is certain;
> that, although the excellency of the power is of God, this great work is to be accomplished by human instrumentality;
> that but for lamentable and criminal apathy of the church, it might have been accomplished ages ago;
> that as Christendom now possesses ample resources and ability, she is solemnly bound in the name of God, and with the least possible delay to set up her banners in every heathen land. And,

that the aspects of Divine Providence are peculiarly auspicious to the missionary enterprizes of the day.[58]

Humphrey reminded his congregation of the urgency of the divine mission of the American church, saying that the mount on which the church stands, overlooks the whole Land of Promise.[59] The figure of the church on a mountain overlooking the Land of Promise wavers between a literal reference to the Holy Land of biblical promise and a general allusion to the tremendous task of evangelizing the whole world. The figure becomes more potent with Humphrey's use of scriptural idiom, in which the church takes on the metaphysical aspect of Zion Hill, addressing its members:

> surely the Isles shall wait for me, and the ships of Tarshish, first to bring thy sons from far, their silver and their gold with them, unto the name of the Lord thy God, and to the Holy One of Israel, because he hath glorified thee.[60]

Thousands, said Humphrey, were answering the call of the church and were coming to the aid of the Lord, proclaiming with one voice: "For Zion's sake we will not hold our peace, and for Jerusalem's sake we will not rest."[61]

Missionary quarters resounded with the trumpet call urging believers to go forth and bring the heathens and Muslims to the light of the Gospel, with the realization of Zion as the ultimate goal. Many of the missionaries were aware of this sacred duty and some advocated the priority of the rebuilding of Jerusalem and the restoration of the Jews. One prominent missionary, J.T. Barclay, said that

> the American Christian Missionary Society (under whose auspices the mission to Jerusalem is conducted), in entering upon the prosecution of the missionary enterprise, resolved—as wisely as unanimously—in imitation of apostolic example, to make the offer of salvation to Israel, that noble race from whom it came—for salvation is of the Jews.[62]

Barclay based this priority for the missionary efforts on the Messiah's address to a Syro-Phoenician heathen when he said "I am not sent but unto the lost sheep of the house of Israel." According to Barclay, Christ gazed at the great city and exclaimed: "O Jerusalem! Jerusalem! how often would I have gathered thy children together, as a hen doth gather her brood!" Christ's instructions to the twelve

Apostles were to "go—not into the way of the Gentiles—but rather to the lost sheep of the house of Israel." The missionaries who were commissioned by Christ were charged especially "to witness for him first in Judea, 'beginning at Jerusalem.'" The acts of the Apostles, said Barclay, prove that they showed special preference for the Jews, and the Apostle Paul, in particular, stated that his "heart's desire and prayer to God [are] for Israel."

Thus Barclay recognized that the first concern for the American Christian society was "to plant its first mission in Jerusalem, mainly in reference to the Jews—not unmindful, however, that Jerusalem possesses various other claims upon our consideration as a field of missionary operations."[63] The first few missionaries and missionary leaders in America were aware of that responsibility. Samuel Worcester, for example, prefaced his "Two Discourses" which he presented in connection with missionary activities with these lines:

O ye seed of Israel his servant, ye children of Jacob his chosen ones;

Be ye mindful always of his Covenant, the word which he commanded to a thousand generations;

Even the Covenant which he made with Abraham, and of his oath unto Isaac;

And hath confirmed the same to Jacob for a law, and to Israel for an everlasting Covenant.

That the Gentiles should be fellow heirs, and of the same body, and partakers of his promise in Christ by the Gospel.

Paul[64]

The combination of the "everlasting Covenant" given to the "chosen ones," and Paul's statement that "the Gentiles should be fellow heirs," reveals the place which American religious leaders felt that Christians had in the Promise, and the responsibility they held to bring about its fulfillment. References in missionary quarters to the exact geographical location of the Promised Land were quite clear from the beginning, unlike the spiritual metaphors of America as "God's Israel." As early as 1819, the active missionary evangelist and theologian Moses Stuart[65] gave a sermon at the ordination of some missionaries who were on their way to the Levant: "Shall the happy days of Christian triumph no more return to bless the earth; to animate the exertions, and exalt the hopes of those who love Zion?" Stuart ended his sermon on a more literal reference: he exhorted the prospective missionaries to go to the midst of Jerusalem to plant, once again, the standard of the Cross.[66]

The missionaries were not to labor alone in the cause of Zion. As a result of the factors already described, there also developed a popular zeal among American Evangelists and moderate Christians to prepare for the Coming Kingdom in the Promised Land. There are many examples of Americans who left the United States to establish settlements in Palestine—where the great event was expected to take place. A new surge of activities took place in search of the literal fulfillment of prophecy. Numerous references were made by travelers to colonies in the Levant which were established in the Holy Land in expectation of the coming of the Messiah.[67] One such reference is the humorous account by Robert Barr of his encounter with some "colonists" towards the end of the nineteenth century. Barr met with a Mr. Rollo Floyd in the Holy Land, and the latter undertook to guide him through the sacred places. Floyd's interesting career, said Barr, "is a striking example of the genius of this great people." The American nation, to which Floyd belonged, was the most inventive of all nations, "having cut itself loose from the traditions of the old world."[68] Americans are credited by Barr with many new scientific and technical inventions, but,

> when the inventive brain of America disdains anything so material as machinery, it turns naturally toward the constructing of religions. I suppose there are more religions invented in America in a year than exist in all other parts of the world put together ... While the broad East is content with one or two religions, the broad West numbers hers by hundreds. Thus we have Mormonism, Spiritualism, Shakerism, and dozens of other isms.[69]

Rollo Floyd, whom Barr met in Palestine, was there because "in his youth he fell a victim to one of the numerous ephemeral religious inventions." The sect to which he belonged started "in cold and stormy Maine, of all places in the world." They believed "that Christ was about to return to the Holy Land, and it was necessary for those who wished to be saved to be there to meet their Redeemer. This was thirty or forty years ago, and enough devotees were got together to equip for themselves and their families a sailing ship."[70] The arrangements for their removal to Palestine were made by the American Consul, who, according to Barr, was a Jew. The pilgrims' hopes were disappointed, and many of them had to be taken back to the United States by arrangements made by Secretary Seward, not before augmenting the Consul's "thrifty bank account."[71]

An account of a similar nature is that given by Annie DeWitt Shaw of Baltimore, Maryland, who visited the Holy Land with "Uncle Will" about the year 1897. On arriving in Jerusalem, Annie recited the scriptural description of the city: "Beautiful for situation, the joy of the whole earth, is Mount Zion, on the sides of the north, the City of the Great King."[72] The next morning the party's dragoman took them on a tour of the city, starting with "a house which is the residence of a community that is awaiting the fulfillment of the prophecies as to the restoration of Jerusalem."[73] The community was called "the American Colony," although it included some other nationalities. Shaw, with childlike innocence, said "I had not the least idea of what they were staying in Jerusalem for; and when they said to me that several of their brethren had gone to Chicago, I innocently asked if they were going to form a community of the same kind there. Uncle Will thought that was something to laugh at."[74]

Not all travelers in the Holy Land, however, looked with humor or innocence at these American colonies. The general attitude was that of veneration for the devotion and self-denial showed by the colonists. The author of *The City of the Great King*, for example, commented that "the unpretending but efficient colony of Americans, first organized under the zealous advocacy of the late Mrs. Minor, has by no means proved an aberration as is sometimes asserted, ..."[75] As for the colonists themselves, there is no better expression of their zeal and self-denial than that of a young American woman, Lydia Schuler, who offered in a series of letters to the *Gospel Visitor* a good example of the sentiments of Adventists waiting for the Messiah in the Holy Land.

In simple, almost unlettered language, but with absolute belief in the literal fulfillment of prophecy, Schuler wrote to her "Dear brother in Christ" on May 10, 1854, from the "Plains of Sharon" explaining the reasons for her removal to Palestine:

> You express a desire to know what has provoked me to forsake my father, mother, brother, sisters and friends and come to this land.—When I felt my sins heavy upon me and no one could take them away but he whose blood was spilt here in this land, he said, come unto me, I will comfort thee; and indeed I found him precious to my soul. I then laid myself and all that was near and dear to me on the altar and prayed that I might only do the Lord's will and be useful in his vineyard.[76]

She went on to relate how she became inspired by the Scriptures and convinced that the duty of the Gentiles was to restore Israel to the "Lord of the Bible." Through her acquaintance with a Philadelphia nonsectarian group, she made her way to the Holy Land to address what she called "the suffering of the Jews."

Five years later, Schuler, still persistent in her quest for the Kingdom of God, revealed an even stronger belief in the approaching millennium. In July, 1859, she summed up in one letter the conditions which prevailed in the Holy Land seen through the eyes of prophecy. The most important condition to be fulfilled in order to bring about the Coming Kingdom was the restoration of the Jews to Palestine. Schuler said:

> The Jews' wailing place was to me the most interesting place in Jerusalem. My dragoman, an East Indian Jew, of Moorish skin, who, by the way, is an English subject, and speaks English well, conducted me thither. We threaded our way through the usual narrow and dirty lanes, misnamed streets, of Eastern cities, and came to an area in the form of a quadrangle, near the bridge where the dwellers in Zion were once wont to pas over, to worship God in the Temple on His holy mount, Moriah. In the ancient foundation wall of the Temple are several courses of large, leveled stones, upon which the Jews lavish their kisses and embraces and through the crevices of which they pour up their prayers to God for the restoration of His Temple, and their early coming triumph in Jerusalem.[77]

Her graphic prose describes her newfound brotherhood with the Jews who brought their prayers to this place that had been defiled by the Muslems, but which would some day be regained as their rightful inheritance.

By the 1850s the transfer of the vision of Zion to the new geographical location in the Holy Land was complete. The second half of the nineteenth century was a period of consolidation of that vision. The number and nature of accounts written by American travelers to the Holy Land are evidence of the process.[78] For example, the "Publishers Announcement" to Barclay's *The City of the Great King* stated that the book "is presented to the public, believing that much will be found in it of great interest and value to all classes of the religious world, and to those who would see the hand of Providence in the history and fortunes of Israel, and the nations with whom they have been associated, for more than three thousand years."[79]

Representatives of the religious world were interested in Israel and the untiring efforts of travelers in the Levant who followed the footsteps of the Tribes of Israel from Egypt to Palestine; these diverse men and women felt compelled to explore that route for themselves. One of these was Samuel Colcord Bartlet, a prominent clergyman and President of Dartmouth College, who first did a good deal of research on the route of the Israelites, then made that trip himself. The result was a work whose title bespeaks his mission: *From Egypt to Palestine, Through Sinai, the Wilderness and the South Country: Observations of a Journey Made with Special Reference to the History of the Israelites* (1879).

Another person who followed the footsteps of Moses to the land of Canaan was Margaret Bottome, a zealous believer, who described her trip in a series of all-but-mystic letters.[80] There was also Beverly Carradine, whose *Journey to Palestine* (1891) reveals the fervor with which a Southern clergyman colored his personal account of his trip from Egypt through Sinai to the Promised Land.

American travelers in the Holy Land heard an irresistible call to trace the path of the Israelites. These pilgrims and travelers identified their past experiences with that of the Hebrews in crossing the wilderness in search of the Promised Land. One distinguished traveler, Stephen Olin, who called himself an enlightened Christian, and looked with scorn on the "superstitious rites of the Christian crowds in Jerusalem" during the pilgrimage season, had nothing but praise for Leider, who worked diligently "in the discharge of his duties, to visit several places very interesting from their connection with sacred history." Olin described these efforts with zeal and admiration. He traced Leider's peregrinations in imitation of the route of the Israelites in order to check the historical journeyings which led to the point where they miraculously crossed the Red Sea, and to confirm what he called "the sacred geography."[81]

THE PLACE OF THE JEWS IN THE VISION OF ZION

Schuler's sentiments toward the Jewish people and their association with the Holy Land were shared by many of her compatriots. These sentiments were an integral part of the Western Judeo-Christian heritage, and in this sense they became characteristic of American religious thinking. Gradually, during the nineteenth century, the Jewish people were injected into the American myth of the vision of Zion whereby Americans began to recognize a central position occupied by the true "chosen people" of Scripture in the Second Kingdom, although still clinging to what they perceived to be their own sacred commission to bring about that Kingdom. There was a noticeable change in the role to be played by America; from "God's Little Israel," America became the instrument in the realization of prophecies and in the fulfillment of promises. Perhaps coming in contact with the Holy Land was responsible for the relocation of the Kingdom of God from the New World to Zion Hill, and consequently it brought to the forefront another people who were supposed to be beneficiaries of the promise.

Contemporary opinion on this matter varied from one extreme to the other. For example, the American edition of Buck's *Theological Dictionary* mildly stated under the subtitle, "Jews, restoration of," that "from the declaration of Scripture we have reason to suppose the Jews shall be called to a participation of the blessings of the Gospel, Rom. xi; 2 Cor. iii.16; Hos. i.11, and some suppose shall return to their own land, Hos. iii.5; Is. 1xv.17, etc.; Ezek. xxxvi."[82]

The time of the return, said the *Theological Dictionary*, is not certain: "some think about 1866 or 2016; but this, perhaps, is not so easy to determine altogether, though it is probable it will not be before the fall of Antichrist and the Ottoman empire."[83] A similar, though more forceful, view was expressed in the *Hand-Book to All Religions* which saw the "Lands of Judea" in light of "the promise to the Jews," and the prophecies which were expected to be fulfilled. The *Hand-Book* realized that the worst obstacle to be overcome was that "the stronghold of Zion" was under the domination of "Turks and Mohammedans."[84]

There were some organizations, and many activities, in both America and England, urging the conversion of the Jews as a step towards their restoration. In fact, one of the earliest American missionary ventures was that of the Boston Female Society for the Promotion of Christianity among the Jews. This society sent Josiah Brewer to the Holy Land to investigate the condition of the Jewish people there and the method to be followed for their conversion to Christianity.[85]

The conversion of the Jews, however, was not always insisted upon. Some of these organizations started using the term "amelioration and reformation of the conditions of the Jewish people," and more efforts were directed to the restoration process. The *Theological Dictionary*, for example, advised that Christians should

> avoid putting stumbling-blocks in their [the Jews'] way. If we attempt any thing for their conversion, let it be with peace and love. Let us, says one,

propose Christianity to them, as Christ proposed it to them. Let us lay before them their own prophecies ... Let us never abridge their civil liberty, nor ever try to force their consciences.[86]

In the Holy Land, the predominant American attitude toward the Jewish people was that of sympathy for their plight and dispersion, and a genuine commitment to the cause of Israel. Schuler's opinions were not those of the extreme Adventists only. An Episcopal minister, Charles Andrews, wrote the editors of the *Episcopalian Recorder* from Jerusalem on February 25, 1842, remarking on "the extreme sparseness of the population" in the whole region of the Holy Land. The only occupants he saw were "a few miserable Arabs with their flocks ... [in] a rich, extensive and beautiful country." The scene evoked in Andrews a long cultural tradition of religious education. "Where," he asked,

were the many thousands of Simeon and Dan to whom this faithful region was assigned! Alas not one of their descendents is here to be found. Prophecy is fulfilled. The country "without inhabitants" sits solitary. But is it not so kept by providence, waiting for its own people? They are indeed long absent.[87]

Andrews' statement was part of the continuing cultural dialogue of the myth of Zion. When writing a historical account of the development of Palestinian explorations, Frederick Bliss said that the history of "the Hebrew conquests" and the

establishment of the Jewish kingdom, its subsequent division, the growing influence of Asyria, the scattering of the tribes in Exile, the return of the Jews to their native land ... these points must be at the tip of the tongue of every Sunday-school scholar.[88]

It is not surprising, therefore, that one of the standard activities of American travelers and missionaries in the Holy Land was a visit to the Wailing Wall and to the Jewish quarter in Jerusalem; the persistence and strength of this cultural tradition can be seen in their chronicles. In 1896 Lee S. Smith was on a pilgrimage from Egypt to Palestine, and when he arrived in the Land of Canaan he "proceeded 'to do' Jerusalem in true American style."[89] His party first visited the Church of the Holy Sepulchre. But he could not for a moment believe that this was the site of the Crucifixion and Resurrection of the Savior. Yet, he said,

> remembering that it has been so considered throughout hundreds of years, and that millions have visited and worshiped there because of that belief; and that the blood of hundreds of thousands had been spilt in fighting for its possession—recollecting all this, we entered it with a feeling of reverence.[90]

Smith was happy to say that the possessors of the church were "Latin and Greek Catholics, and Armenians ... no Protestants, not only because of the necessity of a band of [Turkish] soldiers to preserve the peace, but because of the mummery and the foolery surrounding the place."[91] The party then proceeded to the "Tower of David, the Jewish Wailing Place, and to David's and Solomon's tombs on the crest of Mount Zion." Smith's reaction to these sites sums up the traditional sacred associations of the Judaic history of the Holy Land:

> What emotions filled our breasts as we stood on Mount Zion, and looked upon the group of buildings known as the tombs of David and Solomon—the sweet singer of Israel, and the wise man who so basely abused his God-given wisdom. In this group of buildings is shown a large upper room in which it is claimed that the Last Supper was eaten. As to this there may be doubts, but as to the tombs of those two mighty kings of Israel being somewhere under these buildings, I think there can be no doubt; but unfortunately, the Turk rules here also, and permits no Christians to do more than enter the buildings.[92]

American encounters with members of the Jewish religion on the sacred soil of the Holy Land during the nineteenth century evoked certain emotions which resulted from that same Hebraic tradition which Bliss talked about. They were especially strong and sympathetic emotions because of the transfer of the original American myth of Zion to the Promised Land of Scripture. Thus Lydia Schuler's sympathetic comments on the Jews at the Wailing Wall[93] were matched by many other accounts of American travelers. The Hebrews occupied a special position in the Western Christian tradition, and travelers to the Levant saw them face to face, not as they had seen and dealt with the Jewish people in their own country. One of those American travelers was Barclay who, in Jerusalem, reflected on the situation of the Jews and their special value, saying: "That the Hebrew race is the noblest that has ever adorned the annals of humanity, will not be questioned even by the proud Anglo-Saxons themselves." But in addition to their racial superiority, Barclay saw their value in other respects. For, he said, there could be no doubt that, "if converted—speaking as they do, all the languages of earth, habituated to all customs, and acclimated to every region— they would make the best missionaries on the face of the globe."[94]

A great deal of this adulatory attitude toward the Jewish people, however, was not utilitarian in nature, but resulted from the religious educational tradition in America. One of the people described by Bliss as "every Sunday-school scholar," Marion Harland, devoted two long chapters in her account of travel to the Levant to the condition of the Jews, identifying that same religious education as the source of her feelings. In the chapter entitled "Thine Ancient People the Jews," Harland said

> under this name I heard them prayed for every day throughout my infancy and girlhood. The phraseology in which the patriarch of the household remembered them at the family altar varied little in all those years: "We pray Thee to have mercy upon Thine ancient people the Jews, and bring them into Thine Everlasting Kingdom, together with the fullness of the Gentiles. May they look upon Him whom they have pierced, and acknowledge Him as King of kings and Lord of Lords."[95]

Harland said this prayer "over to herself" on a murky afternoon as she walked through the Jewish Quarter, not mindful of the "corrugated soles" of her shoes, as she slipped and slid "upon the greasy mud of the Jewish quarter in the City of David." She was guided by a Mr. David Jamal (who had been in the service of the Church Missionary Society for 20 years) to the residence of the Chief Rabbi of Jerusalem and then to the house of a lesser Rabbi. Both interviews were, each in its own way, enriching to the spiritual well-being of the American lady and had a salutary effect on her belief in biblical prophecy. Here is a summary of the visits as related by Harland.

Harland exchanges a few ceremonious preliminary remarks and then enters into what she calls "catechizing" with the learned Hebrew. She asks "If he attaches any significance to the influx in late years of the Jews from other lands into Palestine. Also if he can give me an approximate idea of the number who have thus immigrated within ten years." To which the Rabbi answers in a matter-of-fact manner: "If you would know how many have come in the past sixty years, I should answer that there were but one thousand Jews in Jerusalem and the vicinity in 1833. There are thirty thousand now." Harland tries to elicit from the Chief Rabbi an answer which would confirm her understanding of the prophecy. She asks whether they are all drawn by the same motive. He answers, unimpassioned, "The Jews come to Palestine because they love it as the land of their fathers and their country. Some have come expecting the Messiah. They are foolish. When He comes, He will rule the whole earth, not merely this little corner of the globe."

As for the signs that will usher in the Messiah's personal advent, the Rabbi can only suggest that the political horizon is dark and may mean much. But no man can tell. And, anyway, the advent will be prefaced with "the Great Fight of Armageddon ... Gog and Magog will appear and be overthrown. There will be a terrible bloody conflict of all nations in the Valley of Decision." The Messiah's first appearance, says the Rabbi, will be upon "Mount Safed, the highest point of Galilee, so say the holy writings." The American lady recalls in an aside that Safed is indeed called the "city set upon a hill." Perhaps the learned man is right, although, she says, "we are told by Zechariah that when 'the Lord shall go forth and fight against those nations as when he fought in the day of battle, His feet shall stand upon the Mount of Olives which is before Jerusalem on the east.' "

The dispute gets a little more heated when Harland suggests that some of America's most learned Rabbis did not actually expect a personal Messiah. "They believe," she tells the Chief Rabbi of Jerusalem, "that the prophecies relative to His comming point to the perfectibility of human nature; to an advanced state of morality and subjugation of whatever is base and vicious in man's nature and conduct; to the cessation of war and crime ..."[96] This statement ruffles the dignified Rabbi's complexion for the first time, and he retorts in a nervous, loud voice: "No devout Jew believes such a monstrous thing! The men who assert it are infidels—materialists. The Messiah will be a real personage, great, holy, powerful, perfect, and He shall reign in the Mount Zion, forever and ever."[97]

Harland then is taken to visit another religious leader of the Jewish community. He is a man after her own heart. Says Harland, "far from eluding such queries as I have put to his superior in office and worldly gear, he talks enthusiastically of his belief that the Kingdom of the Messiah is near at hand." His explanation of the prophecy of the battle of Armageddon is interesting to his American visitor. He says that

> Gog and Magog are, I am inclined to think, Russia. All nations will be engaged in the Valley of Jehoshaphat. The right will conquer, the God of Israel

fighting for it. A congress of nations will be held and decide to restore Palestine to the Jews, who will thence forward possess and cause the waste places to break forth into singing, the desert to bloom as the rose.[98]

Harland, coaxing her host into more predictions, comments that "there is not room in Palestine—or in all Syria, for that matter—for one-half of the Jews now alive upon the earth." The Rabbi "smiled benignantly and with the calmness of his convictions" answers his guest, basing his conviction on the prophecy:

> You forget that they have never yet had all the Promised Land—"from the river of Egypt, the Nile, unto the great river, the river Euphrates." The promise is "ordered in all things and sure." The whole world will then be at peace; nations shall learn war no more. All will worship one only and true GOD, the GOD of Israel.

Putting out her hand "impulsively" and shaking his hand, the American pilgrim says to the Rabbi: "You are a Protestant!" Obliquely, he answers, "We serve the same Lord."[99]

THE CITY OF THE GREAT KING

During the first half of the nineteenth century, Adventists in the United States of America felt sure of the approaching millennium and called on their fellow countrymen and all Christians to be ready for it. Signs of the times, as we have seen, were unmistakable, and confirmed their expectations. Americans who went to the Holy Land had committed to memory a great number of prophecies and scriptural statements on the future of the Holy Land. They saw in the current state of affairs a confirmation of these signs of the Coming Kingdom, and they pondered with awe and anxiety what was to become of the declining Ottoman Empire.

The most articulate expression of the vision of rebuilding Jerusalem is that voiced by the American doctor and missionary, J.T. Barclay, in 1858. His book *The City of the Great King: Jerusalem As It Was, As It Is, and As It Is To Be* explores with apparent scientific accuracy the geographical and historical realities of the "promise" and prophecies. Barclay, and many of his fellow Americans, recited at the site of the literal Kingdom the prophecies of Isaiah that "the Lord shall arise upon thee, and his glory shall be seen upon thee; and the Gentiles shall come to thy light, and kings to the brightness of thy rising" (ix, 1, 3); and "then the moon shall be confounded and the sun ashamed, when the Lord of Hosts shall reign in Mount Zion, and in Jerusalem, and before his ancients gloriously" (xxiv, 23).[100] Recited by Barclay on Mount Zion, this clearly was no longer a dream of Mexico City or Salt Lake City as the New Jerusalem. It is, as Barclay and others thought, "Jerusalem as it is to be."

The City of the Great King, although not as well-known as the works of Robinson, Thomson and Lynch, expressed the beliefs and aspirations of many religious Americans of the time. Its painstaking, seemingly scientific exploration of the sacred sites, the conviction which informed its description of the present state of affairs in the whole area, and the certainty with which it predicted the future, mark the total transformation of a national myth into a vision of the immediate future.

The sacred sites of the Coming Kingdom evoked expressions of ecstasy and fulfillment from pilgrims to the Holy Land. Such is the beautiful apostrophe which flowed from the pen of Barclay, the medical doctor working for the cause of Zion:

> Jerusalem! "Name ever dear!" What hallowed memories and entrancing recollections spring at the mere mention of that name! There is music and magic in the very thought! Jerusalem, the joy of the whole earth! The city of the Great King! Zion, the city of solemnities—an eternal excellency! The hill which God desireth to dwell in; yea, will dwell in it for ever!: The theater of the most memorable and stupendous events that have ever occurred in the annals of the world. Jerusalem! the world-attracting magnet of the devout pilgrim of every age, and the stern warrior of every clime; not the least of whom were the chivalrous Crusaders of our noble ancestry! a spot at once the focus and the radiating point of the strongest emotions of three powerful religions! …
>
> What are the recollections associated with the monuments and antiquities of Memphis, Babylon, Nineveh, Athens, Rome, London, or the cities of the Azteks, compared with those that cluster around the City of the Great King! … where the son of Jesse tuned his soul-stirring harp, and penned his Psalms for the saints of all ages; where Solomon reared a house for the Lord of Hosts to dwell between the Cherubim; where the Son of God suffered and died, and rose again—whence he ascended on high, and whither he will come again on the clouds of heaven in like manner as he went up … and "Jehovah of Hosts shall reign in Mount Zion and in Jerusalem, and before his ancients gloriously," sitting upon his throne in the sublime metropolis (then brought near)—the New Jerusalem above. Then shall the Holy City truly become "the joy of the whole earth!"

> "Glorious things of thee are spoken,
> Zion, city of God!"[101]

Similar feelings were often stirred by the sight of the sacred city despite its deteriorating condition and the abuses of its various churches. In an "attempt to discriminate between truth and error with regard to the sacred places of the Holy City,"[102] George Jones, a chaplain in the US Navy, showed great excitement at the first view of Jerusalem,[103] and when visiting the Temple, he lost himself in a reverie of vision and biblical longing. Jones recalled that "the Lord is in his Holy Temple, let all the earth keep silence before Him." The Temple represented, said Jones, a "gorgeous edifice," which was "raised to such a stupendous height, wrapped in a splendor that the eye can scarcely look upon."[104] His imagination united with religious emotion as he visualized in the depth of the great Temple "a spot of mysterious darkness and solitude" where one felt "the presence of Jehovah." "This Temple," he wrote

> belongs not to Jerusalem, but to the whole world. And He, the Diety, whose very name is awful, and should be used with reverence, hath blessed this spot with his peculiar presence; and it is meet that man should look upon it with deep and solemn feeling.[105]

The scene evoked Jones' memory of the Psalms of David, no doubt part of his early religious training. "How amiable," Jones repeated, "are thy tabernacles, O Lord of Hosts."[106]

It was not only in the City of the Great King that such emotions were evoked in pilgrims and travelers. Every step on the way from Egypt or Syria to the Holy Land was a reminder of a Patriarch or a Scriptural prophecy. Even traveling down the Nile from Luxor to Cairo was a thrilling religious experience for Charles Andrews, Episcopal minister from Virginia. "My dear wife," he wrote home, "I can scarcely believe my own eyes when I see myself upon the sacred river."[107] And a fellow countrywoman, Sarah Haight, wrote of the view which she had of Cairo from the vicinity of the Citadel which overlooks the city. Her remarks on the view are significant for the perspective which the viewer had:

> From this elevated terrace we had a magnificent view. Beneath our feet lay the whole city, sufficiently distant to prevent its disagreeable details from fending the eye. The domes and minarets of all the mosques were seen at

one glance. Beyond the city, towards the west, were the river and the green valley, bounded by the hills of the Libyan desert, on the edge of which rise the mighty Pyramids. To the north was the Land of Goshen, and the solitary obelisk of Heliopolis is all that now remains of On, that once proud city of priests, where Moses became "learned in all the wisdom of the Egyptians." ... To the east lies the road taken by the Children of Israel at the time of the Exode.[108]

With such a realization of Scriptural analogy and prophecy, Barclay did not find it surprising "that the result of Protestant missionary effort has not been more cheering." However, he took consolation in the obvious fact that "Moslem opposition, it is confidently believed, is now at an end—indeed, the impression is almost universal among themselves that the days of Islamism are numbered—at least for the present."[109] Barclay cited the Muslem's peculiar views of destiny which "can but prove as certainly paralyzing under the waning moon, as they were irresistibly stimulating under its crescent. It is now far too late in the day for Muslem prestige to avail, as in days of yore!"[110]

From 1843, according to Barclay, the governance of Christians in Jerusalem was in the hands of the consuls of foreign powers, especially those of France, Prussia, and Sardinia. Spain and the United States established official consulates in the 1850s and "as far as his own subjects are concerned, a Consul is virtually 'King of Jerusalem,' and plays the despot with perfect impunity."[111] Describing the results of these developments, Barclay concluded that

> as far as Moslem rule is concerned in its exercise towards Christians, Jerusalem is no longer trodden down of the Gentiles. Nor can the least doubt be entertained as to the early enfranchisement and complete enlargement of the Jews. A better day has already dawned upon Zion.[112]

A fellow countryman of Dr. Barclay, J.V.C. Smith, who wrote *A Pilgrimage to Palestine*, and who crossed paths with the doctor in Jerusalem, reached the same Scriptural conclusion based on the moral conditions of the Muslems in the Levant. Smith saw no hope of reforming and converting Muslems because "Christianity offers nothing acceptable to the depraved conquerors of Syria."[113] Smith also noticed the analogy with Scriptural history, remarking that

> the Canaanites were crushed on account of their idolatries, and the cities of the plain destroyed by the fire from heaven for the very abominations

now as common here and notorious as possible; and it is certain, that till the present inhabitants are rooted out of the land, and a new race of men introduced in their stead, the gospel will only be precious with a few, who can have little influence in changing the manners and customs of the whole.[114]

Both Smith and Barclay displayed a remarkable compatibility of political and religious thinking.[115] Both of them sought the rebuilding of Zion and both saw the hand of Providence in the social and political events which were taking place. Furthermore, in common with many other Westerners, Americans not excluded, both saw the prospect for re-establishing Zion as the principal outcome of these events. At the core of the Eastern Question lay the fulfillment of Scriptural prophecies concerning the future of the Land of Promise. Each saw in the power politics of the Western nations clear indications that these nations all agreed, or at least should agree, on the priority of establishing a Jewish commonwealth in the Holy Land. J.V.C. Smith discounted the possibility of individual efforts, and called for collective action by the governments of the Western powers. He said, in part:

> As frequently expressed in the course of preceding observations on the future destiny of the Land of Promise, I fully believe in the final restoration of the Jews, and the re-establishment of the nation. That greatest of all events to the reflecting Christian, who sees the hand of God in the eventful history of the descendants of Abraham, must be brought about by the concurrence and guarantee of all the Christian powers of the earth, who will thus be instrumentalities in fulfilling the intentions of Divine Providence.[116]

Barclay, in turn, quoted the "very just remarks" made by a Dr. Durbin in describing the situation in the Holy Land and the efforts of the foreign consulates to establish a Hebrew diocese in Jerusalem. The statement which Barclay favored is of special significance for the paramount theme of the fulfillment of prophecy within the context of political developments:

> But the prospective political bearing of this Hebrew diocese is perhaps a matter of much greater interest than its immediate religious results. It is doubtless intimately connected with the restoration of the Jewish commonwealth in Palestine, chiefly under the auspices of England and Prussia. It is not to be affirmed that these governments instituted this measure with the sole, or even chief intent to accomplish this great prophetic event; yet

without doubt they looked to the state of the Jewish and Christian mind, which these prophecies have produced with regard to the restoration, as a material, perhaps an essential element in their success. That the measure is considered by the five great powers as having an important political bearing, is evident from the fact that, since the organization of the diocese, France, Russia, and Austria have sent their consuls to Jerusalem, where there is neither trade nor commerce to be encouraged or protected ...[117]

An earlier account of the political situation in the Holy Land was one by Sarah Haight, the "lady of New York." Haight also saw a unique chance for the Western powers, especially England and France, to intervene and divide the area among them. The ambitious policy of Muhammad Ali in Egypt was a reminder of older days. "A faint parallel" appeared to her "between the ancient Pharaoh and the one who now sways the sceptre of Misraim." Muhammad Ali, "like his prototype," had an insatiable thirst for conquest of other countries, and he had already

subjugated all Ethiopia, Libya, and part of Arabia, and has lately overrun Palestine and Syria. This last conquest was to satisfy his rapacious desire for plunder; and though the treasurers of Tyre and Sidon no longer excite the cupidity of the invader, and the gold of the temple of the Lord has long since disappeared, yet the "golden fleece of Serica" yields a rich and tempting crop ...[118]

She went on to warn that the day would come when he will bring about his premeditated plan to conquer the whole Islamic World.

These reflections reminded Mrs. Haight of some "remarks" written by her husband, Richard Haight, in correspondence with a friend back home "on the present affairs and future prospects of the East." The extensive excerpts quoted by Mrs. Haight from her husband's remarks show political insight and prophetic wisdom. Richard Haight was a member of the fledgeling American Oriental Society[119] and must have also had some official position, judging from the warm reception accorded him by the American consuls in Alexandria and Cairo. This, and the fact that he wrote his reflections on the state of affairs in the East before the end of the first half of the nineteenth century, give them added significance. Haight said that Russia had an eye on India, and was capable "at any moment she pleased [to] seize upon the key of the Euxine gates, and close them against the combined efforts of all the West, and hold them, too, in spite of all the navies in existence."[120] On another front, Haight warned that

unless some more decided measures be soon taken by England and France conjointly, Russia would have obtained so firm a foothold in Persia and Kurdistan, that the Punjab would offer but a faint resistance to her arms and wiles. Then the Euphrates and Indus would be as free for her myriads as they were for those of Timurlane and Genghis Khan.[121]

Haight credited Russia with inciting the Greek rebellion against Ottoman rule "to execute her purpose against the Turk." But when the Greek seemed to be gaining the upper hand, Russia gave secret aid to the Turk, "inciting him to use the most cruel measures in the barbarous warfare, until the people of Christendom ... compelled their governments to combine for the rescue of fallen Greece from her cruel oppressor." Thus the Ottomans were weakened and sank deeper in the arms of Russia for protection. Haight added:

Russia had accomplished her purpose; she had prostrated Turkey, and there-fore made a merit of magnanimously sparing a fallen foe. The seeds of discord have taken too deep root in the great empire of Islam for all the diplomacy of the West ever to eradicate them; and all its members are too much disjointed for England to succeed in reconstructing a powerful empire on the ruins of the one she (so foolishly for herself) assisted in overturning.[122]

All of this, said Haight, went on while the nations of Europe were playing a useless game of diplomacy. What surprised him was that England did not, "seize upon Turkey in Europe, and portion off the remainder of the empire to satisfy the cupidity of the other nations."[123] But Haight's plan was not based on political considera-tions only and on the power struggle among Western countries. Here and there the proposal revealed the influence of the vision of Zion and the biblical prophecy. In Europe, said Haight, the Turk was a "usurper" anyway, "and there would be no crime in unseating him by any of the powers." And as for the rest of the Ottoman Empire, "the same may be said of him who ruffianly lords it over the land from the Nile to the Euphrates."[124] Haight did not neglect to propose a solution for the population of this area. "From Constantinople to Cairo," he suggested, "the Turks ... should be politely escorted across the Euphrates, and there permitted to recon-struct an empire on the former territory of the califs, making old

Baghdad's walls once more resound with the glories of Haroun al Raschid."[125]

Haight's analysis of the situation in the East rested both upon his assessment of the political power struggle over the possessions of the Ottoman Empire and on his American Western heritage of the vision of Zion as translated into a geo-political reality. Haight told his correspondent that if he could not "erect empires in Asia," he could "at least build chateaux en Espagne."[126] He then launched on his dream: "I will now carve up the East," he said, "and give to each hungry expectant such a share of it as I think would be most conducive of his own good; after which I will settle the future constitution of Asia as I understand it."[127] England and France, according to Haight, should be the first beneficiaries "of the Eastern banquet which has been so long waiting their pleasure."[128] The proposed division as drawn by Haight gives

> to France all the southern coast of the Mediterranean, from Morocco to the borders of Egypt, with the privilege of making conquests as far into the interior of Africa as she might choose, always excepting the Atlantic coasts. Egypt should be England's, with the right to carry her arms to the Cape of Good Hope. Syria should go to France, as far as the Euphrates on the East and the Taurus on the north. Asia Minor to England, with the right to march to Bucharia if she saw fit.[129]

This accomplished, the Muslim population of these territories should be "politely escorted" across the Euphrates to establish their Caliphate in Baghdad. And once these preliminaries were "settled in secret conclave," Haight, in a chilling foreshadowing of the secret Sikes-Picault Treaty, would have England occupy Persia, Bucharia, Bengal and the Punjab, "thus surrounding the new calif, and preventing him from communicating with the Muslims of Hendustan."[130]

Haight's vision of the future was obviously a yearning for the fulfillment of the literal prophecy of the New Jerusalem—an East where

> Throughout all the Holy Land the sacred monuments are surrounded by thousands of pilgrims from the farthest west; and the pious female devotee returning to her home, nourishes her roses of Sharon with the water of Jordan. The descendant of Ishmael now visits in peace the bazars of Cairo and Damascus, and his hand is no longer against every man, nor every man's hand against him.[131]

Richard Haight's design for the Orient, especially the Holy Land, was unique in that it came so early in the American rediscovery of that part of the world. But it was certainly not an isolated dream. It fits in with Smith's scheme of rooting out the local population and planting in its place a superior race of men, with Schuller's personal participation in the preparation for the Coming Kingdom, with Barclay's City of the Great King as the core of the solution to the Eastern Question, and with scores of other schemes and dreams by Americans who did or did not visit the Holy Land. Some of these persons were practical and some were idealists, but both types had a clear conviction of the possibility, and ultimately in the inevitability, of the realization of their dreams.

William Lynch, navigator of the Dead Sea and the River Jordan, was one of the practical men of action. He came back from his expedition with a detailed official report which he submitted to the Secretary of the Navy, and with an equally detailed narrative of the journey. The latter was printed and reprinted many times. In addition, Lynch led a group of people who advocated the dispatch of excavation and exploration teams to the Levant with an ultimate scheme for the fulfillment of scriptural prophecies—especially those of Isaiah—of populating the desert, restoring the Jews to Zion Hill and making the area a thoroughfare for East–West commerce. As part of this campaign Lynch gave a lecture entitled "Commerce and the Holy Land" which was endorsed by a number of missionaries and prominent Americans.[132]

Barclay's "Millennial Jerusalem," on the other hand, is the pure Scriptural vision of Zion, which was nonetheless based on a practical awareness of the political and social conditions in the area. He looked at some current phenomena and events and saw them as containing preliminaries to the ultimate event. Such a phenomenon is "the Russo–Turkish war—that most anomalous of wars—the significant issue and results of which will tell mightily upon earth's destiny, and invest the Jews and their capital and country with unspeakable interest."[133] Other signs were just as significant, although some of them were in the nature of internal policy and everyday occurrences. Otherwise, he asked,

What mean the various lines of steamers now traversing the length and breadth of the Mediterranean and Red Seas—placing Palestine in such direct, constant, and intimate communication not only with other parts of Asia, but with Europe, Africa, America, and the Isles of the Gentiles?

> What the railways now projected between Jaffa and the Persian Gulf, via Neapolis, with which a branch from Egypt is to unite—passing through Jerusalem, a "highway" from Egypt into Assyria? (S. xix.23.) And what the electric telegraph at the Holy City—the great central metropolis!—to say nothing of the stupendous scheme of converting the great depressed basin of Arabia Deserta into an inland ocean by letting in the waters of the Red Sea![134]

Barclay's vision of the future of the Holy Land agrees totally with the literal interpretation of Scriptural prophecies and promises. To begin with, "the city of cities" will cover more than a hundred square miles and will have millions of inhabitants. There will be railways from Al-Arish, Askalon, and Ghaza. The city will be on the track route between East and West, no doubt the Great Highway to Egypt of Scriptures. To this City of the Great King—the joy of the whole earth—"supremacy is assigned in the coming age by Him who is Governor among the nations—the King of Kings and Lord of Lords."[135] Furthermore, from Zechariah (xiv.8), Barclay learned that "at the coming of the Lord two most copious perennial streams of water shall burst forth from Jerusalem—, one going forth towards the Mediterranean or 'hinder sea,' and the other towards the 'former' or Dead Sea—developed apparently by the great earthquake."[136] An earthquake may have in the past opened the great valley near Jerusalem, and this, said Barclay, may be ready to become the future river-bed. The author, then concluded that although there was no positive information on the size of the river,

> if it be as large as that emptying into the Dead Sea, it may be rendered very serviceable not only for the irrigation of a large district of country, but for internal boat navigation. If it be true that the desert of Arabia was once an inland sea or lake, and is still depressed below the level of the sea, may it not be re-filled either from the sea or by this river? It will be recollected that while Jerusalem is 3927 feet above the Dead Sea, its elevation above the Mediterranean is only 2610 feet; and that Jehovah Shammah will be much more depressed.[137]

Should these two rivers gush forth into the Mediterranean and the Dead Sea, what wondrous prospects of progress awaited this region! One of them, running into the Dead Sea "would produce a succession of rapids, cascades, and cataracts unequalled in all the world …

What inconceivable power for the propulsion of machinery! What teeming luxuriance must crown the banks of this fertilizing and vivifying stream …!"[138] The barren desert would bloom, and then indeed "the wilderness and the solitary place be glad, and the desert rejoice and blossom as the rose!" The Psalmist's "vision," according to Barclay, had predicted all of this in speaking of the gladdening waters of the river "the streams thereof shall make glad the city of God, the Holy Place of the tabernacles of the Most High (Ps.xlvi.4.)."[139] As for the river issuing to the West, Barclay did not find positive information that it would have the greatness of the eastern river, but he considered it a "legitimate inference," that it would be similarly endowed. If on the banks of this river

> the Highway of Holiness shall lead from Yehoval Shammah to the Holy City and Temple, through the desert of Tekoah, thus really become "an house of prayer for all nations," what a paradisaical avenue would conduct the millennarian pilgrim up to the House of the Lord! Thus shall "the ransomed of the Lord return, and come to Zion with songs and everlasting joy upon their heads!"[140]

The temporal blessings of this millennial age will be great: Satan will be bound, the Lord's presence will be felt, the waters of the Dead Sea will be healed, its evaporation will be restricted, and there will be considerable geological changes. Truly, concluded Barclay, as he envisioned this millennial age, "how glowingly is the prosperity of the land and nation of Israel set forth by the prophets, when Judah and Israel shall have been restored and brought in complete subjection to their prince, David—the Beloved—i.e. the Prince Messiah (Is.1x, etc.)."[141]

These, however, are only a few of the glorious events of the millennium. The last few pages of Barclay's *City of the Great King* present a picture of the ideal state over which the Messiah will rule upon his second coming:

> There is no aspect in which the Millennial age can be regarded, that is not richly suggestive of the most pleasing and profitable themes of contemplation. Satan being bound, and man brought into complete subjection to Jesus Emmanuel, the whole creation, which had hitherto groaned in travail on account of man's sin, is vocal with praise—"the times of the restitution of

all things" having now arrived! Who, that has a heart to feel, can refrain from praying and laboring for "a consummation so devoutly to be wished!"[142]

Barclay's is the ideal religious picture of the realization of the vision of Zion, as interpreted literally from Scriptural passages, and applied with total conviction to future developments in the lands of the Bible.

6
Zion and the African-American Experience

It is singularly ironic that as the Puritan immigrants compared their journey from England to the New World with that of the Israelites from Egypt to Canaan, the Africans enslaved in America sought solace in the same biblical symbolism. The slaves, who were abducted and forcefully removed to a life of exile from their home to bondage in a strange land, found some hope of freedom that could only be provided by the "Promised Land" of the Scriptures.

The slave community formed its own biblical discourse of freedom out of their white masters' religious imagery of "home," the "Land of Promise," the "land across Jordan" and the "mountain." This is the region of spiritual geography sought by Africans in America when they realized that they were destined for a life of bondage with no hope of "returning home." It was sought by slaves as they tried, and often failed, to run away to freedom. It was also the symbolic goal of the struggle for emancipation and equality with white Americans.

In a certain sense, this was a process of finding solace and, at the same time, exacting some kind of revenge; solace and comfort in the "Promise" which the God of all humanity made to those who receive Christ as their Redeemer, and a secret sense of revenge in the equality that this faith forced on both blacks and whites, slaves and masters. Thus in this spiritual refuge, this Promised Land, there was to be freedom from slavery and oppression and ultimately, perhaps more probably in death, equality with the oppressors. In fairly recent times, the passionate cry by Martin Luther King, Jr., "I have reached the mountain top. I see the Promised Land" is reminiscent of the subject at hand and it still echoes in the circles of freedom-loving people. Yet this is a far cry from the screams of anguish and pain which issued forth from earlier generations of African-Americans; those who struggled and suffered through a life of slavery and cruel discrimination and those who fought for the abolition of this ugly institution.

THE INSTITUTION OF SLAVERY

It has puzzled many students of American history that the nation which has always prided itself on its principles of human rights and equality, whose Constitution begins by celebrating man's "inalienable rights," and which has historically judged others on the basis of their human rights record, should have tolerated and sustained the institution of slavery for almost three centuries. Perhaps Dr. Samuel Johnson's brief rhetorical question sums up the riddle: "How is it that we hear the loudest *yelps* for liberty among the drivers of negroes?"[1]

Undoubtedly, most whites in America—especially the liberals among them—faced a painful dilemma when dealing with the problem of slavery. There were many brave men who raised the banner of emancipation at a rather early stage. To take one notable example from the world of literature, there was John Greenleaf Whittier who lashed out not only at the institution of slavery but also against those who proposed worse solutions for the problem. In his essay, "Man's Property in Man" Whittier said: "We have found that this evil has preyed upon the very vitals of the union." He derided those who claimed that slaves had their *sympathy*: "Can such hollow sympathy reach the broken of heart, and does the blessing of those who are ready to perish answer it?"[2] With about 2 million human beings held in bondage, and with 1 million helpless slave women unprotected from sexual assault by whites, Whittier concluded that slavery was actually protected by constitutional concepts, by a standing army, and by the militia of the free states.

Nor did those who made suspicious proposals to solve the slavery problem escape censure. The American Colonization Society in particular had rather transparent goals of ridding America of Negroes by sending them off to Africa; in today's language, a systematic plan of ethnic cleansing or transfer. Of course the scheme did not work as well as hoped, but that did not prevent many from modeling other plans on it. John O'Sullivan, the author and advocate of America's "Manifest Destiny," supported his call for annexation of more territories with the argument that the regions of Central and South America would be a perfect "receptacle of slaves when we are ready to slough it off" and to ultimately rid ourselves of the race.[3]

There was no dearth of people who joined the fray, but those who stood out were men of the cloth on both sides of the argument. Supporters of slavery used as their argument the example of the Old Testament Jewish patriarchs who themselves held slaves and the fact that Noah had cursed the ancestor of the Negro race, Canaan.

But there were those who argued for the superiority of the white race, or, like Jefferson, were afraid of the Negro's "mental backwardness and shifty habits."[4]

More baffling is the attitude of the majority of patriotic Americans who sincerely believed that their new experiment was even more glorious than the democracy of Greece, and that all nations of the world should strive to emulate it. One wonders if they were really oblivious to the plight of the slaves, or even to their existence. One obvious example of the enthusiasm over the new experiment is Longfellow's "The Republic" in which he took pride in the American "Ship of State:"

> Thou, too, sail on, O Ship of State!
> Sail on, O Union, strong and great!
> Humanity with all its fears,
> With all the hopes of future years,
> Is hanging breathless on thy fate![5]

THE SLAVES AND THE PROMISE

Against this background we can now turn to the experience of the slaves themselves and at the way they resorted to the concept of the Promised Land and its accompanying ideas in their daily lives. And the first question one asks is: Was this concept something they brought with them from Africa, or was it part of their newly adopted religion? Naturally, a very cursory look at the origins and the very early days of slavery in America will reveal that this concept is a basic element of the faith of the slaves' white masters. It will also reveal another ugly aspect of the institution of slavery, which is the conscious effort by whites to completely obliterate any trace of the slaves' African cultures which they may have retained after their removal to the New World. The dominant white community gave the slaves new names—usually those of their owners—they did their best to separate family members by selling them off to different owners, and they prevented slaves from practicing their own religious rituals or traditions.

The situation is described very effectively by Richard Barksdale and Kenneth Kinnamon in their edition of *Black Writers of America*. "Slavery," they say,

> had the negative effect of divesting Africans of a substantial portion of their own culture ... It is clear that whatever literature survived the traumatic

experiences of enslavement, the middle passage on crowded slave ships, and the brutal oppression and forced labor in America was oral in nature, not written.

They continue:

Not only did the agents of slavery attempt, often quite systematically, to obliterate the sense of culture and personality out of which literature usually grows, but slavery by its very nature as an economic institution largely denied the Blacks the opportunity and the occasion to create written literature.[6]

It is this factor, the loss of their cultural identity, coupled with their forced total submission to the white community, which rendered them wide open to influences of the superior culture surrounding them, including its religion.

It was only natural that the Christian concepts that appealed most to the slave community were those associated with salvation through Christ, and the symbolic journey to some haven safe from suffering and pain. This process was strengthened by the religious enthusiasm of the nineteenth century and the rise of numerous churches which placed the concept of the Apocalypse and Jeremiad at the center of their ideology. Gabriel, the hero of James Baldwin's *Go Tell It on the Mountain*, provides an excellent example of this process. His conversion recalls the most basic ideas in the popular religious tradition, those associated with the religious songs, "Swing Low, Sweet Chariot," "Go Tell It On the Mountain," and "Let My People Go," in addition to using the theme of the Israelites in their flight from Pharaoh's Egypt as an analogy to his people's bondage.

This, of course, did not mean a complete understanding of white culture. Rather, as M. Kammen put it, "Under slavery, African forms of social organization, family life, religion, language, and even art were transformed, leaving the slave neither an African still nor fully an American, but rather a man suspended between two cultures, unable to participate fully in either."[7]

The slave community, perhaps subconsciously, was cumulatively selective in adopting certain concepts of the white masters' faith and subsequently adapting these concepts to its purposes and situation. The cultural implications of Martin Luther King's "I have reached the mountain top. I see the Promised Land" and of James Baldwin's *Go Tell It on the Mountain* can best be understood in the context of these developments. The metaphors of the "mountain," the "river," the "ocean," the "promise," the "rock," and others are all part of the complex paradigm of the Jeremiad that so appealed to African-Americans as analogous to their own experience.

This African-American experience is a unique case of an oppressed community which was able to transform a place of bondage into a symbolic Land of Promise. The enslaved Africans gradually and incrementally adopted their captors' faith and turned it into a cure for their life of misery. The cure, the solace provided by ultimate salvation and the hope of a Promised Land, has been present in African-American religious rituals, writings and oral tradition throughout their existence in America. James Baldwin and Martin Luther King are only two modern representatives of those who used these metaphors to protest against the white oppressors.

The story, however, has a twisted beginning. For the first three Black literate voices in America, Phillis Wheatley, Jupiter Hammon and Alouda Equiano, rather surprisingly, found in their experiences of being captured, removed forcibly from the land of their birth and being held as slaves a way to salvation. And yet this may not be so surprising, after all. That experience, they were taught in the context of their masters' religion, was what brought them to "see the Light of the Gospel" and that of civilized society, thus making them deserving of the saving Grace of Christ. In this faith they too found their promised land. The following verses by Equiano illustrate this point:

> Strivings and wrestling seemed in vain;
> Nothing I did could ease my pain:
> Then gave I up my work and will,
> Confess'd and owned my doom was hell!
>
> Like some poor pris'ner at the bar,
> Conscious of guilt, of sin and fear,
> Arraign'd, and self-condemned, I stood—
> "Lost in the world and in my blood!"
>
> Yet here, 'midst blackest clouds confin'd,
> A beam from Christ, the day star shin'd:
> Surely, thought I, if Jesus please,
> He can at once sign my release.
>
> I, ignorant of his righteousness,
> Set up my labors in its place;
> "Forgot for what his blood was shed,
> And pray'd and fasted in its stead."

When sacrifices, works, and pray'r,
Prov'd vain, and ineffectual were—
"Lo, then I come!" the Saviour cried,
And bleeding, bow'd his head, and died!

He died for all who ever saw
No help in them, nor by the law:
I this have seen: and gladly own
"Salvation is by Christ alone!"[8]

Wheatley, in her turn, not only expressed gratitude to captivity and slavery, but used the same imagery used by whites and taken directly from the biblical story of the Israelites:

While an intrinsic ardor prompts to write,
The muses promise to assist my pen;
'Twas not long since I left my native shore
The land of errors, and Egyptian gloom:
Father of mercy, 'twas thy gracious hand
Brought me in safety from those dark abodes.[9]

In fact, Wheatley's attitude was not only that of a sincere acceptance of the white folks' religion, but also a total repudiation of the old ways of Africa, with the obvious layers of meanings of the biblical "Egyptian darkness." The loss of cultural identity and the adoption of the newfound faith became complete for her only when she acknowledged the errors of her old faith and proposed to atone for the collective sin of the whole continent of Africa:

'Twas mercy brought me from my pagan land,
Taught my benighted soul to understand
That there's a God, that there's a Saviour too:
Once I redemption neither sought nor knew.

Some view our sable face with scornful eye,
"Their colour is a diabolic die."
Remember, *Christians, Negroes*, black as *Cain*,
May be refin'd, and join th' angelic train.[10]

Thus, as a result of this drastic cultural transformation, these early writers believed that atonement was not to be only for the individual's past sins; there was need of redemption for the soul of Africa which was steeped in darkness and ignorance. The fruits of redemption were realized for them in this land of promise, in Samaria, as a former fellow-slave, Jupiter Hammon, told Phillis Wheatley in these verses:

> Oh, come, you pious youth! Adore
> The wisdom of thy God,
> In bringing thee from distant shore,
> To learn His holy word,
>
> Thou hast left the heathen shore;
> Through mercy of the Lord,
> Among the heathen live no more;
> Come magnify thy God.
>
> Come, dear Phillis, be advised
> To drink Samaria's flood;
> There nothing that shall suffice
> But Christ's redeeming blood.[11]

This total acceptance of Christianity notwithstanding, there was another aspect of the slaves' adoption of their oppressors' faith. This is the logical use of that faith as an argument against the inhuman treatment meted out to them by the very Christian community whose religion they had adopted. An early example of this aspect is this incident related by Equiano in his autobiography:

> One Mr. D— told me that he had sold 41,000 Negroes, and that he once cut off a Negro man's leg for running away. I asked him if the man had died in the operation, how he, as a Christian, could answer for the horrid act before God? And he told me, answering was a thing of another world, what he thought and did were policy.[12]

This argument has become a constant practice in African-American struggle against injustice. In the mid-twentieth century, for example, Martin Luther King went a step further by proposing that ultimately the Negro would provide salvation for white Americans. He said:

> This is a great hour for the Negro. The challenge is here. To become the instruments of a great idea is a privilege that history gives only occasionally. Arnold Toynbee says in *A Study of History* that it may be the Negro who will give the new spiritual dynamic to Western civilization that it so desperately needs to survive. I hope this is possible. The spiritual power that the Negro

can radiate to the world comes from love, understanding, good will, and nonviolence. It may even be possible for the Negro, through adherence to nonviolence, so to challenge the nations of the world that they will seriously seek an alternative to war and destruction. In a day when Sput-niks and Explorers dash through outer space and guided ballistic missles are carving highways of death through the stratosphere, nobody can win a war. Today the choice is no longer between violence and nonviolence. It is either non-violence or nonexistence. The Negro may be God's appeal to this age—an age drifting rapidly to its doom. The eternal appeal takes the form of a warning: "All who take the sword will perish by the sword."[13]

Just as potent are the verses by the African-American poetess Gwendolyn Brooks in which she condemned all kinds of cruelty—including Israeli practices—of man towards fellow man, all in the context of Christ's walk to Calvary:

> I recollect the latter lease and lash
> And labor that defiled the bone, that thinned
> My blood and blood-line. All my climate my
> Foster designers designed and disciplined.
>
> But my detention and my massive strain,
> And my distortion and my Calvary
> I grind into a little light lorgnette
> Most sly: to read man's inhumanity.
> And I remark my Matter is not all.
> Man's chopped in China, in India indented.
> From Israel what's Arab is resented.
> Europe candies custody and war.
>
> Behind my exposé
> I formalize my pity: "I shall cite,
> Star, and esteem all that which is of woman,
> Human and hardly human."
> Democracy and Christianity
> Recommence with me.[14]

NEGRO SONGS AND SPIRITUALS

Preoccupation with the dream of a Promised Land where misery and pain end and a safe haven is found has been a permanent feature in African-American songs and spirituals and other forms of written and oral tradition. Undoubtedly, the use of spirituals and songs had psychological and social therapeutic benefits. In spite of adversities, the African-American community in general remained close-knit, helped mainly by the church and religious activities. Whether on the cotton fields, at social events or at church activities, African-Americans chanted songs and danced to their tunes as a means of alleviating their burdens and getting some comfort and relief. In short, these songs and spirituals formed an essential part of their daily lives. There must have been some kind of comfort for the slaves working the cotton fields to sing together something like "Swing Low, Sweet Chariot":

> Swing low, sweet chariot, Coming for to carry me home;
> Swing low, sweet chariot, Coming for to carry me home.
>
> I looked over Jordan, and what did I see
> Coming for to carry me home;
> A band of angels coming after me,
> Coming for to carry me home.
>
> If you get there before I do,
> Coming for to carry me home;
> Tell all my friends I'm coming there too.
> Coming for to carry me home.[15]

Or, when overwhelmed by the trials of slavery, to dream of freedom and hum to oneself "I Want to Be Ready":

> I want to be ready, I want to be ready,
> I want to be ready to walk in Jerusalem just like John.
>
> O John, O John, what do you say? Walk in Jerusalem just like John.
> That I'll be there at the coming day, Walk in Jerusalem just like John.
>
> John said the city was just four square, Walk in Jerusalem just like John.
> And he declared he'd meet me there, Walk in Jerusalem just like John.
>
> When Peter was preaching at Pentecost, Walk in Jerusalem just like John.
> He was endowed with the Holy Ghost, Walk in Jerusalem just like John.

They sang in the field and they chanted in church, usually as a psychological relief from their unbearable situation. It was a means of transcending the pain of bondage and oppression and reaching for a goal, usually expressed in religious terms. These songs also helped to provide a bond to members of these communities, thus giving one another moral and spiritual support.

Transcending the pain and misery of this life, the spirituals, in particular, promised better things to come which would bring happiness and peace. And, given the fact that in most cases there was no end to slavery in this life, the promise had to be something of a spiritual nature, usually referred to as "home," "Glory," "freedom," sometimes "death" as a place of peace and salvation. The following verses picture such a dream:

Ev-ry Time I Feel the Spirit

Ev'ry time I feel the spirit moving in my heart, I will pray, oh
Ev'ry time I feel the spirit moving in my heart, I will pray.

Upon the mountain
When my God spoke,
Out of His mouth
Came fire and smoke.
Looked all around me
It looked so fine,
Til I ask my Lord
If all was mine.

Jordan's River runs
Chilly and cold,
Chills the body
But not the soul.
Ain't but one train
On this track,
Runs to heaven and then right back.

This is the realm of spiritual geography traveled by the Negroes during the time of slavery; in the twentieth century, the promise developed to include liberty and a life of justice and equality. The geographical zones in these songs were mainly derived from the Judeo-Christian heritage of the Kingdom of God.

It was that process of psychological transcendence that must have inspired the phrase "chains do not make a slave" in Albery A. Whitman's epic *The Rape of Florida*:

The negro salve by Swanee river sang;
Well-pleased he listened to his echoes ringing;
For in his heart a secret comfort sprang,
When Nature seemed to join his mournful singing.

Song is the soul of sympathy divine,
And hath an inner ray where hope may bask;
Song turns the poorest waters into wine,
Illumines exile hearts and makes their faces shine.[16]

This is not an expression of defiance as much as a way of clinging to the prospect of moral and spiritual salvation. And, the worse the cruelty and oppression inflicted, the stronger the certainty of reaching that Promised Land. One senses that certainty in the power of the refrain, 'soldiers of the cross' in the following spiritual:

We Are Climbing Jacob's Ladder

We are climbing Jacob's ladder, We are climbing Jacob's ladder,
We are climbing Jacob's ladder, Soldiers of the cross.

Ev'ry round goes higher, higher, Ev'ry round goes higher, higher,
Ev'ry round goes higher, higher, Soldiers of the cross.

Sinner, do you love my Jesus? Sinner, do you love my Jesus?
Sinner, do you love my Jesus? Soldiers of the cross.

If you love Him, why not serve Him? If you love Him, why not serve Him?
If you love him, why not serve Him? Soldiers of the cross.

And, indeed, sometimes one senses a timid saber-rattling, only to see it couched in religious metaphor, such as appears in songs on the battle of Jericho:

Joshua Fit De Battle of Jericho

Joshua fit de battle of Jericho, Jericho, Jericho;
Joshua fit de battle of Jericho, an' de walls come tumb-lin down.

You may talk about the man of Gideon,
You may talk about the man of Saul,
But not like good old Joshua,
At de battle of Jericho. Dat mornin'.

Up to the walls of Jericho He marched
With spear in han';
"Go blow ram horns," Joshua cried,
"For de battle is in my hand." Dat mornin'.

It was a revelation for me to see how pervasive the theme of the Promised Land is in these songs and spirituals, and, to a lesser degree, in other kinds of expression. This dream of a Land of Promise took on a number of forms and metaphors in these writings. The haven sought by slaves could be as ephemeral as "the bosom of Abraham"; the resting place after death, as we see in the following song:

> Rock-a-my soul in the bosom of Abraham,
> Rock-a-my soul in the bosom of Abraham,
> Rock-a-my soul in the bosom of Abraham,
> Oh, rock-a-my soul!
>
> Why don't you Rock my soul.
> The Bridge so high you can't go over it.
> So low you can't go under it.
> So wide you can't go around it.
> You must come in at the door.

Tied more closely to the biblical tradition, the dream of peace in the "bosom of Abraham" takes on an added dimension in Baldwin's *Go Tell It on the Mountain* where Gabriel dreams of "climbing the mountain" in order to reach a land of peace and comfort where only the "elect" may go. Baldwin's conversion to the Pentecostal church and his service as preacher for three years must have helped form this Calvinistic view of the universe. Thus, the "promise" which he hears a voice give him is in line with that religious tradition. His hypocrisy makes Gabriel believe that he, and he alone, has arrived at the Kingdom of God. The Promised Land has been achieved, only because Gabriel is one of the "seed." I believe that Martin Luther King's "Dream" is in part a reflection of the search for the "bosom of Abraham." King's speech also ends with this passionate statement:

> When we let freedom ring, when we let it ring from every village and every hamlet, from every state and every city, we will be able to speed up that day when all of God's children, black men and white men, Jews and Gentiles, Protestants and Catholics, will be able to join hand and sing in the words of the old Negro spiritual, "Free at last! Free at last! Thank God Almighty, we are free at last!"[17]

This is confirmed also by the last paragraph of King's "Letter from Birmingham Jail":

> One day the South will know that when these disinherited children of God sat down at lunch counters they were in reality standing up for what is best

in the American dream and for the most sacred values of our Judeo-Christian heritage, thereby bringing our nation back to those great wells of democracy which were dug deep by the founding fathers in their formulation of the Constitution and the Declaration of Independence.[18]

I do believe that King's universal human appeal is genuine; yet, one cannot overlook the exclusion from his dream of all but those who qualify for the promise. Jews and Gentiles, in the context of Western culture, are members of what has been commonly described as followers of the Judeo-Christian tradition. All other members of the human family are technically excluded from the promise.

In many of the Negro spirituals and songs the search in this realm of spiritual geography ends with physical death and spiritual rebirth. Where misery and the trials of life come to an end, bliss and salvation commence. The spiritual "I Want Jesus to Walk with Me" is an expression of the certainty of salvation in the midst of the troubles of life:

> I want Jesus to walk with me;
> I want Jesus to walk with me;
> All along my pilgrim journey, Lord,
> I want Jesus to walk with me.
>
> In my trials, Lord, walk with me;
> In my trials, Lord, walk with me;
> When my heart is almost breaking, Lord,
> I want Jesus to walk with me.
>
> When I'm in trouble, Lord, walk with me;
> When I'm in trouble Lord, walk with me;
> When my head is bowed in sorrow, Lord,
> I want Jesus to walk with me.
>
> Walk with me, Lord; Lord, walk with me
> Walk with me, Lord; Lord, walk with me
> All along my pilgrim journey,
> Lord, I want Jesus to walk with me.

The symbolic journey of life, the pilgrimage, which ends in peace, is often associated in these songs with the topology of physical geography; metaphor and reality come together in "Down by the Riverside":

> Going to lay down my sword and shield, Down by the riverside,
> Down by the riverside, Down by the riverside;

Going to lay down my sword and shield, Down by the riverside,
Study war no more. I ain't goingt' study war no more,
Ain't goingt' study war no more, Ain't goingt' study war no more,
I ain't goingt' study war no more, Ain't goingt' study war no more,
Ain't goingt' study war no more.

2. Going to lay down my burden, Down by the riverside, ...
3. Going to try on my starry crown, Down by the riverside, ...
4. Going to meet my dear old father, Down by the riverside, ...
5. Going to meet my dear old mother, Down by the riverside, ...

Going to meet my loving Jesus, Down by the riverside, ...

The battle of life, as seen in such a song, ends in a resigned appeal to meet the Savior by the riverside. "River" is a term used frequently in Negro spirituals as a reference to the River Jordan. This is the theme of the following song where the journey ends in the peaceful repose of the Jordan:

Deep River

Deep, river, my home is over Jordan.
Deep, river Lord, I want to cross over into campground.

O don't you want to go to that gospel feast,
That promis'd land where all is peace?

The metaphor is extended further in some spirituals to include added elements from physical geography in the context of the biblical story of the escape from Egypt to the land of Canaan, the Promised Land. The spiritual "Oh Mary Don't You Weep" is a good illustration of this:

Oh, Mary, don't you weep, don't you mourn,
Oh, Mary, don't you week, don't you mourn,
Pharaoh's army got drowned
Oh, Mary, don't you weep.

Jordan's River is chilly and cold
Chills the body but not the soul
Pharaoh's Army got drowned
Oh, Mary, don't you weep.   (Chorus)

One of these mornings it won't be long
Look for me and I'll be gone.

> Pharaoh's army got drowned.
> Oh, Mary, don't you weep.   (Chorus)

> If I could I surely would
> Stand on the rock where Moses stood.
> Pharaoh's army got drowned.
> Oh, Mary, don't you weep.   (Chorus)

The story in its metaphorical form is very common in African-American writings of all times. Baldwin's Gabriel in *Go Tell It on the Mountain* quotes the following verses to strengthen his claim to "election":

> On Jordan's stormy banks I stand,
> And cast a wishful eye
> To Canaan's fair and happy land,
> Where my possessions lie.
> I am bound to the promised land ...

Though obviously taken directly from the religious text, the story of Moses and Pharaoh has clear symbolic references to the Negro community and the white masters. The refrain "let my people go" in the song by the same title has been for a long time on the repertory of church choirs as well as demonstrators against racial injustice:

Go down, Moses

> Go down, Moses, way down in Egypt land,
> Tell ole Pharaoh, Let my people go.

> When Israel was in Egypt's land, Let me people go.
> Oppressed so hard they could not stand, Let my people go.

> Go down, Moses, way down in Egypt land,
> Tell ole Pharaoh, Let my people go.

> "Thus saith the Lord," bold Moses said, Let my people go.
> "If not, I'll smite your first-born dead," Let my people go.

> Go down, Moses, way down in Egypt land,
> Tell ole Pharaoh, Let my people go.

> No more shall they in bondage toil; Let my people go.
> Let them come out with Egypt's spoil, Let my people go.

> Go down, Moses, way down in Egypt land,
> Tell ole Pharaoh, Let my people go.

I stated at the beginning that this chapter is part of a project that deals with the general topic of American Orientalism. How does African-American symbolic use of this spiritual paradigm of the Promised Land contribute to a study of America's attitude to the Arab Orient?

Two rather important theories of the development of human culture come to mind in this connection: T.S. Eliot's suggestion that in the accumulation of a national culture "the historical sense involves a perception, not only of the pastness of the past, but its presence," and that all works of literature belonging to a certain culture "have a simultaneous existence." "Works do not signify in a vacuum; they are part of a system of relations and cannot acquire their complete meaning alone."[19]

T.S. Eliot and Northrop Frye express the firm belief that Western culture had as its principal wellspring the Christian religion with its sacred texts and all the myths and concepts derived from them. Words, especially those loaded with mythological and religious connotations, have a tremendous power in the structuring of a nation's thought and culture.[20]

The cumulative use of the paradigm of the Jeremiad and the terms and words associated with it, such as "Israel," the "Promised Land," "going home," "Egypt," "Moses," "Pharaoh," "Jordan" and many others have had a tremendous effect on America's self-image in relation not only to the historical Orient but also to modern developments in the area. The use of this paradigm by African slaves in the nineteenth century was an ironic but convenient extension of its American precedents.

Part III

The Promised Land

7

American Travelers in the Orient: The Quest for Zion

In the wondering footsteps of the children of Israel.
John Lloyd Stephens, *Incidents of Travel in Egypt,*
Arabia Petraea, and the Holy Land, 1837

On May 4, 1840, the correspondent of the *New York Herald* reported from Alexandria that the number of American visitors to Egypt and the Holy Land was noticeably increasing. Observing that he had seen Americans in Alexandria during that year more than he could "ever recollect to have heard of before," he added that "upwards of twenty are now on their way to Mount Sinai, Petra, and Jerusalem." In fact, the *Herald* correspondent decided that, "should the Turco-Egyptian question be amicably settled, it is likely we shall have more visitors to Egypt next year than we have had this."[1]

Many remarks made by travelers to the Orient indicate that by the 1830s the number of Americans making the journey was on the increase. The famous American traveler John Lloyd Stephens, while in Smyrna, decided to give only a brief description of the city because, he said, "I need not attempt to interest you in Smyrna; it is too every-day a place; every Cape Cod sailor knows it better than I do."[2]

Americans contemplating a trip to the Orient did not lack company. There were regular trips from Europe which took travelers to Constantinople, Smyrna, Alexandria or Beirut, and Americans exercised their options depending on which European port they wanted to leave from and what route they wanted to take.[3] A letter from an American named Charles Edwin Bergh, for example, informed his father that he would have no trouble finding a fellow-traveler for his visit to the Orient despite having been abandoned by his first companion.[4] There are no complete official records of the names and numbers of Americans who visited the Orient during the nineteenth century, although many contemporary sources indicate that the tour was becoming increasingly popular among Americans. A list of those Americans who made the Oriental journey would include persons from all walks of life: it would include David Dorr, a black slave from Tennessee; Ulysses Grant, President of the United States; an uneducated farmer, [McI.] Robertson; the renowned educator-statesman Henry Adams; Commodores Read and Patterson of the United States Navy, and Navy Chaplain George Jones; and some drunken tourists whom Robertson met in Cairo.

Others who made the popular pilgrimage were William Cullen Bryant, the poet and arbiter of cultural taste; newspaper editors like George William Curtis, and writers in the best tradition of American humor; Sarah Haight, the sophisticated "lady from New York," and the devout down-to-earth wife of a missionary, Sarah Smith; Stephen Olin, theologian and President of Wesleyan University, and William Thomson and Edward Robinson, biblical scholars and researchers. Finally, the list would include a long line of men of letters such as Emerson, Taylor, Melville, Twain, DeForest, Stoddard and Warner.[5] The impact on the American public of their writings and of the impressions communicated by them (and by a thousand others) must have been significant. What is remarkably striking to the modern reader is the relatively similar attitudes and conduct displayed by this heterogeneous group of persons, both in their tours of the Orient and in the impressions brought back home.

For a number of reasons the principal source of information on American travel to the Orient remains those accounts, both published and unpublished, which were written by some of the persons who made the journey. Travel accounts were very popular with the reading public; they revealed the travelers' reasons for undertaking the trip and for recording their experiences. These travelogues are an invaluable source of information because of the numerous references to other Americans encountered along the way. In addition they show the extent of active involvement of ordinary American citizens in the Orient—the degree of which might otherwise have been unknown to the modern researcher. Most important is the realization that these travel accounts reveal some kind of collective logic—a pattern—which, perhaps consciously, attaches itself to the itinerary or general route traversed by many of the travelers to the Orient and to their all-but-common feelings. For these compelling reasons, travel accounts will be used extensively in the course of this chapter.

POPULARITY OF TRAVEL LITERATURE

There is clear evidence that travel literature, especially that which dealt with the Orient, enjoyed tremendous popularity. Publication dates and the numbers of editions of these books indicate immediate success and continued demand. Stephen Olin's *Travels in Egypt, Arabia Petraea, and the Holy Land*, for example, came out in 1843, but by 1844 a fourth edition became necessary. William Lynch's *Narrative of the United States' Expedition to the River Jordan and the Dead Sea*, which was published in May 1849, was issued in a second edition in November of the same year. By 1853 Lynch's *Narrative* ran into a ninth edition.

Among other books which gained immediate renown and netted their authors considerable profits are those by John Lloyd Stephens, George William Curtis and Mark Twain. Stephens's *Incidents of Travel in Egypt, Arabia Petraea, and the Holy Land*, originally published in October 1837, was issued in six consecutive editions by the next year. Stephens acknowledged popular favor in the sixth edition by stating that "the preface of a book is seldom read, or the author would express his acknowledgements to the public for having so soon demanded a sixth edition of his work."[6] A contemporary of Stephens, William Lynch, who made the Oriental trip in 1847–49, expressed his gratitude for a letter of advice and information he received from "Mr. Stephens of New York, the author of one of the most interesting books of travel which our language can produce."[7] The modern editor of the *Incidents* shows that Lynch's opinion was well founded. "Arabia Petraea," Victor Wolfgang von Hagen says, "was widely reviewed, and without exception it was widely praised."[8]

Even the British, in spite of their lack of admiration for American writings, praised Stephens' work and continued to print it until 1866. But the *Incidents'* sales in America were phenomenal. "Within two years," says Stephens's editor, "Arabia Petraea had sold 21,000 copies," and the book continued in print until 1882. Stephens' royalties amounted to $25,000 in the first two years.[9] Mark Twain's book of travel, *The Innocents Abroad* (1869), sold more than 30,000 copies within five months and about 67,000 copies during the first year.[10]

Authors and publishers repeatedly showed their awareness of this popularity and often revealed a sense of frenzied competition and fear of piracy. Sarah Haight's *Letters from the Old World* was prefaced by a "Publishers' Notice" and an "Author's Notice to the Reader," both of which offer reasons for rushing to press soon after the *Letters* were published serially in periodicals. The publishers said that portions of the letters were published "within the present year in columns of the New-York American, and have been copied thence into several other journals." The "Notice" went on to say that "the publishers confidently anticipate for the letters in their present form a reception from the public not less cordial than that which was bestowed upon a portion of them when they appeared weekly in the columns of a newspaper."[11] The author herself stated that she was reluctant to allow her letters to be published, but she ultimately had to agree.[12]

Competition led William Lynch to rush his *Narrative* to press, "induced," as he said, "by hearing of the proposed publication of a Narrative of the Expedition, said to be by a member of the party."[13] Lynch made sure to get the approval and blessings of the Secretary of the Navy, John Mason, who had commissioned the expedition and to whom the *Narrative* was dedicated. He also expressed confidence in a favorable reception of the book by the public in spite of the wealth of materials on the Orient. The same confidence is seen in George William Curtis's playful "letter to the Pasha" with which he opened his second "Hawadji" book. "My Dear Pasha," Curtis said to his imaginary companion,

> In making you the Pasha of two tales, I confess with the Syrians, that a friend is fairer than the roses of Damascus, and more costly than the pearls of Omman.
>
> You of all men, will not be surprised by these pages, for you shared with me the fascination of novelty in those eldest lands,—which interpreted to us both that pleasant story of Raphael. When his friend, Marc Antonio, discovered him engaged upon the Sistene picture exclaimed, "Cospetto! another Madona?"
>
> Raphael gravely answered,
>
> Amico mio, my friend, were all the artists to paint her portrait forever, they could never exhaust her beauty.[14]

This inexhaustible beauty of the Orient was often anticipated before the journey. Haight expressed such anticipation in her letter from Alexandria, upon leaving for Cairo, when in expectation of a rich field ahead of her, she told her correspondent that "however often it may have been reaped by others who have preceded me, there is, doubtless, an abundance of rich gleanings which I may be able to gather into my garner."[15]

The field was open, and the public was very receptive. There were, in addition to the travel books, scores of articles in periodicals describing travel experiences. Mark Twain's trip was commissioned by the *Alta California*, and William Cullen Bryant and George William Curtis did a great deal to popularize this form of daily reading among the American public. In the handwritten letters of Charles Wesley Andrews and Charles Edwin Bergh we see the curious phenomenon of letters sent by travelers and subsequently published in periodicals under the signature of the paper's "correspondent."[16] Many of the travelers, moreover, upon their return home, went on lecture tours fascinating their audiences with tales of their experiences in the exotic Orient. Bayard Taylor, a traveler-poet of note, is said to have delivered his lectures wearing a full outfit of Arabian clothes. He earned an average of $5,000 per lecture season.[17]

AMERICAN PRESENCE IN THE MUSLEM WORLD

Travel accounts by Americans tell the story of frequent crossings of paths and curious meetings in Oriental localities. Some Americans were in the service of the Ottoman authorities in Constantinople and its surrounding area or of the local authorities in various provinces of the Ottoman Empire. The most obvious examples are Henry Eckford and Porter Rhodes, who successively were in charge of building Ottoman naval vessels in the 1830s and 1840s. Another conspicuous group of Americans are the soldiers of fortune who left the States after the Civil War and rendered services to the Egyptian armed forces, especially to train and rebuild these forces.[18]

There are many contemporary references to Eckford and Rhodes by Americans who visited Constantinople, but one very proud reference is by a United States diplomat at the High Porte. David Porter recorded with pride in his *Constantinople and its Environs* that one of the ships ordered by the Sultan, "a despatch boat, which was to beat every thing on the Bosphorus in sailing," was built by Henry Eckford. When the boat was ready for the Sultan's review, Porter said, "I went on board of her, on her first trial, and we beat up to the truely magnificient palace of Beglerbeg, just finished, and the present residence of the Sultan." In a typically Oriental scene, the Ottoman Emperor stood at the window to watch the parading ship; following a Lear-like scene of jesting Foster recorded that the Sultan, "cast his eyes around among us, and immediately asked who I was? They told him. He then inquired who my nephew was, and on being informed called Mr. Eckford to him, and gave him a snuff-box set with diamonds." The scene ends with the Sultan showering the group of Americans who accompanied Porter with "individual gifts of money."[19]

Another traveler in the Orient, Mrs. Sarah Haight, confirmed the efforts made by Eckford and Rhodes, and their great reputation in Constantinople. On one occasion she observed that the port of Constantinople was full of ships of all nationalities, but that the Sultan's navy had the best ship in the harbor, "the proudest of them all, ... a Yankee frigate [which] rides here a proud monument of the skill of our lamented fellow-citizen, Henry Eckford."[20] Haight, however, took consolation in the fact that Eckford's successor, Foster Rhodes, was also an American who distinguished himself in building ships for the Sultan.[21]

There were other American nationals, although not so distinguished, who worked for the Ottomans. We learn from William Lynch, commander of the official American expedition to the Dead Sea and the River Jordan in 1847–48, that while in Constantinople, he met a Dr. Davis from South Carolina who was there with his family, his brother, and a number of slaves. Dr. Davis was part of a United States official agricultural cooperation program and worked as superintendent of a farm and agricultural school in nearby San Stephano. Besides Dr. Davis, his slaves, and his family, "including his intelligent brother," Lynch also met "Dr. Smith, who holds the important office of geologist to the Ottoman government to whom we are indepted for many scientific suggestions."[22]

Other American expatriates who impressed Lynch, Haight and most other travelers to the Orient were those belonging to the missionary establishments. Missionaries often operated "hospitality houses" to which travelers came for help and advice. In Constantinople, for example, Lynch recorded that "from Bishop Southgate, of the American Episcopal mission, we received many kind offices, including a present of his work on Armenia, Persia, and Mesopotamia. By the gentlemen of the Evangelical Mission and their families, we were also welcomed with cordial hospitality."[23] The nature of David Porter's position as a government representative made it necessary for him to have a good deal of association and cooperation with the missionary establishment. Regarding the wide-ranging activities of the missionaries in the Ottoman Empire and his involvement with it, Porter stated in a letter written on December 25, 1833, that

Mr. Goodell has established everywhere schools on the Lancastrian plan for the Greeks and Armenians, with the approbation of the patriarchs and bishops; and two Turkish schools of the same kind, have been established by him at the desire of the Sultan; one, at the barracks of Scutary, containing one hundred young soldiers; and the other at the barraks near Dalma Bashi, with four hundred and fifty scholars of the same kind. I visited both these schools three months after they were established, and saw the young soldiers first go through the exercise of their arms, with all the precision of veteran troops; after which they took their places in their classes in the school room ... It was a college for soldiers, what West Point is for our officers.[24]

Many other Americans had occasion to visit these schools, and they had every praise for their work. Sarah Haight commented on the excellent work done by "the veteran labourer in the good cause, the Rev. Mr. Goodell, and his coadjutor, the Rev. Mr. Dwight." Their admirable schools and establishments, she added, "fully persuaded [me] of its immense utility, and firmly convinced [me] that they have adopted the right and only course to penetrate the darkness that over-shadows this heathen land."[25] In Jerusalem, Haight was visited by "two American gentlemen, connected with the missionary establish-ment in this city. One was the Rev. Mr. Whiting, from the State of New York, and the other the Rev. Mr. Lannean, of Charleston, South Carolina."[26] And in Beirut Haight commented on the excellent house of the resident missionaries, adding:

We dined with them and visited their school. Mr. Smith is, no doubt, one of the best qualified persons for this important service throughout the East; his amiable and indefatigable companion is making herself extremely useful by teaching a school of small children. All her books and exercises are in the Arabic language.[27]

American missionaries and residents in the Orient were active in many circles, including the military and agricultural communities and young children's schools. They seemed also to be present every-where, even in the least expected places. In Damascus William Lynch "dined with Dr. Paulding, who with his brother-in-law, the Rev. Mr. Barnet, belong to the American Evangelic Mission in Syria."[28] While Lynch and his party were on their way from Damascus to Beirut, some of his companions became very ill: "at eleven, Beirut and the sea in sight, but the sick scarce able to keep their saddles, when fortunately we met our countryman, Dr. De Forest, of the Evangelical Mission, who prescribed some medicine to be administered as soon as possible."[29] The matter-of-fact manner in which the author recorded meeting "our countryman" in as unlikely a place as the road to Damascus indicates the frequent presence of Americans in the area. On arriving at Beirut, one of Lynch's party, a Mr. Dale, died at the house of the Rev. Eli Smith "of the American Presbyterian Mission." Lynch recorded with gratitude "the kindest attention" received from Smith, his wife, Dr. DeForest, Dr. Vandike, the Rev. Mr. Thompson and many others.[30]

Dale was not the first American to be buried in the Orient. That was also the fate of John Ledyard, a young adventurer from Connecticut who died in Cairo early in 1788. He was remembered by Mrs. Haight who, while in Cairo, met a Mr. Bota, "son of the historian," and when she "looked upon him," she said, "I thought of the tomb of our own enterprising young Ledyard, who lies buried in the desert."[31] Two other Americans traveling in the Orient recorded memories of such sad events. Charles Edwin Bergh of New York wrote to his mother on February 13, 1842, telling her that he visited the American cemetery in Jerusalem and that on Mount Zion he visited the Tomb of David and "prayed by the graves of W. Costigan who lost his life at the Dead Sea in 1830, and a young American who also died here the same year."[32] Charles Wesley Andrews of Virginia also mentioned in a letter to his wife that the Rev. Mr. Gober died in Cairo "on Friday from Typhus fever ... at a time when a stranger might well expect such a result."[33] Of the missionary establishment, a number of persons died in the Orient during their service there. Eli Smith's wife died in Beirut, working for the missionary cause to the last minute.

Perhaps because of its sacred associations, the Orient was sought by many Americans for what was believed to be its healing power, both physical and spiritual. In the Orient, a *New York Morning Herald* correspondent decided, "an invalid has every thing he can desire or wish for."[34] At about the same time, Charles Wesley Andrews, the Episcopal minister from Virginia, was convinced of this beneficial effect on his health when he wrote his wife from Paris to tell her of his plan to visit the Holy Land. His letter, written September 6, 1841, shows a man torn between the duty of going back to his wife and children and the promise of spiritual as well as physical healing which would result from the intended journey. He finally decided to "comit my way unto the Lord that he may direct my path," and to go to Marseille, where he would wait for his wife's reply. He suggested gently that "the atmosphere of the holy land may invigorate my decayed constitution and give strength to preach again the unsearchable riches of Christ."[35] Andrews' health did improve during his Oriental journey, especially on his trip through the Holy Land.

The same fate was not to be the lot of two prominent Americans, Herman Melville and Ralph Waldo Emerson, both of whom made the journey to regain their physical and mental health. We learn from the editor of Melville's *Journal* that by the end of 1856 he was "severely ill physically (and evidently not a little mentally)."[36] His father-in-law, Lemuel Shaw, attested to this in a letter to his son explaining that the author's state of mind and body made the trip necessary.[37] With this resolve, the editor said, "the voyage through the Levant and Europe was projected in the hope of recuperating his failing health, and, perhaps, of restoring his spirits from a mood of profound skepticism, disillusion, and gloom."[38] Judging from the prevailing mood of his *Journal* and *Clarel*, the two works which directly resulted from the trip, Melville must not have received the salutary effect expected. Emerson's trip to the Orient in 1872 was a present from his friends and disciples, and was meant to raise the spirits of the aging Concord philosopher following a series of calamities which had culminated in the destruction by fire of his house and library. Emerson did not seem to have been inspired by Egypt, where "he did not find the Nile of his imagination,"[39] and although he temporarily recovered his health and spirits, he finally succumbed to illness and old age in 1882.

TRAVELERS' EXPECTATIONS OF THE ORIENT

For the majority of Americans, however, the Orient presented a prospect that was quite thrilling and very different from what they expected to see on a European tour. There was something about that part of the world—quite apart from its religious associations—which promised an experience which was as novel as it was exciting. Expectations were high even before the beginning of the journey, and were to a certain degree preconditioned by an accumulation of cultural as well as personal memories. We listen, for example, to Melville's enthusiasm as he recorded his reaction to an earlier plan to visit the Orient: "This afternoon Dr. Taylor and I sketched a plan for going down the Danube from Vienna to Constantinople; thence to Athens on the steamer; to Beyrouth and Jerusalem—Alexandria and the Pyramids ... I am full (just now) of this glorious Eastern jaunt. Think of it! Jerusalem and the Pyramids—Constantinople ...!"[40]

There was a uniqueness to the very prospect of that first visit to the Orient.

And if Melville combined both Europe and the Orient in his joyous vision, many other travelers made a clear distinction between the European world and the Orient. The rapture of excitement was reserved for the latter, if only because Europe was more familiar. Yet there was also something familiar about the Orient—a preconceived notion of what was awaiting the traveler.

Such was the expression in Sarah Haight's first letter from Constantinople in which she apologized for the dull letters she had sent from Europe. She told her correspondent that her impatience at receiving more compelling descriptions of the Orient could not have exceeded Haight's impatience. But, she said, she hoped that the letters she had imposed on her correspondent from Europe "may have served to stay your craving appetite for sketches of Oriental wanderings." Continuing the gustatory metaphor, Haight said "I only hope that, like caviare before the feast, they may have been the means of whetting it to a keener edge. It will be impossible for my imperfect descriptive powers to mete out to you such a portion as you may expect, of the mental feast which I now begin to realize is before me." The "feast" was so sumptuous that Haight could only send "fragments, crumbs which fall from the table." Her aim, she said to her correspondent, was "to captivate your fancy, and subdue your judgement with the weapons of enthusiasm."[41] All of this anticipation, and she had been in Istanbul for a mere two days!

But Haight's expectations are justified, for the novelty and uniqueness of the experience are nothing like what the United States or Europe could offer. The catalog of opposites is long, as one look at the "Queen of the Orient" demonstrated to her. Departing, she said

> from a modern European city (Odessa) ... in two days I found myself in Turkey, with everything differing so materially from what I had ever before seen. The turban in lieu of the hat, flowing robes and wide trousers in place of short coats and pantaloons, red and yellow slippers instead of boots, long beards and curled mustaches instead of shorn faces, and veiled heads in lieu of the female face divine ... minarets in the place of towers and steeples, and the cry of the Muezzin [sic] instead of bells ...[42]

A hundred other opposites are listed which transport the traveler to a world which has existed only in the imagination. The mood is one of joyous expectation and a craving for more of the same.

Such contrast is made all the more striking on the return trip to Europe, and the traveler felt the let-down which results from returning to a familiar European life. Charles Edwin Bergh recognized this contrast on arriving in Vienna from Smyrna and in his travel account warned his readers of the change which was inevitable.[43]

The first serious modern attempt at a detailed study of the archeology of Palestine was made by an American, Edward Robinson, who prefaced the published results of his labors in the Holy Land with the statement that the journey "had been the object of my ardent wishes, and had entered into my plans of life for more than fifteen years."[44] The Holy Land, in fact, was part of the plan of life, dreams and ardent wishes of many Americans in the nineteenth century. And the desire to make the journey was not limited only to religious scholars and missionaries. The naval officer William Lynch, who headed what was ostensibly a scientific expedition commissioned by the United States government, admitted in his account that he had entertained the trip for a long time. "The yearnings of twenty years," he said at the start of his journey,

> were about to be gratified. When a young midshipman, almost the very least in the escort of the good Lafayette across the ocean, my heart was prepared for its subsequent aspirations. ...
>
> Twice, since, at distant intervals, I contemplated making the desired visit. But the imperative calls of duty in the first instance, and a domestic calamity in the second, prevented me. As I have before said, in the spring of the present year I asked permission to visit the lands of the Bible, with the special purpose of thoroughly exploring the Dead Sea; the extent, configuration, and depression of which, are as much desiderata to science, as its miraculous formation, its mysterious existence, and the wondrous traditions respecting it, are of thrilling interest to the Christian.[45]

The lands of the Bible were, in a sense, considered to be the sacred spiritual property of church-going and devout Christians. They saw these lands graphically presented in every chapter of the Bible, in religious hymns, in Sunday-school instruction, at revival meetings, and in the stories of the early Christian community in Palestine. The mental picture of Palestine was deeply impressed on their thoughts. These sentiments were expressed by Edward Robinson in his work on the Holy Land:

> As in the case of most of my countrymen, especially in New England, the scenes of the Bible had made a deep impression upon my mind from the

earliest childhood ... Indeed in no country in the world, perhaps, is such a feeling more widely diffused than in New England; in no country are the Scriptures better known, or more highly prized. From his earliest years the child is there accustomed not only to read the Bible for himself, but he reads or listens to it in the morning and evening devotions of the family, in the daily village school, in the Sunday school and Bible class, and in the weekly ministrations of the sanctuary.[46]

This shared communal interest gave added incentive to explore the actual geographical area. When Lynch, for example, planned his expedition, he kept his plans secret (with official approval, especially that of the Secretary of the Navy) for fear that not enough financial support could be mustered. Nonetheless, Lynch himself had no doubt that support would be forthcoming. In the preface to his *Narrative* he said:

I had an abiding faith in the ultimate issue, which cheered me on; for I felt that a liberal and enlightened community would not long condemn an attempt to explore a distant river, and its wondrous reservior,—the first, teeming with sacred associations, and the last, enveloped in mystery, which had defied all previous attempts to penetrate it.[47]

These sacred associations in the minds of Americans were what led many seek verification on the spot. In one brief statement, a devout American, David Millard, summed up the attraction the Orient held for Westerners, particularly Americans. He introduced his *Journal* thus:

In later years, my profession led me to study and contemplate everything connected with sacred history. The reading of the Sacred Scriptures often awakened in me an ardent desire to visit the principal places of their historical scenery ... By too much study and intense labor, my health had been seriously impaired. Suffering greatly under an affected state of the nervous system, I was advised by physicians to take a voyage to sea. I chose the direction of the Mediterranean, with the intention, should my health permit, of visiting Egypt and the Holy Land.[48]

A more emotional expression of the opportunity to visit the land of Scriptures came from the pen of Charles Wesley Andrews in a letter to his ailing wife. Torn between the sense of duty to return to her bedside and the temptation of a visit to the Holy Land, the

Episcopalian minister wrote from Paris:

> Tuesday morning, September 7, I have been thinking more and more about my journey and trying to commit my way unto the Lord that he may direct my paths. I think I will at last go to Marseilles and wait for yr: next letter. There I shall know again of yr: state and hope if you really wish me to come back this fall, that letter may contain an expression of your wish and you will see me by the 25th of October:, but in the workings of my mind upon the subject I sometimes think I hear you advising me to go on, that you will wait very cheerfully until I come home and wd rather that I wd see Thebes and home and Jerusalem and that you might hear of those wonderful cities from my mouth.[49]

A less personal, but no less emotional, response upon actually reaching on the land of Scriptures was made by George Jones, Chaplain of the US Navy, in his *Excursions to Cairo, Jerusalem, Damascus and Balbec*. In Jones's apostrophe on the Holy Land we have a rare combination of the land of childhood memories and the wanderings of the imagination, together with discovery of the physical location itself. While approaching the coast of Palestine, Jones said:

> Early on the morning of the 12th we had the pleasure of seeing the hills of Palestine emerging from the waters. What a thrill was occasioned by the sight!
>
> The birth-place of a wide-spread and wonderful religion—the land of a thousand miracles—the original home of a people now spread every where, and every where a miracle; and every where, from Lapland to India, still yearning towards their fatherland—the mountains, the plains of Judea were before us. In our earliest infancy we had tried to picture them—they were mingled with the deepest and warmest feelings of our maturer years; in imagination how often had we wandered over the hallowed ground, and here before us was now the reality itself.[50]

The feeling of joy which came over the traveler as he set foot in the Holy Land made the journey more of a pilgrimage than a pleasure trip. The idiom and imagery which inform accounts of these pilgrimages are reminiscent of the symbolic Christian final journey to the Kingdom of Heaven, as well as those of the first migrations of English immigrants to the New World. One of the first Americans to undertake a religious mission to the Holy Land, Josiah Brewer, used language similar to that of the Pilgrim Fathers:

> The Atlantic I have expected to find like Israel's "waste howling wilderness," spread out as a trial of patience, before entering the promised land. Short be our passage, is the prayer of the voyager, and shorter still, you may add, be the story of it. Yet, since you have requested to share in the benefits of my pilgrimage, think not to stand with me on Mount Zion, without first learning something of the inconveniences and trials encountered by the way.[51]

THE JOURNEY AS PILGRIMAGE

A number of dominant factors in American travel idiom can be seen in this statement, especially in the context of travel to the Orient. The journey, from the traveler's viewpoint, was a pilgrimage to the Promised Land, the earthly Canaan; and crossing the howling wilderness was an essential requirement for the pilgrimage. Time had run full cycle: the Pilgrims first journeyed west across the expanse of the Atlantic in search of the Land of Promise; their descendants were now on a journey east—crossing other distances to reach the Promised Land. "In all thy ways acknowledge Him, and He shall direct thy paths (Proverb iii, 6)." This was Thomson's "traveling motto, roving or at rest, ever since I left the banks of our bright Ohio for this 'Land of Promise.'"[52]

The Pilgrim Fathers sought to establish the Kingdom of God, an earthly Canaan, in the New World—perhaps in Boston or New Mexico. That was the Canaan of spiritual geography which colored the speeches of so many of the settlers and inspired them to give their settlements names like New Jerusalem, New Lebanon, and Bethlehem. Thomson and his generation, in their turn, made the journey to the Promised Land "with the cheerful hope and fervent prayer that our pleasant pilgrimage through the earthly Canaan may hereafter be resumed and perpetuated in the heavenly."[53] When he actually arrived in the Holy Land, Thomson exclaimed:

> Our first walk in the Land of Promise! To me a land of promises more numerous and not less interesting than those given to the Father of the Faithful, when the Lord said, "Arise, walk through the land in the length of it and the breadth of it; for I will give it unto thee." It is given to me also, and I mean to make it mine from Dan to Beersheba before I leave it.[54]

This was the Pilgrim's Progress of every ardent Christian. The American Canaan was a prelude to another earthly Canaan, itself representing for most American Christians the real Second Kingdom. It was not out of keeping with the setting that Charles Andrews took along *The Pilgrim's Progress* on his journey to the Holy Land,[55] or that Charles Edwin Bergh, a less devout Christian, reached for "the little Bible," which his mother had packed in his luggage, and read passages from Exodus while at the Convent of St. Catherine on Mount Sinai.[56]

In the accounts of travelers to the Orient they demonstrate a sense of déjà vu—a shock of recognition—a rediscovery of previously explored regions. It is as though these pilgrims were renewing an acquaintance with the land of their spiritual birth and nativity.[57] This is the ecstatic high that we hear in Stephen Olin's words upon approaching the city of Jerusalem and the Mount of Olives, a site, he said, which

> yielded up my mind to recollections and emotions which rushed upon me with irresistible force. I had trodden the ground, and in all probability the very path most frequented by the blessed Redeemer and his apostles. The Garden of Gethsemane, through which I had passed in my way from the city, and which lay in the deep valley below me in full view, the declivity of the mountain which I had just ascended—its elevated summit, upon which I was now standing, were the favourite haunts of the Savior of the world ...
>
> With the exception of Calvary, no spot on earth is so historical and so rich in holy associations as the Mount of Olives.[58]

It became very difficult for the American divine to leave the city:

> It was indeed painful to tear myself away from the sacred objects to whose power I had for several weeks so unreservedly yielded my imagination and my heart, and my thoughts still lingered upon Calvary and Olivet, and in the Garden of Gethsemane. Happy and swift were the hours spent in communion with these hallowed scenes, and deep and enduring the lineaments in which they have impressed their images and subduing associations upon my mind.[59]

Less eloquent, though sincere, are the words of a Tennessee farmer traveling in the Holy Land, showing that these emotions emanated from the less-educated masses as well as from sophisticated clergy. In fact, the shock in the case of [McI] Robertson resulted from his inability to recognize in the actual locations the hallowed images of his religious imagination. "On our way to Jerusalem shortly after we had lost sight of Hebron," Robertson said, "we observed the tree under which Abraham is supposed to have communed with the Angels; it is called ... by the Arabs Oak." Furthermore, Robertson was disappointed by the barrenness, and marveled at the great change that "must have taken place since it was the land flowing with milk and honey."[60] However, he was awed by the realization that he actually was standing in that most sacred land which saw the birth of the Savior and was revered by Christians all over the world.

These ecstatic outbursts were the result of a host of sacred memories which rushed to the mind of the pilgrims as they traveled through the Holy Land. There was the sense of a fulfilled vision, a realization of a cultural historical past. The expression at times became a derivative of biblical experience, as when Sarah Haight wrote:

> While I was returning to our tent, the impression made on my mind when I first landed on the coast of Syria returned to me with increased interest, now that I felt myself actually treading in the soil of Palestine, the theatre of so many mighty events. All my historical recollections, sacred and profane, came fresh to my memory; and I fancied I saw in every face a patriarch, and in every warrier chieftain an apostle.[61]

Every stop on the way was the scene of some biblical or early Christian event: while sailing from Smyrna to Constantinople, Josiah Brewer recalled the journey of St. Paul, conscious that he was in a sense, another apostle on a mission, even though he "reversed the order of the Apostle Paul's last voyage to Jerusalem."[62]

The land and the book came together with intensity and clarity in the experiences of travelers in the Orient. This was partly a result of their memories of childhood Bible-reading exercises, but they were made more vivid because many a traveler brought his Bible along on these journeys and spent hours reading the textual explications of sacred geographical locations. In fact, William Thomson, in his work *The Land and the Book*, stated in the preface that his aim was, "to illustrate the Word of God [which] is in itself commendable. On this fundamental fact the author rests his apology for obtruding the present work upon the notice of the public."[63] Thomson sought to guide his readers in the "good land" of Scriptures where they could read his words as a supplementary illustration to the Bible and thereby relive the "adventures and life of Christ and his disciples in the Holy Land."[64] Even those who might be reading the Bible in the comfort of their American homes could relive its events by viewing Thomson's illustrations which identify the sacred scenes where "in this identical land, amid the same scenes, the author of this work earnestly cultivated communion and intimate correspondence with this divine Teacher, and with the internal and external life of the Book of God."[65]

A contemporary review of *The Land and the Book* emphasized the important position occupied by the Bible in the life of Christians in America. Thomson's writings were praised because, by describing the sacred stage on which the events of the Bible took place, he helped Christians understand the Word of God. On the other hand, for travelers in the Holy Land, including Thomson himself, the Bible acted as a guide to the land. The Bible was used to verify the authenticity of some places or to disprove others. If there was doubt regarding any site, the Bible offered the higher proof; thus places were recognized by their Scriptural rather than by their current names.

As Sarah Haight toured the suburbs of Cairo, she paused at the site of Heliopolis and recalled that this was "the On of Scriptures." Although nothing was left but the remains of a ruined wall which had enclosed the temple, she stated that the visit to the site aroused in her "feelings no other place in the world did." Even she could not explain the reason of that enchantment by a ruined place. But then her memory was aided by her "eye of imagination" and some passages from the Bible.[66] As she read "chapter after chapter" from the Scriptures, she realized that the attraction of the place was the result of her feeling that it "identifies with the earliest history of our sacred scriptures."[67]

The Bible was also useful on these voyages as a suitable source of topical materials for sermons and preaching. For example, when in Sidon, in South Lebanon, Haight cut short a letter she was writing, saying,

> The above must suffice for this evening, for the hour has come for our scriptural lecture. Mr. R's text tonight is in Genesis xLix, verse 13. "Zebulon shall dwell at the haven of the sea; and he shall be for a haven of ships; and his border shall be unto Zidon," ... tomorrow our journey from Beyrout to this place, and our visit this day to Sidon.[68]

One of the biblical sites most celebrated by travelers in the Levant was Idumea of Scriptures, and Americans made every effort to identify the area, to find out its religious significance, and to be among the first to "walk through" it. Stephens in his *Incidents of Travels in Egypt* mentions that he decided to strike "directly through the heart of the desert from Mount Sinai to the frontier of the Holy Land." And in spite of the dangers and difficulties of this route, it would spare him the quarantine and would present "another consideration ... which, in the end, I found it impossible to resist."[69]

When Edgar Allan Poe reviewed Stephens's book for the *New York Review* (October, 1837), he found it "of more than ordinary interest—written with freshness of manner, and evincing a manliness of feeling, both worthy of high consideration." But in spite of Poe's high praise, he found reason to quarrel with Stephens's and Keith's interpretations of the Scriptural prophesy concerning Idumea. In fact, Poe concluded, after a tortuous analysis of the text, that the Hebrew words of Scripture meant that the curse will fall on "he that passeth and repasseth therein," not those who pass through the land. Poe said that,

> The prophet means that there shall be no marks of life in the land, no living being there, no one moving up and down in it: and are, of course, to be taken with the usual allowance for that hyperbole which is a main feature, and indeed the genius of the language.[70]

So important was this subject that when in August, 1841, Poe reviewed Stephens's *Incidents of Travel in Central America*, the bulk of that review was devoted again to Stephens's passage through Idumea. Poe again concluded that the reference in prophesy is "to the inhabitants. The prophet speaks only of the general abandonment and desolation of the land."[71] Perhaps because of that "error" in interpreting the Scriptures, Poe changed his mind about Stephens's earlier book, and considered its high "reputation not altogether well deserved."[72]

Not all Americans, however, shared Poe's opinion of Dr. Keith's *Evidence of Prophesy*. In fact, this book was a constant companion for some travelers in the Holy Land and was their chosen guide through the sacred sites of the Bible. Sarah Haight, for example, said that, "The Rev. Doctor Keith, in his Evidence of the Truth of the Christian Religion, derived from the literal fulfillment of PROPHECY has been invaluable to me in my travel, and was borne out in the details of my experience."[73]

Millard may not have cared for the literal interpretation of the references in the Bible to certain places in the Holy Land. He did however, carry with him Dr. Robinson's *Researches*, for which he had the greatest respect. Millard also used Thomson's *The Land and the Book* and Keith's *Evidence*. Another traveler in the Levant, Stephen Olin, himself a man of the cloth, paid attention to these references and to the truth of the geographical locations of biblical places and events.[74] Even the liberal and politically minded Charles Edwin Bergh read the 20th Chapter of Exodus at the Convent of St. Catherine on Mount Sinai, "especially the ten commandments." He also remembered to break "a piece of the granite rock on which I stood" and took it home as a souvenir.[75]

This literal interpretation of biblical texts in identifying certain sites was carried to such absurd extremes that at one point William Lynch admonished those who spoiled the moment by quibbling over the text. Overlooking the Sea of Galilee, and recalling its sacred associations, he said:

> I neither put implicit faith in, nor yet, in a cavilling spirit, question the localities of these traditions. Unhappy is that man, who instead of being impressed with awe, or exultant with the thought that he is permitted to look upon such scenes, withholds his homage, and stifles every grateful aspiration with querulous questioning of exact identities. Away with such hard-hearted scepticism—so nearly allied to infidelity.[76]

There were many unpleasant experiences encountered on the journey, ranging from the scorching heat of the desert to the lack of bare necessities. These conditions spoiled the religious delight of travelers as they trod in Moses' footsteps or roamed among the sacred places of the Holy Land. But the most unpleasant experience—one which evoked almost universal repugnance—was the discovery that the area was actually populated, indeed dominated, by people whose culture and beliefs differed from those of the traveler. There was a sense of injured pride, of molested personal property, when the Western Christian traveler arrived in Hebron, Jerusalem, or Constantinople after a long journey, with great expectations, only to find that the guardians of "his" holy places were either Muslims, or, at best, Eastern Christians and Catholics. These alien natives, "occupiers" in the eyes of the travelers, were deluded intruders in a land which the American traveler considered his own possession. For some of them the Muslim presence in the Holy Land, indeed in the whole surrounding area, evoked bitter historical memories of the spread of Islam and raised the persistent hope of evicting these Muslims from the land which "belonged" to the Christian West. Reflections like these, superimposed on current realities in the Ottoman Empire, urged the repossession by the West of the Holy Land and the speedy demise of Islam.

Even as the traveler set foot on the first port of entry to the Orient, his mind became preoccupied by these reflections. Constantinople, the European gateway to the Orient, capital of the Ottoman Empire, provided a rich source of Christian associations. Standing by the old wall of the city, Josiah Brewer forgot everything around him and saw only "the cannon gate, by which Muhamet entered the city in 1453."[77] Peacefully, but certainly, Brewer predicted that

> a holier cross than that borne by the crusaders, shall take the place of the crescent which we now see around us, on the top of the minarets; and instead of the blood-red flag, with its drawn sword in the midst, there shall float on these walls, the white banner and branch of peace.[78]

And at that same spot, Sarah Haight imagined a weak point in the wall of the city which reminded her that

> in that breach perished the last of the emperors, bravely defending the remnant of this once great empire. Through that breach first poured into the beautiful city those Tartar hords, who, thirsting for the blood of Christians, bade the cimeter do its worst, and over the bodies of the prostrate Greeks was raised the standard of Islam.[79]

In fact, all of Haight's historical, political and religious knowledge was evoked as she sailed across the Bosphorus towards the Eastern part of Constantinople. "At that point," she said,

> where hostile Asia approaches nearest to Europe, two more castles mark the spot, where, when the Christian forces were worn out by constant watching, and weakened by dissensions, the proud Osmanlies descended like a torrent upon Christian Europe, never to be driven back until their empire of rapine shall have consumed itself, and its weak residium be trampled under foot by indignant Christendom.[80]

Until then, however, "St. Sophia and her sisters churches" will wear "the degrading chains of the triumphant crescent."[81]

The anguish expressed by Haight at the sight of Constantinople suggested the feelings of a former owner. The first great dome she saw was the mosque of St. Sophia, "once the magnificent temple of Constantine, and dedicated to the worship of the religion of Christ."[82] But many of these "splended structures," said Haight, had been "converted into mosques."[83] Constantinople had been desecrated by Muslems, and "every hill is covered with them [mosques], and the tortuous skyline of this beautiful panorama is everywhere broken by their swelling domes and lofty minarets."[84] The changes which had befallen the city of Constantinople could be seen only through the eyes of one who had had preconceptions and personal feelings toward it. The "lady of New York," who had never before set eyes on the city, let go a cry of pain at her first sight.

> Is not this the land by Nature blessed beyond her pale, and where "all save the spirit of man is divine?" and yet is it not here that those blessings are least appreciated, and left to run fallow through the sheer neglect and inanity of the lazy and stupid possessors of the soil? Is not this once splendid capital of a Roman empire now the mere rendezvous of a horde of beastly Tartars? …
>
> At that perhaps not distant epoch the crescent will fall from each proud minaret, and the emblem of the Christian faith resume its former place, and these swelling domes shall again resound with loud Hosannas to the Lord of Hosts.[85]

Stronger feelings of dismay and antagonism were expressed by American travelers in the "Bible Land proper" when they saw Muslems, Arabs or Turks hold sway over the land and exercise authority over Christian sacred places. The Black American, David Dorr, for example, exclaimed on arriving in Hebron:

> after thirty-five days in the Desert, we came to Hebron, the burial ground of Abraham, Isaac, and Jacob. Here we were quarantined for three days. After traveling all these thousands of miles, the Arabs would not let us enter the Mosque built over these distinguished men's bodies.[86]

Here was an insult that could not be tolerated! And in Jerusalem, the mere size and height of a mosque in the Holy City offended him:

> The mosque of Omar's dome glittered in the sun beam, and this Mohammedan sanctum towered above all the other buildings in this city, that was once the "glory of the world," because of its godliness. Yes, the mosque of the Turk looked down upon our glorious sepulchre, as it were with contempt.[87]

Another fellow American traveler suffered the hardships of the desert route of the Israelites only to arrive at Hebron and find that the

> walk through its dirty streets did not make a very favorable impression on me. The most prominent point as seen from the distance is the large mosque—a large building which covers the cave of Macphelah but into the building no "christian dog" is allowed to enter. The people of the town are the most bigoted musselmen in the world and scorn the Christian with a most disdainly smile.[88]

Robertson, nonetheless, supplied his readers with a list of references to these holy places in Scripture, "as it would occupy too much time and space to quote."[89] And when Robertson and his party arrived at a spot overlooking Jerusalem, they paused to admire "the most beautiful city in the world ... [the] city of God's chosen people on whose temple he consented to visit his Divine Presence." But alas! the temple was not clearly visible, "its place was filled with a Mohammedan mosque and instead of the [illegible] of the glorious temple the dome and minarets have [illegible] their copious heads."[90]

In Jerusalem many American travelers were turned away from the Mosque of Omar, especially during prayers. This aroused feelings of resentment and called forth expressions of hatred against the Muslim population. Almost identical statements came from the pens of such different persons as Robertson, J.V.C. Smith, William Millard, Charles E. Bergh, Charles W. Andrews and many others, who protested against this Muslim "intrusion" on "their" rights. Smith called on the "Pasha, the Turkish military governor in command" whose residence, according to Smith, adjoined "the wall surrounding the square prepared by Solomon for the temple, now desecrated by a mosque and a college of dervishes." Smith then described the interesting interview with the Pasha:

> On a low bench against the ceiling, cushioned very indifferently, sat the great man, a mild, pleasant-looking personage, who may have been sixty years of age. He was sitting cross-legged, and smoking. An interpreter stated that we were Americans, and that the object of the call was to look into the holy enclosure. His pashaship salamed gracefully, spun out a long wiry stream of tobacco smoke, remarked with becoming solemnity, "God is great," and readily gave permission.[91]

Smith proceeded to give a description of the mosque and of the religious treasures which the Western travelers could expect to find. (At the risk of being caught, Smith broke off a piece of the corner of a stone of the mosque to take back home as a souvenir.[92]) The same experience evoked a burst of anger from Millard against Muslems. When he was prevented from entering the mosque which, he said, occupied the site of the ancient temple, he shouted: "Shame on Mahommedanism!"[93]

Bergh and Andrews, two Americans with different turns of mind, reacted similarly to the experience. Bergh, the enlighted man of the world, followed the religious sites accurately and suggested that "the Moslem wretches" should be driven away from the land.[94] Andrews, the zealous missionary, was pained to see the sacred sites dominated by Muslims and ascribed their attitude to the teachings of "the false prophet."[95]

IN THE FOOTSTEPS OF THE CHILDREN OF ISRAEL

The most important part of the pilgrimage to the land of the Bible was the trip across the Sinai desert from Egypt to Palestine. This was a long stretch of desert track which the travelers took on camelback, following "the route of the tribes of Israel." A grueling trip even with a convenient means of travel, it was very trying and dangerous in the nineteenth century. Yet most American travelers considered the trip an essential part of their pilgrimage and insisted on taking it. In February, 1842 Charles Edwin Bergh wrote to his mother from Jerusalem describing his feelings about that part of the journey. Despite the dangers encountered in the desert from Cairo to Akaba, Bergh said that he and his companions were anxious to be the first Americans to cross the Sinai desert and go through the "land of Edom" after a two-year interval during which no traveler dared make the trip:

> I was aware that this journey had not been made for the last two years by any traveler in consequence of the disturbed state of the country—but concluded that I had come almost too far to be disappointed. Notwithstanding the discouraging accounts we received from all quarters, we determined that Americans should be a second time the pioneers through the land of Edom.[96]

Bergh, like Olin, Stephens and others, was meticulously discriminating in following the exact track of the Israelites. In a letter to his

father written on March 6 from Beirut, he described how the drom-
edaries were "around the head of the gulf of Suez" while he and his
party made sure to "cross the sea in a boat that was pulled across the
whole distance where it was a half a mile wide." After reaching the
Asiatic shore, the party had difficulty meeting up with the rest of
the caravan, and by the time they did, it was too dark to continue.
They pitched tents and spent the night where, said Bergh,

> having consulted the various opinions of our writers relative to the mirac-
> ulous exodus of the Israelites, the next morning we walked down to the sea
> and continued several miles along shore until we came to a point of land
> opposite to the valley between two mountains and which is generally sup-
> posed to be the place where the Hebrews crossed and the armies of
> Pharaoh were overwhelmed—although some fix the passage at Suez where
> our boat was pooled over.[97]

At about the same time, in December, 1841, David Millard was in
Cairo preparing to make the journey to Palestine, where he "providentially met two American gentlemen who had recently returned
from the cataracts of the Nile, and had been making some arrangements to go to Palestine by the way of Suez, Mount Sinai, Akabah,
and the ruins of Petra," and then to Hebron and Jerusalem. The
news from Palestine and Syria, however, indicated that a "civil war"
was raging, and "not a Frank traveler had ventured through the
proposed route for about two years." Even the "American consul
spake of such a journey in rather discouraging terms."[98] The two
Americans were willing to take any risk rather than lose the opportunity of crossing Sinai and following the route of the Israelites.
Millard also

> was indeed anxious to pass over that interesting route. It would lead
> through a country which, aside from the Holy Land, I considered from its
> sacred historical and prophetic scenery, the most interesting portion of our
> globe. Our route would embrace a very large part of the road traveled by
> the Israelites in their journey from Egypt to the promised land ... Finally, I
> encouraged the enterprise, and said, "I will go."[99]

This "most interesting portion of the globe" was punctuated with
sacred sites: Idumea, the land of Esau, the inheritance of Ishmael,
the passage across the Red Sea, the Holy Mount—the list was quite
extensive, and throughout the journey travelers drew on Scriptural

evidence to guide them to these sites. Bergh consulted various writers on the subject; Haight loaded her camels with a complete library of related materials; and Millard, attempting to ascertain the exact route carried with him the findings of meticulous American researchers. In fact, Millard did so much reading on the subject that he felt qualified to agree with Dr. Robinson on some points such as "the miraculous passage of the Israelites through the Red Sea [which] must have taken place but a few miles at farthest south of Suez." In a remarkably authoritative note, Millard stated that

> Professor Robinson, in his "Biblical Researches," fixes the land of Goshen from whence the Israelites fled, on the Pelusiac arm of the Nile, directly east of the Delta, constituting the part of Egypt nearest to Palestine. Having carefully examined his reasons for fixing that land where he does, I consider his arguments entitled to, at least, a good degree of credit ... [100]

Robinson's attempts to explain the miraculous crossing in rational scientific terms, however, did not serve or strengthen Millard's devout faith. This, he thought, was a futile exercise which did not lead to any satisfactory results, and, in spite of his admiration for the *Researches* of Robinson, he expressed the opinion that

> All that kind of reasoning which has for its object the means of dispensing with a direct miracle in causing the waters of the Red Sea to divide for Israel to pass over, I regard as savoring too much of direct scepticism. Nor is it without regret that I see so much of this kind of argument in Dr. Robinson's valuable "Researches." It has been contended that "a strong east wind" caused the entire water at the north end of the gulf to recede southerly for miles, thus offering a way for the Israelites to pass over. 1. An east wind would not naturally drive the water in the gulf south, as the gulf itself leads off in nearly a south direction. 2. If this were possible, it would not agree with the sacred account of the event ... In whatever way, therefore, "the Lord caused the sea to go back" by "a strong east wind," it was in no other way than to leave the waters a wall on either hand. Nothing but a direct miracle could have effected this. [101]

The text of the Bible, not the process of scientific rational research, remained the only true guide. That text said: "for Pharoah will say of the children of Israel, that they are entangled in the land, the wilderness hath shut them in." So, Millard reasoned while on his journey, the logical conclusion regarding the geographical location of the crossing went like this:

> Had the children of Israel marched in any other direction than along the narrow stretch of shore between the present Gibbel Ataka and the sea, I cannot see how it could, with any propriety, have been said they were "entangled in the land," or that the wilderness had shut them in. But here the entanglement was complete.[102]

The pilgrim went on tracking the miraculous route, visiting various sites along the way with the aid of the sacred text. At one point Millard observed with great satisfaction that "Mount Hor, with Aron's tomb on its top, had been in sight nearly the whole day. Late in the day we turned east into a valley called Waddy Mequrader, which divides the range of Mount Seir." There they pitched their tents and spent the night outside the city of Petra "in sight of Mount Hor."[103] At night, Millard and his company watched the wild Arabs sitting around the campfire and thought of their plans for the next day. In the morning they went up the mountain to inspect the tomb. This was an exhausting, dangerous adventure but one which had to be included in the pilgrims" itinerary, and the only fitting statement he could think of, to crown the achievement of the day, was the quotation from Scripture:

> And the children of Israel, even the whole congregation, journeyed from Kadesh and came unto Mount Hor. And the Lord spake unto Moses and Aaron in Mount Hor, by the coast of the land of Edom, saying, Aaron shall be gathered unto his people; for he shall not enter into the land which I have given unto the children of Israel, because ye rebelled against my word at the water of Meribah ... "Numbers," XX.[104]

Then, and only then, could Millard conclude with certainty: "that this is the true Mount Hor of the Scriptures, I believe is not disputed by any traveler who has visited it. Its peculiar adaptation to the display of such an event 'in the sight of all the congregation,' is conspicuous to the observer."[105]

For Millard, and for most American pilgrims to the Holy Land, there was no disputing Scriptural geography as evidence of geographical research, especially when the matter concerned the route taken by the tribes of Israel. In fact, even for those who could not exactly be described as reverent pilgrims, the very context of their journey was Scriptural. John Lloyd Stephens, for example, illustrated not only the total acceptance of the Scriptural text as his guide, but also a willingness to relive the text in every step he took. So, having crossed the borders of Edom, Stephens stood on the shore of the Red Sea and contemplated "the doomed and accursed land" which stretched out before him:

> The theatre of awful visitations and their more awful fulfillment; given to Esau as being the fatness of the earth, but now a barren waste, a picture of death, an eternal monument of the wrath of an offended God, and a fearful witness to the truth of the words spoken by his prophets.[106]

And as he stood there, Stephens looked at the emptiness and barrenness of the land as a test of Scriptural truth and recited the words of the prophets:

> "For my sword shall be bathed in heaven: behold, it shall come down upon Idumea, and upon the people of my curse, to judgment." "From generation to generation it shall lie waste; none shall pass through it for ever and ever. But the cormorant and the bittern shall possess it; the owl also and the raven shall dwell in it; and he shall stretch out upon it the line of confusion and the stones of emptiness."[107]

"I read," said Stephens,

> in the sacred book prophecy upon prophecy and curse upon curse against the very land on which I stood. I was about to journey through this land, and to see with my own eyes whether the Almighty had stayed his uplifted arm, or whether his sword had indeed come down "upon Idumea, and the people of his curse, to judgment."[108]

He quoted further from the Scripture and then witnessed that a work by Keith proved beyond doubt that the great trade routes to Mecca were laid waste and that no traveler had ever traversed the land upon which the Almighty's judgment was called down by the prophets.

Sacred history became a personal experience for Stephens when he embarked on his journey in the land of Idumea where, he said, the Bedouins roamed and terrified pilgrims and travelers. Quoting a number of historians and travelers, he established the fact that the "opposition and obstruction" of the Bedouins resembled "the case of the Israelites under Moses, when Edom refused to give them passage through his country. None of these [travelers] had passed through it, and ... when I pitched my tent on the borders of Edom no traveler had ever done so."[109] It was now time for him to put to practical and hazardous test the words of the prophets. Stephens mounted his horse and gazed from the shore of the northern extremity of the Red Sea at "an immense sandy valley, which, without the aid of geological science, to the age of common observation and reason, had once been the bottom of a sea or the bed of a river." Without the aid of science, Stephens came to the conclusion that

> it was manifest, by landmarks of Nature's own providing, that over that sandy plain those seas had once mingled their waters, or, perhaps more probably, that before the cities of the plain had been consumed by brimstone and fire, and Sodom and Gomorrah covered by a pestilential lake, the Jordan had here rolled its waters ... The land of Idumea lay before me, in barrenness and desolation; no trees grew in the valley, and no verdure on the mountain-tops. All was bare, dreary, and desolate.[110]

Scriptural idiom and prophecy overwhelm the narrative of personal experience, and the two become inseparable. The "extraordinary fit of enthusiasm" exhibited by Stephens and his companion, Paul, at the beautiful sight of the temple of Petra and its great theatre was soon replaced by a sombre reflection on the great city which had once stood there "in the earliest periods of recorded time, long before this theatre was built, and long before the tragic muse was known." At that time,

> when Esau, having sold his birthright for a mess of pottage, came to his portion among the mountains of Sier; and Edom; growing in power and strength, became presumptuous and haughty, until, in her pride, when Israel prayed a passage through her country, Edom said unto Israel, "Thou shald not pass by me, lest I come out against thee with the sword."[111]

Stephens documented his narrative with quotations and notes from Jeremiah xlix and Isaiah xxxiv as he observed the results of the Lord's terrible denunciations against the land of Idumea, "her cities and the inhabitants thereof."[112] After personally witnessing the fulfillment of prophecy in the perpetual waste, the absence of the city's nobles, Stephens burst out in an angry cry:

> I would that the skeptic could stand as I did among the ruins of this city among the rocks, and there open the sacred book and read the words of

the inspired penman, written when this desolate place was one of the great-est cities in the world. I see the scoff arrested, his cheek pale, his lip quiver-ing, and his heart quaking with fear, as the ruined city cries out to him a voice loud and powerful as that of one risen from the dead; though he would not believe Moses and the prophets, he believes the handwriting of God himself in the desolation and eternal ruin around him.[113]

A concluding serene note—"Paul and myself were alone"—comes as a quiet confirmation of his belief set against the doubts of the imaginary skeptic. After all, Stephens was there with the Apostle.

Part IV
Religion in America

8

The Judeo-Christian Tradition: Prelude

> The Gospel is the book of Christianity, and Christianity is
> the Religion of the West.
>
> Frederick Carpenter, *Emerson and Asia* (1930)

On the domestic political, social and religious levels and in the
foreign policy regarding the Arab–Israeli conflict, it can be said that
the modern period in American history sums up the entire course
taken by the Judeo-Christian tradition in American history. The
impact of the Judeo-Christian set of beliefs has appeared in many
public and private activities and policies. This can best be illustrated
by a few public events which have taken place in recent years.

On January 25, 2001, the Inauguration ceremony of George W.
Bush was held in front of the Capitol, and on the next day a prayer
service was held for the same occasion in the Washington National
Cathedral in the American capital. The religious convocation was
given by the Baptist minister Franklin Graham, and, like the
Inauguration of the previous day, the church service was carried live
throughout the United States and many parts of the world.

Holding a religious service and prayer on a major political occasion like the inauguration of a new president, although not an
uncommon practice, took on added significance this time because it
ushered in a new administration with avowedly strong religious
convictions and leaning to the political right. It is more significant,
however, in its association with the Judeo-Christian tradition in
America because of the sermon given on this occasion and the person who was "invited" to give it. The Reverend Franklin Graham is
the son of the world-famous and highly respected Reverend Billy
Graham. Franklin Graham is also slated to succeed his ailing father
in the leadership of the powerful Southern Baptist Convention.

This sermon given by the Reverend Graham derives a great deal
from the American version of the Judeo-Christian tradition. After a
brief introduction on the significance of the event and on "Christ as

the source of all wisdom," Graham proceeded to prescribe an antidote for the present "restlessness within the soul of America." To "once again ignite the soul of America," Graham presented a model from the Old Testament, where "God worked in a mighty way through the life of King David, the greatest king of Israel, most likely all of human history."

The stories of King David and Israel are mentioned in one paragraph after another in connection with the Inauguration of the American President. But only verbatim quotes could give the accurate theme and implications of the sermon. Graham reminded the congregation that

> God said that David was a man after His own heart. Throughout David's life, from the time he was a small boy tending his father's flocks, he inquired of the Lord what he should do, regardless of whether the decision was great or small. David did not test the political winds of the day to see which direction he should go. David's only concern was to find the will of God for his life and then to do it. God blessed him and God blessed the nation of Israel because of David. Today I believe that God will bless our President and Vice President and our nation if we will humble ourselves before the Almighty and seek his will and then to do it.

On the day before, Graham reminded the audience, "the entire nation [came] together here in this great city to inaugurate our President," and

> when David was anointed king, all the tribes of Israel came to David at Hebron; he came to the throne after a great struggle and great controversy. The king united the *country of Israel* by inquiring of the Lord. God strengthened David and his army and led them to defeating the *enemies of Israel*. By doing so, King David secured peace and prosperity for the nation. He did not gain victory because of his might; it was because David sought the Lord and the Lord responded to David's plea for help, direction and guidance, and David obeyed. (Italics added)

America, said Graham, needed to drop on its knees and pray "just as King David did long ago." For Kind David's prayer is "one of the great prayers of the Bible." David's prayer begins with the expression "Blessed are you, Lord God of Israel, our Father forever and ever." This is the example Graham set for many of the prominent persons who "today will have decisions of state, perhaps greater than any of those made by your predecessors. May the life of King David, his prayers and praise to God be a source of inspiration to guide you."

Graham's references to the lessons to be learned from Christ are, by comparison, very few, and although Graham quoted Christ's statement that "No man comes to the Father but by me," he concluded that "on this solemn occasion, my prayer is that we will turn our hearts towards the living God as King David and our forefathers did long ago." Throughout the sermon, the emphasis is placed on the analogy of David and Israel to President Bush and America. The model for Americans and their leaders is King David and his prayers and exemplary behavior and principles.

One has to be totally oblivious to the current state of the world and the nation not to notice the messages embedded in this sermon. On the domestic front, would the President and his Administration take stands or make decisions regarding the issues of abortion, school prayers, gay marriage, faith-based policies without "testing the political winds of the day"? And on the foreign policy front, how was the new Administration to deal with the Palestine question? "The country of Israel" (so mentioned by Graham to refer to an era where the concept of "country" was nonexistent) has been constantly in the news and in the consciousness of millions who were watching or listening to the sermon, and so have "the enemies of Israel." On a strictly national American occasion, the preacher saw fit to devote the bulk of his sermon to forcing an analogy between King David of Israel and President Bush and America, with "David" and "Israel" mentioned more than any other names. The metaphor and the real situation are so skillfully fused that no open statement of intention is needed, especially if one recalls Graham's continued support for the country of Israel and his blunt opinions against Islam and Arabs, "the enemies of Israel."

Another example from American public life of this Judeo-Christian factor came on the occasion of two tragic incidents in the American space program. The two incidents were separated by 17 years, but the statements and activities that followed them derived some of their symbolism and essential forms from the same tradition.

The first event was the explosion of the Challenger space shuttle on January 28, 1986. President Reagan addressed the nation on television shortly after the accident; he told the nation that faith in God's Providence will help them get through the tragedy. He then added the very eloquent and very symbolic statement that the American astronauts who died on board the Challenger had left this earth and gone up "to touch the face of God."

The second tragic accident happened on January 31, 2003 when the shuttle Columbia disintegrated minutes before landing after a successful space trip. Six American and one Israeli astronauts were lost in this accident. Here again, President Bush addressed the nation on television, quoting from Isaiah some expressions of the rapture of the saved, and adding that the seven astronauts did not come back to earth, but that they were safe at home.

The spontaneous reactions of the two presidents were couched in comforting end-times, symbolism that may have triggered certain responses in the collective cultural consciousness of their audiences. This is especially true since the remarks came from two avowed right-wing born-again Christians.

The more studied reaction to the second event came in the open-air ceremony held in Houston a few days later. The ceremony was begun by the Navy Captain Rabbi Harold Robbinson who read a poem in Hebrew and then an English translation of the poem. The Rabbi then recited a prayer in English and a Hebrew translation.

There followed a friend of the astronauts who praised every one of them, and, when he came to the mission commander, Joshua Husband, he emphasized his deep faith, adding that at a family gathering a few hours before the shuttle takeoff, Commander Husband's final activity was reading with family and friends from the Gospel a text on God's promise to give the Holy Land to the Israelites.

President Bush also gave a very touching speech in which he mentioned by name every one of the astronauts. Then, when he came to the Israeli member of the team, Bush showered him with praise because he was a "national hero who fought in two wars in defense of his country." The President added that during the flight the Israeli astronaut passed over his country, over "the Land of Israel."

At the end of the ceremony the audience recited Psalm 23.

It does not matter if Joshua Husband's choice of the "promise" text and George W. Bush's choice of "the Land of Israel" were intended to have topical implications. Perhaps they were part of their casual everyday speech. Yet, because they are casual everyday practice, they carry with them the kind of Judeo-Christian symbols which have become part of the collective cultural memory of the millions of Americans who watched or listened to these events. It is also these cultural habits of thought and speech that feed into the nation's identification with King David and Israel. Franklin Graham referred to "our forefathers" who followed David's example; undoubtedly, he had in mind the Puritans and the Founding Fathers who also used the same analogies and the same cultural habits of thought and speech.

Reverend Graham's disproportionate emphasis on Israeli and Hebraic symbolism on the occasion of the inauguration of the US President must have tremendous implications, albeit indirect, for the current situation in the Middle East and for America's identification with the cause of Israel. So does President Bush's reference to "the Land of Israel." The "order of things" is not difficult to discern in America's official and public constant stand on the Arab–Israeli conflict.

The Judeo-Christian tradition runs deep in American cultural development, but it is the conscious use of this tradition that characterizes contemporary history. Many politicians, political planners and religious leaders have tried to capitalize on this tradition in wooing Jewish and Christian Right voters. A simple example of this trend, this time coming from a Democratic leader, shows the use of Judeo-Christian symbols and idioms in dealing with the conflict in the Middle East. On May 23, 2000, Vice President Al Gore addressed the American–Israeli Public Action Committee (AIPAC) in what was clearly election rhetoric.

In his speech, Gore described Ben-Gurion, the father and first Prime Minister of Israel, as "a modern-day prophet. He was part of a generation that believed it was their responsibility to make the centuries-old long dream of a Jewish homeland a reality." Gore quoted Ben-Gurion's statement: "It appears to me that by the end of this century, the prophecy of Isaiah will be fulfilled." "Today, said Gore, confirming the common Judeo-Christian heritage, "we meet for the first time in a new century—still striving to fulfill that prophetic vision." To further assure his Jewish and Christian Right constituencies, the Vice President said: "I will never, ever let people forget that the relationship between the United States and Israel rests on granite—on the rock of our common values, our common heritage, and our common dedication to freedom."

More explicit statements, not based on mere symbols, were made by the highly decorated American General William Boykin, veteran of the Somali debacle and Deputy Under-Secretary of Intelligence, also in charge of combating terrorism. General Boykin became notorious for a series of speeches he made to evangelical church congregations while wearing his military uniform and his many medals.

On June 30, 2002, Boykin addressed the congregation of the First Baptist Church in Broken Arrow, Oklahoma, where he showed the picture of Bin Laden on a screen and named him "the enemy, the man that hates us." Boykin then flashed a larger-than-life picture of President Bush and added:

And then this man stepped forward. A man that has acknowledged that he prays in the Oval Office. A man that's in the White House today because of a miracle. You think about how he got in the White House. You think about why he's there today. As Mordecai said to Ester, "You have been put there for such a time and place." And this man has been put in White House to lead our nation in such a time as this." Then General Boykin showed a picture of Satan on the screen, adding,

We are a nation of believers. We were founded on faith. And the enemy that has come against our nation is a spiritual enemy. His name is Satan. And if you do not believe that Satan is real, you are ignoring the same Bible that tells you about God. Now I'm a warrior. One day I'm going to take off this uniform and I'm still going to be a warrior. And what I'm here to do today is to recruit you to be warriors of God's kingdom.

A year later, General Boykin was still enthusiastically beating his war drums. On June 21, 2003, he told the congregation of the Good Shepherd Church in Sandy, Oregon:

And we ask ourselves this question, "Why do they hate us? Why do they hate us so much?" Ladies and gentlemen, the answer to that is because we're a Christian nation, because our foundation and our roots are Judeo-Christian. Did I say Judeo-Christian? Yes. Judeo-Christian. That means we've got a commitment to Israel. That means it's a commitment we're never going to abandon. We, in the army of God, in the house of God, in the kingdom of God, have been raised for such a time as this.

In January 2003, Boykin had caused a row over statements he made at a church meeting in Daytona, Florida, where he described America's military actions in Somalia, reminding this audience of "a man in Mogadishu named Osman Otto" who appeared in the film *Blackhawk Down* bragging that the American enemy would never get him because, he said, "Allah will protect me." Boykin commented:

Well, you know that I knew that my God was bigger than his. I knew that my God was a real God, and his was an idol. But I prayed, Lord let us get that man. Three days later we went after him again, and this time we got him. Not a mark on him. We got him. We brought him back into our base there and we had a Sea Land container set up to hold prisoners in, and I said put him in there. They put him in there, there was one guard with him. I said search him, they searched him, and then I walked in with no one in there but the guard, and I looked at him and said, "Are you Osman Otto?" And he said "Yes." and I said, "Mr. Otto, you underestimated our God."

JERRY FALWELL

The best and most vocal adherents to the Judeo-Christian ideology, who also call themselves Christian Zionists, are to be found among the ranks of the Fundamentalists and extreme Evangelicals. A leading figure, whose career embodies the development of modern American Judeo-Christian beliefs, is the Reverend Jerry Falwell.

Approaching the age of 70, Jerry Falwell sits at the helm of a wealthy religious empire and wields immeasurable influence on millions of people, including many right-wing politicians. He also presents in his career as preacher and public figure a perfect example of the Judeo-Christian tradition in modern America and a personification of what has come to be known as Christian Zionism.

Falwell never tires of declaring that he is a Zionist, and claims that there are in America today 70 million Evangelists who also call themselves Zionists. On June 29, 2002, Falwell appeared on the popular television show *Hardball* and told the host Chris Mathews: "We are all Zionists. We are Isreal's best friends. Jews are the children of Abraham. The Bible Belt is Israel's security belt." Falwell's unlimited support for Israel and his hatred of Arabs and Islam (despite his protestations to the contrary) make him especially relevant to the present work. So do his strong views on the inerrancy of the Bible, the emphasis on the Old Testament, and his belief in the special position accorded to the Jews in God's plan.

At the age of 17, Falwell was "born again in Christ" and bought his first Bible; since then he has waged a lifelong campaign of advocating Christian Fundamentalist and Zionist programs. His Liberty University graduates thousands of young men and women who are indoctrinated in Falwell's ideology, and features speeches by US presidents and other prominent persons. Furthermore, his Thomas Wood Church and broadcasting complex employ close to 3,000 persons and his daily *Gospel Hour* program, according to some estimates, reaches 50 million homes. Falwell himself boasts that there

are more than 120,000 church pastors across the country who support his religious, social and political campaigns. To his religious
program, Falwell added the organization he called the Moral
Majority in 1970 as a social and political action organ separate from
his religious organization.

With all of these powerful instruments and organizations at
Falwell's disposal, one can realize the extent of his influence on the
public, especially in Christian Right quarters. Consider, for example,
the statement made by Falwell on the television program *60 Minutes*
that Muhammad was a murderous terrorist who called on his followers to kill and destroy. After repeating this and similar opinions
a number of times, Falwell appeared on the television program
Hardball and, when asked if he wanted to retract his statements, he
replied emphatically, "No, not at all." Then, in a lame, underhanded
appeasement to millions of Muslims, Falwell said that he believed
that the majority of Muslims are good people and do not follow the
teachings of Muhammad.

Vicious attacks on Islam and the Prophet Muhammad have
become an addendum to the basic Judeo-Christian tradition in the
United States. The best illustration of this tradition can be seen in
the book *Jerry Falwell and the Jews*, written by Merrill Simon in a pre-
arranged question-and-answer session with Falwell. In a "Foreword"
to the book, Rabbi Emanual Rackman states that "the lovers of Israel
today are to be found principally in the camp of Protestant
Fundamentalists."[1] Nonetheless, this support is clearly considered
by the author as only a marriage of convenience since Jews can not
be sure of the Fundamentalists' real motives. Simon assures his readers that he "felt very strongly that the basic good will of the
Evangelical community—tens of millions strong—should be the
first to be tapped. Their Fundamentalist view of the Old and New
Testaments gave them at least a theoretical love of the State of Israel,
which possibly could be transformed into a practical political support to offset the growing influence of the Arabs." The author cau-
tions his readers that the book

> cannot answer the question so often asked of me, "Does Jerry Falwell really
> mean what he says?" My answer to those of you who ask such a questions
> is a quote from the Talmud which says that man can only judge another man
> by his deeds, but only God can interpret what is in man's heart. (p. xiv)

But Falwell's answers to Simon's probing questions about his
Christian Zionist beliefs are so emphatic and consistent that the
reader comes out totally convinced that they are genuine.

The story of Falwell's "conversion" to Christian Zionism reveals a combination of the literal interpretation of the Scriptures, the belief in the inerrancy of every word of the sacred text and the curiously tortuous application of the text to the present political developments. On his first visit to the Holy Land "in the late 1960s," Falwell says, he felt deep affinities with "the land of Israel…because of the fact that Christianity had its beginnings there." He explains, "As I went from site to site re-reading my Bible and the Biblical occurrences that transpired there, everything took on new meaning" (p. 60). With emphasis on his belief that this land is the rightful inheritance of the people of Israel, Falwell draws the all-too-common analogy with the experience of the immigrants to the New World:

> The people, like the land, also made a great impression on me. The most impressive remembrance I have of the people is the kindness and courtesy they showed to Christian Americans who were making their first pilgrimage there. The patriotism of these people was astounding indeed. What had happened to their land in such a short time was amazing. As I visited town after town and went up and down the land of Israel, I marvelled at the commitment of the people to the rebuilding of their homeland. I imagined that our early American founding fathers must have had a similar commitment to carving a nation out of the wilderness and paying whatever price was necessary to do so. I left the land and the people of Israel with a greater commitment to the Bible, and a greater commitment to God's land and people.

In an attempt to assure his Jewish readers that Christianity is not a rival religion to Judaism, Falwell states that the Christianity does not present even an improvement on the message of Moses. "The New Testament," he says,

> teaches that Jesus Christ is actually the fulfillment of the Old Testament Messianic prophecies (John 1:45). Jesus clearly taught that He was the expected Jewish Messiah (John 4:25–6; Luke 24:25–7, 44–8). Christianity accepts the veracity of that claim. Thus, the entire background of Christianity is Jewish. We believe in a Jewish Messiah as prophesied in a Jewish book written by Jewish authors. We do not improve on Judaism, because it is the foundation for all Messianic fulfillment.

The Old Testament is obviously the basic tome in the Christian Zionist creed, if only because "the New Testament takes only fifteen hours to read" (p. 17). The main point which Falwell emphasizes is that both Jews and Christians have "common goals such as the preservation of the State of Israel and the well-being of Jewish people everywhere" (p. 18).

"I am a Zionist," says Falwell, "and have acquired this dimension to my beliefs from studying the Old Testament" (p. 62).

Falwell never tires of repeating his identification of Israel with the Old Testament prophecies and the consequent duty of Christians to stand firmly with Israel. He says:

> I feel that the destiny of the State of Israel is without question the most crucial international matter facing the world today. I believe that the people of Israel have not only a theological but also a historical and legal right to the land. I am personally a Zionist, having gained that perspective from my belief in Old Testament Scriptures. I have also visited Israel many times. I have arrived at the conclusion that unless the United States maintains its unswerving devotion to the State of Israel, the very survival of that nation is at stake. I think that the 1980s are going to be very critical times for Israel. Every American who agrees that Israel has the right to the land must be willing to exert all possible pressure on the powers that be to guarantee America's support of the State of Israel at this time.

Falwell has no doubt that Christians have a religious duty to support Israel because it is the fulfillment of prophecy: "Anyone who truly believes in the Bible sees Christianity and the new State of Israel as inseparably connected. The reformation of the State of Israel in 1948 is, for every Bible-believing Christian, a fulfillment of Old Testament and New Testament prophecy."

9
The Role of Religion in American Life

> Then will the trumpet of Jubilee sound, and earth's debased
> millions will leap from the dust, and shake off their chains,
> and cry, "Hosanna to the Son of David."
>
> Lyman Beecher,
> "Address at Plymouth" (1827)

Religion has played an important role in American life. As has been demonstrated, the early Puritan settlements considered religion a basic part of their experiment. During the American Revolution and early Independence, the Founding Fathers frequently expressed in statements, speeches and actions a mixture of patriotic and religious feelings; and when the American nation faced the most dangerous period in its history with the war between the North and the South, both sides quoted religious texts to justify their respective positions. In both camps, churchmen were busy preaching to the soldiers, consoling the wounded and praying over the dead. The eighteenth and nineteenth centuries saw the rise of a number of churches and religious groups, many of which believed in end-times prophecies.

In the twentieth century, especially during the second half, religion played an important role in various aspects of American life and was evident in the behavior and statements of private and public figures. This role was obvious during major conflicts such as World War II, the Korean War and the Vietnam War and during election campaigns. It was more pronounced, however, in the events which preceded the establishment of the state of Israel and ever since.

Today, religion exercises a strong influence on American politics, and with the rise of the political and religious Right to the position of power, religion is becoming more prominent in political affairs. In an electronic conference (Amman, Jordan, the American Embassy, January 16, 2000), Thomas Beyers, Professor of Religion at the University of Kentucky, stated that "the United States is today by far the most religious of the advanced countries in the world." Beyers clarified this statement by adding: "The Christian Right exercises great influence on the American people." Indeed, public polls have shown that many more Americans regularly read the Bible and go to church than Europeans.

What kind of religion is this that is so prominent in American life? Is there such a thing as an American religion, or an American Church?

There has been in America a general acceptance—if not belief—in a supreme power—often referred to as God—which governs the affairs of the universe. Furthermore, Americans down the centuries have expressed a good deal of confidence in being favored by this supreme power and in playing a central role in a divine plan for human history. This role assigned by Providence included, in addition to establishing the ideal American state, extending to others the benefits of their experience. Expressions of these beliefs have often been couched in Old Testament Hebraic myth and metaphor which many Americans studied in Sunday Schools and heard at religious services. This is a brief description of the outlines of what has come to be known to some historians as "civil religion" which is generally accepted by the majority of Americans. The following pages will attempt to elucidate the point.

According to Winthrop Hudson,

> the first Americans thought that God had "sifted a whole nation" in order to plant his "choice grain" in the American wilderness, but His purpose was more far-ranging than merely to enable them to escape the inhibitions they had suffered at home. They were not fleeing from persecution; they were executing a flank attack upon the forces of unrighteousness everywhere. Their role, John Winthrop had reminded them, was to be "a city on a hill" to demonstrate before "the eyes of the world" what the result would be when a whole people was brought into open covenant with God. As part of God's program of instruction, they were to provide the nations with a working model of a godly society and by the contagion of their example were to be God's instruments in effecting the release from bondage of all mankind.[1]

The notion is confirmed by Philip Hosay, Professor of History at New York University, who said:

> For its part the United States sees itself as a model that the rest of the world should emulate. The idea of America as a model goes back to the

17th Century when the first substantial group of Puritans emigrated from East Anglia to that section of the United States now known as New England. In 1630, the leader of the Puritans, John Winthrop, gave a speech in which he envisioned the new settlement as a "City Upon a Hill." Leaving what they regarded as a corrupt society, they envisioned building a new society that would bring man closer to God and to God's purpose. They believed that this new society would serve as a model which would lead to the reformation of the rest of the Christian world.[2]

During the American Revolution, Americans became more convinced that theirs was the ideal system, the "model state" whose citizens enjoy full freedom and democracy, and which has the responsibility of spreading the benefit of their experience to the rest of the world. When the leader of the Revolution and first President of the United States, George Washington, addressed the American nation on retiring from political life, he emphasized the importance of protecting their freedom, avoiding the corruption of the Old World and giving the rest of the world a model to emulate.

This utopian self-image which appeared early in American history was often interlaced with the biblical thinking that provided the myth of the "American Israel" and the religious model of the virtuous community. Increase Mather (1639–1723) wrote in 1677 that there had not been in the history of humanity a generation that was so able to shake off the "dust of Babel" as that which immigrated to the New World.[3]

As we have seen, the writings of the Pilgrim Fathers clearly show that they were working and thinking in terms of the biblical discourse of the "Chosen People" and the "New Canaan," and the biblical references in early American experience have been described by Vernon Parrington as a search for the "Canaan of their hopes."[4]

The early Puritan settlers believed in divine dispensation for the universe, and that God in his infinite wisdom drew out a grand plan for history and placed America in the center of it. America had been there since the beginning of creation and was now ready to appear and play the central role decreed by God. Hudson summarized this dispensational belief:

Since every Englishman had been taught from childhood to view the course of history as predetermined by God's overruling providence, no one could regard the colonizing activity in America as an ordinary venture. As early as 1613, William Strachey was insisting that God had kept America hidden for a purpose and that those who had established the small settlement in Virginia were but pursuing a course of action which God had foreseen and willed and was now carrying to its foreordained completion. This purpose of necessity was related to God's final act of redemption, for this was the end toward which all history was directed.[5]

Many American and foreign writers have recognized that the Puritan brand of Protestantism has had a lasting influence on the development of American religious thinking and on the shape of subsequent American Protestantism. The French historian Andre Seigfried looked at this American brand of British Protestantism in light of the development of the American religious experience. Seigfried said: "If we wish to understand the real sources of American inspiration we must go back to the English Puritanism of the seventeenth century."[6] And the nineteenth-century German visitor to the United States Philip Schaff remarked that "Puritan Protestantism forms properly the main trunk of our North American church." He added that this American church "owes her general characteristic features to the Puritans of New England," and that these New England religious beginnings had "a powerful influence upon the religious, social and political life of the whole nation."[7]

The nineteenth-century French traveler in America Alexis de Tocqueville realized in 1836 that "there is no country in the world in which the Christian religion maintains a greater influence over the souls of men than in America."[8] De Tocqueville's description of the rise of the American brand of religion is an early recognition of what came to be known as "civil religion":

> The greatest part of British America was peopled by men who, after having shaken off the authority of the Pope, acknowledged no other religious supremacy: they brought with them into the New World a form of Christianity which I cannot better describe than by styling it a democratic and republican religion.[9]

Religion in America took a different turn from its European roots, and thus became markedly different from the Anglican Church and from European Protestantism. The Anglican Church, according to the Puritans, was not completely cleansed of the vestiges of the Church of Rome; their goal was to "purify" the Protestant Churches of England and Europe. The Puritans of the New World, furthermore, derived from John Calvin's ideology of Predestination—fate preordained by God—and added to it the American factor.

Early American Protestantism, then, was a unique development from the start, especially with regard to dispensational beliefs, and to America's role in God's plan. These unique developments provided the bases of the modern American Christian Right. The collective experience which Americans went through down the centuries gave them, regardless of their different church membership, a unified outlook on their place in the history of the universe. During the seventeenth century, the Great Awakenings and the religious revivals of the nineteenth century, American Protestantism took a course that contributed to this ideology. So, although modern developments in American Christianity grew out of early Puritan theology, they are also the result of the religious movements and churches which branched out of the trunk of American Protestantism. The nineteenth century, in particular, witnessed the rise of end-times sects such as the Adventist groups, Jehovah's Witnesses, the Mormon Church and others. And, although these sects caused some divisions in American society, they also gave the nation common goals and bonds. The strongest bond which brought the American nation together has been the religious interpretation of America's history, its past and future.

This was the factor which unified the goals of the leaders of the Revolution during the War of Independence. It was the factor which inspired the Founding Fathers' statements that derived from religious symbolism and discourse. During the Civil War, the same factor informed Abraham Lincoln's central statement "One Nation under God," becoming in the mid-nineteenth century part of the "Pledge of Allegiance."

The leaders of the North during the Civil War believed that the war against the South and the institution of slavery was God's judgment against the iniquities committed by His people. It was the means to cleanse this "American Israel" and return it to the right path. President Lincoln's summational statement indicated that this was God's call to the American people. It was in Daniel Aaron's words, Jehovah's decision to rebuke His American people. Recently Pat Robertson and Jerry Falwell gave a similar reason for September 11.

We need only read the Inaugural Addresses of United States presidents to realize the pervasiveness of public expressions of the belief in God's hand in America and in America's sacred mission. There is also a general agreement on America's special role in the divine plan for the universe. America and the American nation are principal actors in the Divine Will. Lyman Beecher's eloquent expression of this concept should illustrate this point:

> Changes in the civil and religious condition of the world, revolutions and convulsions are doubtless indispensable ... To the perfection of this work a great example is required of which the world may take knowledge, and which shall inspire hope and rouse and concentrate the energies of man. But where could such a nation be found? It must be created for it had no existence upon the earth. Look now at the history of our fathers and behold what God hath wrought ... a powerful nation in full enjoyment of civil and religious liberty, where all the energies of men ... find scope and excitement of purpose to show the world by experiment of what many are capable ...
>
> When the light of such a hemisphere shall go up to the heavens it will throw its beams beyond the waves; ... it will awaken desire and hope and effort and produce revolutions and overturnings until the world is free.
>
> From our revolutionary struggle proceeded the revolution in France and all of which followed in Naples, Portugal, Spain, and Greece. And though the bolt of every chain has been again driven, they can no more hold the heaving mass than the chains of Xerxes could hold the Hellespont vexed with storms. Floods have been poured on the rising flame, but they can no more extinguish it than they can extinguish the fires of Etna. Still it burns, and still the mountain heaves and murmurs. And soon it will explode with voices and thunderings and great earthquakes. Then will the trumpet of Jubilee sound, and earth's debased millions will leap from the dust, and shake off their chains, and cry, "Hosanna to the Son of David."[10]

A more permanent, if only symbolic, expression of this concept of God's favor was placed by the Federal Congress on the National Seal: "God Has Favored Our Undertaking." Later on, a symbolic statement of similar intent, "In God We Trust," was placed on American currency. It is obvious that one of the factors which have given the American nation (regardless of regional, ethnic or church orientation) a sense of unity is this firm belief that it has been called upon to fulfill a divine mission, as shown in the previous statement by Lyman Beecher and others like it.

The fact that the Constitution bans the adoption by the state of a certain church or religion has prompted students of American history to conclude that the United States is a strictly secular state where religion does not influence politics and the government, and where the state does not interfere in religious affairs. Furthermore, the presence of so many churches and sects, in addition to non-Christians, agnostics and atheists, makes it appear inaccurate to speak of an American religion, official or public. Nevertheless, a number of prominent scholars have plausibly advanced the concept of an "American civil religion" which is an expression of a set of beliefs subscribed to by a majority of Americans regardless of church or sect affiliation.[11]

Robert Bellah described civil religion as a

> religion obviously involved in the most pressing moral and political issues of the day ... "God" has clearly been a central symbol in the civil religion from the beginning and remains so today. This symbol is just as central to the civil religion as it is to Judaism or Christianity ... From left to right, all could accept the idea of God.[12]

The concept of God or "the Supreme Being" remains at the core of civil religion, regardless of the religious affiliation of its adherents. This is the concept expressed by American presidents and on the National Seal and the currency of the US. According to Robert Bellah, "few have realized that there actually exists alongside of and rather clearly differentiated from the churches an elaborate and well-institutionalized civil religion in America."[13] What is more, Bellah insisted, "American civil religion is still very much alive today."[14]

The importance of this civil religion can be seen in the self-image Americans have had, especially in relations with others, particularly Muslims. It is also important to the extent that this self-image is seen in the context of America's role in a cosmic plan. This has inevitably affected the policy and behavior of Americans towards the rest of the world.

American civil religion has historically been active in politics as well as in the social and spiritual life of Americans, perhaps mainly because the churches did not take a stand against the Revolution and the efforts to establish an independent democratic state. Indeed, religious beliefs and sentiments played a role in the establishment of democratic institutions. Consequently, despite the separation of state and church, there was no conflict between the two; this is one of the factors which explains the present-day increasing connections between politics and religion.

Although civil religion and spiritual religion work independently in the day-to-day affairs of Americans, there are important bonds between the two. In fact, Americans by and large viewed both of them in the context of divine dispensationalism; both promised some apocalyptic time when believers will achieve spiritual and political salvation. The Founding Fathers and early political leaders described the War of Independence as a battle between the forces and good and evil; England became identified with the Antichrist while Americans were described as the army of the saints and the saved. While the Continental Congress was still debating the Declaration of Independence, one of the members, Samuel Sherwood, spoke of God's work in the Revolution and the establishment of the independent state. Sherwood described the War of Independence in end-times discourse; America's Independence was meant to bring about Christ's return and his millennial reign. In a sermon significantly entitled *The Church's Flight Into the Wilderness: An Address On the Times* (1776) delivered on the eve of Independence, Samuel Sherwood explained America's sacred mission:

> When that God, to whom the earth belongs, and the fulness thereof, brought his church into this wilderness, as on eagles' wings by his kind protecting providence, he gave this good land to her, to her own lot and inheritance forever. He planted her as a pleasant and choice vine; and drove out the Heathen before her. He has tenderly nourished and cherished her in her infant state, and protected her amidst innumerable dangers ... God has, in this American quarter of the globe, provided for the woman and her seed ... He has wrought out a very glorious deliverance for them, and set them free from the cruel rod of tyranny and oppression ... leading them to the good land of Canaan, which he gave them for an everlasting inheritance.[15]

The concept was confirmed by a contemporary of Sherwood, the Continental Congress Chaplain George Duffield, who said that in America vice and sin would be banished and the wilderness would blossom.[16]

At the core of American civil religion is the biblical symbolism of the "chosen people," "the Kingdom of God" and the "Promised Land." The new state represented New Jerusalem, and the people of America were Israel and its kings. Soon after Independence, Pastor Abiel Abbot gave a sermon in which he said that the term "our American Israel" had become a common description of the American Republic, and that "common consent allows it apt and proper."[17]

This concept of the "American Israel" has been a favorite image Americans have had of their situation since Independence. It is this biblical symbol which Winthrop Hudson described as the "religion of the Republic":

> "Civil religion," the "religion of the republic," was public religion, a religion available to all through natural reason. "Spiritual religion" was *private* religion, an "experienced" religion that was intensely personal. The one was preoccupied with the nation and its mission; the other was preoccupied with individuals and their redemption. The one provided a bond which united the nation and gave it a reassuring sense of a God-given vocation; the other rescued individuals from sin and, in reconciling them to God, established them in the paths of virtue.[18]

Hebraic symbolism has appeared in American writings in both religious and political contexts. We have seen that the first two epics written after Independence, *The Conquest of Canaan* and *The Vision of Columbus*, used this symbolism to celebrate America; and on March 4, 1805, Thomas Jefferson said in his Second Inaugural Address:

> I shall need, too, the favor of that Being in whose hands we are, who led our fathers, as Israel of old, from their native land and planted them in a country flowing with all the necessaries and comforts of life; who has covered our infancy with His providence and our riper years with His wisdom and power.[19]

More recently, President Reagan repeatedly warned of the imminent Battle of Armageddon and President George W. Bush spoke of the mission assigned to America by history to save the Free World and spread the ideals of freedom and democracy throughout the world. The rise of civil religion with its biblical discourse since the Revolution and Independence, as Nathan Hatch pointed out, made this religion a useful instrument for political programs and goals. Civil religion entered the political arena and became part of American political history. Thus, the issue of America's freedom became God's cause, and English colonial rule became the cause of the Devil. Independence and democratic rule, in turn, became a prerequisite for the Coming Kingdom. This development of civil religion made the concept of the Millennial Kingdom of Christ come close to what has been described as "civil millennialism."[20]

Recognition of these developments in America's political and religious history will help understand the continuing interaction between the worlds of politic and religion. In this context one should place Herman Melville's statement that "the political

Messiah has indeed come in us" and John Ashcroft's statement that in America "we have no king but Jesus."[21] The Christ who guided the actions and thoughts of the Founding Fathers is essentially the progenitor of Melville's "political Messiah" and of Ashcroft's "King Jesus," each coming in the political context of its time, but a context connected to religious discourse.

This political-religious discourse has succeeded down the centuries in addressing American dreams in biblical language and symbols which Americans understand and identify with. The language of "civil millennialism" crossed the borders of American churches and religions and became a unifying factor especially in times of crises and political campaigns. While the Pilgrim Fathers sought to spread the light of the Gospel in the New World, the Founding Fathers and their descendants aimed at providing a beacon of freedom and democracy for all of humanity. The Kingdom of God evolved into the political reign of Christ in the dream of an American global empire.

The modern American political language has increasingly adopted biblical millennial terminology and symbols, especially in the context of America's relations with other nations. Americans, especially missionaries, in the nineteenth century decided that the Star of the East had spent itself, and that it was the turn of the Star of the West to spread American values around the world. And this Western Star has progressively reflected a Hebraic sun and developed into an ideology which has come to be known as the "Judeo-Christian tradition."

The Inaugural Addresses of American presidents give relevant samples of this political-religious discourse. Many presidents included in their addresses expressions of gratitude for God's favor and patronage of America's efforts on behalf of humanity. In his first Inaugural Address, George Washington thanked the "benign Parent of the Human Race in humble supplication that, since He has been pleased to favour the American people ... so His divine blessing" may include his government.[22]

John Adams, in his turn, prayed to God to preserve and protect America, adding that the American experiment was made according to divine purposes:

And may that Being who is supreme over all, the Patron of Order, the Fountain of Justice, and the Protector in all ages of the world of virtuous liberty, continue His blessing upon this nation and its Government and give it all possible success and duration consistent with the ends of His providence.[23]

A more eloquent modern expression came in Calvin Coolidge's Inaugural Address of March 4, 1925, where he said:

America seeks no earthly empire built on blood and force. No ambition, no temptation, lures her to thought of foreign dominions. The legions which she sends forth are armed, not with the sword, but with the cross. The higher state to which she seeks the allegiance of all mankind is not of human, but of divine origin. She cherishes no purpose save to merit the favor of Almighty God.[24]

More recently, the administrations of Ronald Reagan and George W. Bush have openly expressed religious goals for their political actions and campaigns. President Bush, especially, has considered his election and presidency part of a divine plan. It is reported that when Bush was Governor of Texas and thought of running for President, he told his friends that God told him He wanted him to run, and when he told his mother, Barbara Bush, of his thoughts, she compared him to Moses in leading the Israelites to safety. In 1988, Pat Robertson ran for President at "God's bidding," and in 2004 he said that "God told him" that President Bush would be re-elected in a landslide.[25]

Following the terrorist attacks on New York and Washington, President Bush frequently referred to America's role in the context of a mission assigned by "history" or "fate." On February 8, 2004, President Bush appeared on the weekly program *Meet the Press* where he repeatedly cited America's responsibilities to the world and announced that this is "history's call to America." This self-perceived image of America and its historical cosmic role has led Americans to make historical decisions that have positively affected the whole world. The same self-image may cloud America's judgment and lead to very dangerous policies that can also affect the world. Indeed, it has led on several occasions to disastrous results that have stained America's history with stories of inhumanity; such are the stories of America's treatment of the American Indians, the institution of slavery, the Vietnam War and the question of Palestine.

Through all of these experiences, American statesmen and leaders used the arguments of the concept that John O'Sullivan described in the mid-nineteenth century as America's "Manifest Destiny"; these arguments have also been the justifications for America's missionary efforts to "save souls" and "reclaim the land for Christ."

Now that America is the only superpower, the danger inherent in this tendency is more imminent and can plunge the world into chaos. This danger has been recognized by prominent American intellectuals and statesmen even before the collapse of the Soviet Union. Robert Bellah remarked in 1967 that this is not just a case of imperialist expansionism. It is, he said:

> the tendency to assimilate all governments or parties in the world which support our immediate policies or call upon our help by invoking the notion of free institutions and democratic values. Those nations that are for the moment "on our side" become "the free world." A repressive and unstable military dictatorship in South Viet-Nam becomes "the free people of South Viet-Nam and their government." It is then part of the role of America as the New Jerusalem and "the last hope of earth" to defend such governments with treasure and eventually with blood. When our soldiers are actually dying, it becomes possible to consecrate the struggle further by invoking the great theme of sacrifice. For the majority of the American people who are unable to judge whether the people in South Viet-Nam (or wherever) are "free like us," such arguments are convincing.[26]

It has become quite acceptable today to describe American troops stationed in more than 136 locations around the world as champions of freedom and democracy. And just as Americans in the past identified their cause with divine will and purpose, today America's mission is a "sacred historical struggle to save human civilization," and the enemy is variously described as "the Empire of Evil," the "Axis of Evil" and similar terms.

Traditionally, any opponent of the United States has been relegated to the ranks of the "uncivilized," "rogue states" or "terrorist states"; they are all expected to change their evil ways in order to be allowed to join the community of "civilized nations." The enemy, however, does not have to belong to a specific geographical entity. Today America struggles against "terrorism," the "evil ones" and "those who hate freedom"; and today American champions of freedom and democracy can extend the threshold of their battle to include those who support terrorism, give sanctuary to terrorists, and even those who do not condemn terrorism as defined by Americans.

This sense of superiority and self-righteousness has appeared in many forms in recent years. The "arrogance of power"—as the late

Senator William Fulbright once called it—has prompted top officials in the Bush Administration to warn the United Nations (all 190 nations of the world!) to do its duty (i.e., agree with the US) or render itself "irrelevant." The same sense of self-righteousness has also allowed the American government to pressure, encourage, cajole, arm twist, and use financial aid and the threat of boycott to get other countries to support its policies.

One stark example of this tendency can be seen in statements made by Senator John McCain, an ardent advocate of war. McCain was asked how he felt about the 10 million strong who demonstrated on the same day in many parts of the world against the war on Iraq. The Senator stated that he respected their right to voice their opinion, and also respected "their right to be foolish and unwise"!—a clear departure from Jefferson's "decent respect to the opinions of mankind."

In this climate of thought, everyone is either "with us" or "against us." Consequently, the possibility—indeed the right—to resort to military action can be used against any enemy of choice, in defense of the "free world." This often happens, as Bellah put it, when

> in a moment of uncertainty [we have] been tempted to rely on our overwhelming physical power rather than on our intelligence, and we have, in part, succumbed to this temptation. Bewildered and unnerved when our terrible power fails to bring immediate success, we are at the edge of a chasm the depth of which no man knows.[27]

Written in 1967, Bellah's words ring so true in 2005.

Yet there is hope in the political wisdom and level-headedness of moderate Americans who have the moral courage to stand up to this dominant extremism of the Christian and political Right. Former President Jimmy Carter wrote a letter to the *Washington Post* (September 5, 2002), in the middle of frenzied attacks on Islam and Muslims, praising President Bush's reassuring statements to the Muslim community but expressing fear that

> formerly admired almost universally as the preeminent champion of human rights, our country has become the foremost target of respected international organizations concerned about these basic principles of democratic life. We have ignored or condoned abuses in nations that support our antiterrorism effort, while detaining American citizens as "enemy combatants," incarcerating them secretly and indefinitely without their being charged

with any crime or having the right to legal counsel. This policy has been condemned by the federal courts, but the Justice Department seems adamant, and the issue is still in doubt. Several hundred captured Taliban soldiers remain imprisoned at Guantanamo Bay under the same circumstances, with the defense secretary declaring that they would not be released even if they were someday tried and found to be innocent. These actions are similar to those of abusive regimes that historically have been condemned by American presidents.

Former President Carter voiced severe criticism of the Administration's cruel and illegal treatment of detainees and of the laws which clearly violate the basic human rights that America has always espoused. Carter also criticized American policy in the Middle East. "Tragically," he said,

our government is abandoning any sponsorship of substantive negotiations between Palestinians and Israelis. Our apparent policy is to support almost every Israeli action in the occupied territories and to condemn and isolate the Palestinians as blanket targets of our war on terrorism, while Israeli settlements expand and Palestinian enclaves shrink.

At the Nobel Peace Prize ceremony also (December, 2002), former President Carter objected to American unfair policy in support of Israeli occupation of Palestinian lands. Carter said that war is an evil that may be necessary, but it remains evil. Former President Carter expressed the hope that although

belligerent and divisive voices now seem to be dominant in Washington, they do not yet reflect final decisions of the president, Congress or the courts. It is crucial that the historical and well-founded American commitments prevail: to peace, justice, human rights, the environment and international cooperation.

Perhaps the best critical comments on America's image of self-righteousness that lead to acts of belligerencies came from the late Senator William Fulbright. In opposing the Vietnam War, Senator Fulbright described American policies in terms that apply to recent developments:

When a nation is very powerful but lacking in self-confidence, it is likely to behave in a manner that is dangerous both to itself and to others.

Gradually but unmistakably, America is succumbing to that arrogance of power which has afflicted, weakened and in some cases destroyed great nations in the past. If the war goes on and expands, if that fatal process continues to accelerate until America becomes what it is not now and never has been, a seeker after unlimited power and empire, then Vietnam will have had a mighty and tragic fallout indeed.

I do not believe that will happen. I am very apprehensive but I still remain hopeful, and even confident, that America, with its humane and democratic traditions, will find the wisdom to match its power.[28]

RELIGION AND POLITICS TODAY

In 1960, when John F. Kennedy was campaigning for the presidency, he addressed an audience of Protestant religious leaders in Houston, saying

I believe in America where the separation of church and state is absolute—where no Catholic prelate would tell the president (should he be a Catholic) how to act, and no Protestant minister would tell his parishioners for whom to vote.[29]

Almost 40 years later, religious interference in politics reached such a height that President Clinton complained to the *Electronic Magazine* of the United States Information Agency (March issue) of the frequency of public statements by politicians about their religious beliefs and affiliations.

And commenting on religious activism in politics which characterized political developments since the 1960s, Keith Gephart—himself a Fundamentalist preacher—remarked: "When I was growing up, I always heard that churches should stay out of politics. Now it seems almost a sin *not* to get involved."[30] This was in stark contrast to the first half of the twentieth century during which churches and religious leaders seldom openly interfered in the political process or in the affairs of the state. The idealistic dream of President Kennedy remained a dream, while in the real world the religious community, especially what came to be known as the Religious Right, became more and more involved in politics.

In their turn, politicians also have played up to religious groups and constituencies, and sought their support. Ever since the 1980s, politicians and aspirants to political positions became featured speakers at religious functions and on religious television channels.

This has been especially true of the Republican Party leaders on the one hand, and the Southern Baptist Convention and other Christian Right groups on the other. A *Newsweek* writer described this feature of the 1984 election campaign: "[Fundamentalism] is a constituency that the president [Reagan] has assiduously courted, appearing, for example, on Jerry Falwell's 'Old-Time Gospel Hour' last March. Fundamentalist churches are now an integral part of GOP registration drives."[31]

In the 1984 election campaign, the interaction between religion and politics was an accepted fact of life, in spite of the protests that cited the Constitution for their separation. Indeed, many religious leaders and politicians have (until now) been quoting the First Amendment as a guard against official recognition of religion; but in the second half of the twentieth, and into this present century, it has become almost imperative for religion to play a role in the political process.

Leaders of the Christian Right, including the various divisions of American conservative Protestant churches, have been frequent participants in political events. Jerry Falwell and Pat Robertson are only two prominent examples of pastors who enlisted the help of their followers in supporting the candidates of their choice.

Just as the Republican Party has traditionally allied itself with the Christian Right, Democrats have resorted to similar tactics in seeking the support of moderate white Christians, African-American churches and the Jewish vote. Since the 1980s, both white and black churches, especially in the South, became voter registration centers, and preachers used the pulpit to urge their congregations to vote for this candidate or that. African-American congregations were fired up by the emotional sermons and speeches which used the rhetoric of the freedom movement of the 1960s in the political election context. As a result, African-American participation in the political process became quite effective, and voter registration drives by the church yielded good results. In fact, one of the African-American churchmen, Bishop H.H. Brookins of Los Angeles, said of the 1984 campaign: "No black politician of note can say he or she had been elected without the black church."[32]

This statement is also an accurate description of the successive (if unsuccessful) campaigns for the nomination of the Reverend Jesse Jackson for President. Jackson's campaigns have been sponsored and constantly supported by the African-American churches, especially the National Baptist Convention. Jackson's Bible Belt voter registration drive in 1984 resulted in the registration of millions and in a political awareness and activism never seen before in the African-American community. The intensity of the religious involvement in politics can be illustrated by the competition for the Senate seat of North Carolina in 1984 between the incumbent Senator Jessie Helms and Governor Jim Hunt. After a long career as an extreme right-wing Republican, as television political commentator, and as member of the US Senate for many years, in 1984 Helms' position was seriously challenged by Jim Hunt with the backing of Rev. Jesse Jackson and his constituency in the Bible Belt and the National Baptist Convention. Jackson himself was attempting to gain the Democratic Party's nomination for the presidency. This became a joint campaign for Jackson and Hunt.

Helms, on the other hand, received the backing of the Christian Right, including persons like Jerry Falwell, and the support of the Southern Baptist Convention. Helms' and Reagan's campaigns also became a joint effort by the Republican Party and the Christian Right. Falwell's phenomenal efforts made a great contribution to Reagan's and Helms's victories in the 1984 elections. *Time* magazine reported at the time that Falwell's Moral Majority gave Reagan 100 percent backing of its 6.5 million members. The Moral Majority had a plan to register 2 million additional voters that year. Falwell boasted that "they have enough influence to decide the results of the election."[33] The voter registration drive aimed at using 150,000 churches nationwide.[34] Additionally, the Helms campaign headquarters used the mailing list of the Southern Baptist Convention (albeit without permission) to send (18,000) letters to pastors and church leaders. Helms was aware of the power of religious sentiments in the election process, and he played on them. In his Moose Lodge Auditorium campaign speech, Helms told his constituents in a warning tone: "I think the Lord is giving us one more chance to save this country." Echoes of this divine mission resounded on the campaign trail of both parties. In the speech delivered by Jerry Falwell at the Republican Party Convention in Dallas—itself a significant departure from party convention traditions—he announced that Reagan and Bush were "God's instruments in rebuilding America."[35] And Pat Boone, the born-again Evangelist singer, also declared to his fans that "you and I need Jesse in Washington. America needs him. God needs him."[36]

After the 1984 campaign, Americans gradually saw the effectiveness of Falwell's opinion that "it is not only legitimate to advocate basic religious values in the political arena, but it is essential for the health of our republic that believers participate in the debate of the day." His basic belief is that it is the religious duty of a Christian to participate in politics and that he can "be true neither to his country nor to God" if he separates his religious convictions from his political views. After all, as Falwell told his Moral Majority and congregations, this was "the basic belief that drove the Pilgrims to our shores."[37] This kind of involvement of religion in politics set the tone for subsequent political elections and events. In the 1988 presidential elections, Pat Robertson attempted to get the Republican nomination, but Falwell's endorsement of George Bush, Sr., tipped the balance against him. In fact, Falwell's influence on the Christian Right was a major factor which gave Bush the victory.

It has also become acceptable for US presidents to consult with and seek the advice of religious leaders in matters of domestic and foreign policy. It is reported that President Bush, Sr., had a session with Jerry Falwell on the eve of the Gulf War. And when George W. Bush reached 40, his father asked the Rev. Billy Graham to pray with him in the hope that he would mend his ways. After a night-long prayer session with Graham, George W. "found Christ" and became a "born-again Christian." Ever since, Bush has openly adopted the Christian Right agenda and beliefs. The present Administration has committed itself to a religious stand on many issues, and before the dust has settled on the elections of November 2004, this kind of religious rhetoric is more likely to increase. Members of the Administration have at various times made remarks that are consistent with the principles of the Christian Right. The Attorney General had declared on one occasion that there is one king in America and that is King Jesus, and has been reported to compare "Allah" very unfavorably with God. The Secretary of Defense has stated that what is going on at this time is a "war of ideas," and an army general with an influential title has publicly reviled Islam and declared that "they hate us because of our Judeo-Christian beliefs." The President has launched his "Faith-Based Initiative," frequently courted religious organizations such as "The Christian Broadcasters Association," and received in the White House the two "freed" American missionaries to Afghanistan who had lied about the nature of their work there.

These moves also include policies that are consistent with the open statements of faith made by members of the Administration. They also include such issues as the "right to life," school prayers and gay rights. The President has even advocated the extreme suggestion of amending the Constitution to make same-sex marriage illegal. These declared religious beliefs have influenced the self-righteous image that President Carter and Senator Fulbright warned against in the context of relations with other nations.

In a perceptive essay on President Bush's upbringing and education, Michael Ortiz Hill portrayed the President as a person driven by millennial and dispensational beliefs. Hill's essay carries the appropriate title: "Mine Eyes Have Seen the Glory: Bush's Armageddon Obsession," *Counter Punch* (January 4, 2003). According to Hill, Bush was taught by Billy Graham to live in expectation of the Second Coming, but the person who helped shape his ideology was his close friend Dr. Tony Evans. The overlapping of political principles and end-times expectations is at the core of Evans's teachings and of the goals of his "Promise Keepers" organization. Evans taught Bush how to look at the world from the vantage point of the Lord, and that the only way to "save the world" is to return it to the control of the "people of God." So, when following the September 11 terrorist attacks on America, Bush and his lieutenants repeatedly spoke of "ridding the world of evil," they were actually criss-crossing the line between the current political situation of defending America and the larger divine plan of saving the world. In fact, Hill suggested that by going against the opinions of millions across the world, including some of his military and political advisors, "Bush is literally and determinedly drawn, consciously and unconsciously, toward the enactment of such a scenario, as he believes, for God's sake. Indeed the stark relentlessness of his policy in the Middle East suggests as much."[38] The combined efforts of this Judeo-Christian belief and the ideology of Islamic extremists may, according to Hill, push the world to a state of complete chaos.

The call of history, according to the President, has come to the right nation. On studying this Judeo-Christian strain in American culture, one cannot fail to see in the present situation a continuation of the Puritan belief that America was preserved from the beginning of creation to appear at the right time and play a central role in God's plan. The principles of civil and religious millennialism and of the Judeo-Christian tradition are clearly at work today.

THE ISRAEL–ISLAM FACTOR

The central position of end-times ideology in the present Administration's agenda is nowhere more aggressive than in America's policy toward the Arab–Israeli conflict. Yet, the present US Administration does not hold a monopoly on this policy. Judeo-Christian beliefs have been at the heart of statements, behavior and active involvement in the affairs of the Arab World on many levels of the American nation.

Three events marked significant turning points in the modern development of American politics and religion and of America's policy towards the Palestine question. They are:

(1) The establishment of the state of Israel in 1947.
(2) The open participation of the Christian Right in the 1984 American election campaign.
(3) The barbaric attacks on the Trade Center and the Pentagon on September 11, 2001.

Although these momentous events may not seem directly related to America's involvement in the affairs of the Arab World, an analysis of American domestic and foreign policy will reveal a strong, if sometimes latent, connection. The analysis presented here has to be brief and selective, first, because of the wealth of interrelated materials, and, secondly, because at the time of writing events are still unfolding almost on a daily basis which are in part consequences of these three events.

The Judeo-Christian tradition has been a continuous thread that binds many aspects of American life. In modern history, this tradition can be illustrated in these three events in all its literal and symbolic manifestations. The establishment of the political state of Israel was the result not only of foreign policy considerations, but also of the constant Western preoccupation with Apocalyptic visions and the Jeremiad. And the results of this event went far beyond political ramifications and military hostilities. The state of Israel strengthened the belief in an Apocalyptic vision of the world among the increasingly powerful Christian Right in the United States. Since then, there has been a surge of activities on various levels that stem from this Judeo-Christian Apocalyptic vision.

One illustration of this vision merits a detailed analysis. In 1950, three years after the establishment of Israel, the retired Chief Justice of the US Supreme Court, William Douglas, made a trip around the world and recorded his experiences in a book entitled *Strange Lands, Friendly People*. In Syria, Iraq and Jordan, Douglas visited the refugee camps recently populated by Palestinian refugees who were uprooted by the Israelis. Douglas described rather sympathetically the life of misery and destitution led by these refugees. He recognized the tragedy of these homeless people, especially when he visited the Sukhne Refugee Camp in Jordan which housed 16,000 people. Dysentery, malnourishment and the general atmosphere of squalor and poverty were all recognized by the American visitor, but his conclusions did not depart from the manner of Western Orientalist generalizations about Muslims and Arabs; the fact that these refugees were the outcome of the establishment of a state in their homeland for another people did not merit his attention. In fact, throughout his account, Douglas refers to Palestinian refugees as "Arabs" or "Moslems," very seldom as "Palestinians."

Amid this tragic scene, Douglas summed up the situation, together with its causes, in no uncertain terms:

> The scourge of the Arab world, so far as small children and others who have not built up an immunity are concerned, is dysentery. Dysentery and under-nourishment go hand in hand. In the Moslem world if there is not enough food to satisfy the hunger of the whole family, the boys and men are fed first, the girls and women last. It's a man's world; and every advantage from birth on through life is granted the male.
>
> We saw at Sukhneh an example of this. In one of the hospital tents British nurses were giving intravenous injections to some babies less than a year old.
>
> "What is the trouble?" I asked a slim, blue-eyed, blonde nurse.
>
> "These are girls who were about to die from undernourishment and dysentery," she replied.
>
> "Many cases like this in camp?"
>
> "I've been here a month; and I would say we have saved the lives of at least two hundred little girls this way."[39]

The site of the Sukhne Camp stirred the former Chief Justice's cultural memory. In the land where the camels of Arabs were trying to search "the scorched earth for nibbles of nourishment," Douglas was quick to notice that

> this plateau is a part of Moab, sometimes known as the Mount or Mountains of Abarim.
>
> It was from Moab that Moses first saw the Promised Land. This is a land of scorpions and vipers—the region of the fiery serpents of Biblical fame (Numbers 21:6). Moab has little rainfall—from six to ten inches a year.

The land is dry and parched in the summer. Here the Israelites had to dig for water as they sang, "Spring up, O well; sing ye unto it" (Numbers 21:17). Here in the land of Moab at some unknown spot Moses lies buried (Deuteronomy 34:6).[40]

The Judeo-Christian set of beliefs were especially apparent in Douglas's reactions to what he saw in the newly created state of Israel. He was given a tour of the city of Jerusalem by "the famed Colonel Moshe Dayan of the Israeli Army and his wife Ruth." Douglas remarked on the Arabs' determination "to defend with their lives the shrines holy to them," associating it with what he saw as "religious fanaticism [that] grew in the breasts of many." Yet Douglas had nothing but admiration for Dayan's emphatic statement that "these historic spots are ours and we must occupy them."[41]

In stark contrast to Douglas's description of the life of hopelessness and destitution in refugee camps, his narrative of the lives of European arrivals in Palestine is very comforting. Jews were coming out of a synagogue "back to their new homes; children were doing a hop, skip, and jump along the road; a rabbi, bent in meditation, walked slowly through the village. The men and women pouring out of the synagogues had faces that were happy and relaxed." Having "barely escaped death at the hands of Hitler's henchmen, for them," Douglas said, "this was, indeed, the Promised Land. Here refugees from terror and agonizing death had found security, freedom, or peaceful valley ... Their new freedom was reflected in their eyes, in the spring of their walk, in the laughter of their children."[42]

Douglas's admiration of the new Israelites stems both from their determination and his education in the tradition of biblical prophecies. In Jerusalem he met the newly appointed Supreme Court Judges, an incident that recalled his Judeo-Christian education. He said that this place witnessed

an ingathering of exiles from many lands. They had come to reclaim Jerusalem and the Holy Land, to dedicate it to the freedom of man, to make this city a righteous one and thus to fulfill the prophecy. Like the Jews who manned the outposts of the Israeli Army or tilled the fields, these lawyers and judges were also inspired. They had a zeal, a drive, a purpose, a cause. They were dedicating themselves to a crusade in this, the Eternal City. They were laying in Jerusalem the foundations for the capital of the new state of Israel.[43]

The zeal, purpose, cause and dedication to a crusade are admirable qualities in the Jewish settlers. The Arabs' determination to defend their homes, on the other hand, can only be described as religious fanaticism.

Douglas also quoted the statement of Ben-Gurion, the first Israeli Prime Minister, that Jerusalem would be the unified "Eternal" capital of Israel, commenting, "so it was three thousand years ago, so it will be, we believe, until the end of time" (echos of John Barclay's book!). And of the Histadrut, the trade union which helped settle Jews in Palestine, Douglas approvingly described its "invaluable services to the cause of Zionism ... More than any other group, it is responsible for the actual reclamation and settlement of Israel."

In a separate chapter, which he entitled "The Eternal City," Douglas described his tour of a number of Christian ancient sites, and rhetorically asked his guide: "All of Jerusalem seems to me to be a Christian Shrine. How can the Arabs lay claim to it?"[44] Has not this question also been asked by generations of Western Christians who never laid eyes on the Holy Land but who claimed ownership of it by divine dispensation?

In the chapter which Douglas devoted to the description of the conflict over Palestine, he began by presenting Islam to his readers as the "world of Allah reduced by Mohammed to the Koran." Muhammad, according to Douglas, left "behind a militant religion and a group of fanatic followers who used the Book and the Sword to conquer the earth." By contrast, the Crusaders' invasion of the Arab World, for Douglas, came in a "holy cause" because, as Pope Urban II had announced, "God wills it." And the Arabs who fought the Crusaders back had "a leadership driven by a religious fanaticism. With them the jihad (holy war) was a duty."[45]

The Chief Justice of the US Supreme Court, together with the rest of the Judges, is entrusted with the sacred duty of ensuring the separation of church and state and to guard against the trampling of civil liberties by religious prejudice. As Chief Justice, Douglas had conducted himself properly in discharging his duties. Yet, all of this became irrelevant when it came to Douglas's treatment of Islam, and his attitude to beliefs embedded in America's Judeo-Christian heritage.

The idiom used by the former Chief Justice is all-too-familiar. It had been used, as we have seen, by American travelers and missionaries in the Arab World; it is still used by the American Christian Right, with special emphasis after September 11, 2001.

The Legislature in the US has shown even more prejudice and enthusiasm in dealing with the Palestinian–Israeli conflict. Time and again the Congress passed resolutions calling on the government to recognize Jerusalem as the unified capital of Israel and to move its embassy there. The Congress has also on an annual basis voted to give Israel billions of dollars in grants and loans with total disregard to Israel's violations of international law and scores of UN resolutions. These unanimous decisions of the US Congress are matched by statements and actions of its members and other American politicians, religious leaders and public figures.

In 1997, Newt Gingrich visited Israel to celebrate the thirtieth anniversary of the occupation of Jerusalem and to affirm the number of resolutions passed unanimously by the US Congress to recognize Jerusalem as the capital of Israel. The Speaker of the American House of Representatives did not even give a thought to the thousands of Arabs who have been expelled from the city of their birth and ancestors or to the inhuman treatment the Arabs remaining in the city are daily subjected to. Nor did the American chief legislator recall the scores of UN resolutions condemning Israeli annexation of Jerusalem as a violation of international law and of the most basic of human rights. There was no place in dispensational discourse for such mundane considerations.

In the same year, Al Gore, Vice President and presidential hopeful, visited Israel to celebrate the fulfillment of a "three-thousand-year-old miracle," i.e., the establishment of the political state of Israel. When asked by a reporter about his feelings concerning the 4-million-plus Palestinians who have been displaced from their homes where they and their ancestors had been living for over 3,000 years, and who have been suffering the pain and deprivation of exile, Gore's answer was a painfully patronizing: "Let us not dwell on the past, and let us look to a better future for everybody." Only one who has been raised in the cultural tradition and mythology of this idiom can in one breath "celebrate the *fulfillment of a three-thousand-year-old miracle*" and advise the Arabs "*not to dwell on the past.*"

And shortly after the massacre at Qana, where the Israeli army bombed a UN compound, killing close to 300 civilians who were taking shelter there, President Clinton received the Prime Minister of Israel at Whiteman Air Force base. Clinton's welcoming remarks included a warm handshake and a celebration of "our shared values."

Tom DeLay and Dick Armey, both prominent members of Congress, appeared more than once in 2002 on separate TV shows, and made no secret of their desire to have all Palestinians, 4 million or so, removed from Palestine because there is no room for them in the land that belongs to Israel! House Majority Leader Dick Armey (R-Texas), talking to Chris Mathews (*Hardball*, May 1, 2002), referred to the occupied West Bank and Gaza as Israel, and stated that the Palestinians should leave and establish a state somewhere else "just as Jews came from all over the world and established their state in Palestine." Mathews gave Armey many chances to deny that he was calling for an ethnic cleansing operation, but the House Republican Leader insisted that the Palestinians should be removed.

In his turn, Tom DeLay (*Meet the Press*, May 5, 2002) referred to the West Bank as Judea and Samaria, and called for the transfer of Palestinians because "this land belongs to Israel." The two leaders in the nation's highest legislative body had no difficulty calling for an operation of ethnic cleansing on a massive scale because the land "belongs to the Jewish people." No public protest was heard, not from human rights, civil liberties, or any other group.

On February 18, 2000, the 86-year-old renowned long-time news reporter who covered the White House for 52 years, Sara McLendon, told a VOA host that the greatest American president she knew was Harry S. Truman. The reason? "Why, if it weren't for Truman, there would be no Israel!"

On Thursday, February 18, 2000, all three Republican contenders for the nomination of their party—Bush, McCain, and Keyes—responded to a Larry King question about whether they would recognize Jerusalem as the capital of Israel in the following manner:

> Bush: "Immediately."
> McCain: "Definitely."
> Keyes: "I believe we should."

Bush stated that he would commit American troops to action if "America's vital interests" are threatened, volunteering as an example of that eventuality, "if Israel's security is threatened."

During the 2000 presidential campaign, George Bush and Al Gore participated in a debate on October 11, 2000. One of the questions was about their respective positions vis-à-vis the Arab–Israeli conflict. Bush said that peace in the Middle East was part of the United States' vital interests. Gore answered that Syria must release the three Israeli POWs, Arafat must order an end to violence, and that Iraq still posed a threat. He added that Israel must feel safe all the

time, because the relations between America and Israel are permanent and strengthened by traditional ideological bonds that do not
change with events. And Bush retorted that Israel would always be
America's ally and that he would always stand by Israel. He added
that he also thought Arafat should order a stop to violence. The
moderator at that point concluded—not without some sarcasm in
his tone—that neither of them believed that the United States
should take sides!

During the last days of Clinton's presidency, he granted amnesty
to Mark Rich who had been a fugitive in Europe convicted for tax
evasion and fraud. Clinton defended this decision on the basis of
the tremendous amount of money given by Rich to Israel, and cited
the intercession of many Israeli former and present government top
officials.[46] Finally, in October 1994, following the signing of the
Wadi Araba agreement in Jordan, Clinton went to Israel where he
addressed the Israeli Knesset, again celebrating the cultural and
humanitarian values that bond the two nations.

Even after leaving office, Clinton continued his expressions of support for Israel. On July 29, 2002, for example, Clinton, addressing a
fundraising dinner for Israel in Canada, restated his support for Israel
and also offered to carry a gun and be in the frontline trenches to
defend Israel if its security was threatened. This came from a person
who refused to join his country's army during the Vietnam War.

In a long article on the 1984 election campaign, the *Mideast
Monitor* (January 1985) surveyed the promises made to support
Israel in its conflict with the Arabs by those running for seats in the
Congress. In fact, a close look at the political platforms of both
parties will show an unwavering commitment to maintain Israel's
security and its goals in the Middle East. The Republican Party
boasted of the efforts it was making to help Soviet Jews settle
in Palestine, and of President Reagan's personal involvement in
building the Holocaust monument. The Democrats, however, criticized the Reagan Administration's wavering policy regarding the
Arab–Israeli conflict, and promised to be more aggressive in its support of Soviet Jewry. The Democrats pledged to work for a solution
to the Middle East conflict, but without harming "Israel's interests."

On the religious front, the situation is even more aggravating,
especially because all of the players are of the genuinely "compas-
sionate conservative" type. In 1985 the International Christian
Embassy convened the first Zionist-Christian conference on August 27
in Basle, Switzerland—similar to the first Zionist Conference

convened by Hertzel in 1897, and in the same hall. The conference decided that Jerusalem—the City of David—is the unified eternal capital of Israel, and that Judea and Samaria—misnamed by Arabs the West Bank!—are part of Israel by virtue of Old Testament rights.

Pat Robertson, Jerry Falwell, Tim LaHay, Hal Lindsey, William H. Armstrong, Oral Roberts and scores of other religious leaders have always identified the events in the Middle East, especially those connected with Israel, as the acting out of God's millennial plan. Billy Graham, known and highly respected by millions for his humanity and compassion, added his voice early in the game to this chorus of pro-Israel statements based on religious beliefs. One of Reverend Graham's contributions to this cause is a film produced shortly after the establishment of the state of Israel called *His Land*. Alfred Lilienthal's description of the film sums up its beauty and its effect on the viewer:

> A particularly vivid influence has been the beautiful film made by Billy Graham, *His Land*, which has been viewed by fifteen millions across this country and Canada. This superbly photographed visual survey of the land of Israel, accompanied by narrated biblical prophecies and religious songs, celebrates the fact that God has kept His word to the Jew, that He has fulfilled prophetic promises given 2,500 years ago by restoring Israel in the 20th century. As the film's advertisements put it: "Israel today is a living testimony to the words of the Old Testament prophets, and a portent of the triumphant return of Christ." The rebirth of the State of Israel by United Nations decree on November 29, 1947, is by far the greatest biblical event that has taken place during the twentieth century.[47]

The Reverend Graham had no words of compassion or commiseration for the Palestinians displaced from "His Land" in the acting out of God's plan. What is important to note here is the immense popularity and influence of these religious leaders; tens of millions of peoples are reported to tune in to their broadcasts and to turn up at their meetings.

Literal interpretations of biblical prophecies and the application of these prophecies to modern events have been openly and consistently challenged by many religious and political groups and individuals. Many also opposed the vicious attacks on Islam and Muslems, the evil-vs-good rhetoric labeling whole nations and ethnic groups, and the rush to go-it-alone in the "war on terror." Opposition to these trends came from religious groups such as the

National Council of Churches, the Churches for Middle East Peace, the Evangelical Lutheran Church in America and the General Assembly of the Presbyterian Church, USA, to name only a few.

On October 7, 2002, a day after Jerry Falwell made an attack on Islam and called Muhammad a terrorist, the National Council of Churches (representing 36 denominations with 50 million members) issued a statement unanimously condemning and repudiating Falwell's attacks, describing them as hateful and destructive. And on June 27, 2002, the Council joined the Civil Human and Voting Rights Task Force of the Washington Inter-religious Staff Community in issuing a document sent to the US President, the Attorney General and the House and Senate Judiciary Committees. The document acknowledged the necessity "to protect our nation from further danger and harm," but cautioned against adopting "methods by which we compromise the very liberty we seek to defend." Noting that "the right of due process has been eroded since September 11," the declaration stated that "persons must be free from arbitrary arrest and detention; must have a just and open trial with the opportunity to confront accusers; and must have access to meaningful judicial oversight" (www.ncccusa.org).

Elenie K. Huszagh, President of NCC, and Bob Edgar, NCC General Secretary, warned on many occasions against the prejudice and hatred which are bred by dividing the world into "us" and "them," the "good" and the "evil." Bob Edgar, on June 19, 2002, responded to the attacks by pastor Jerry Vines on Islam and the Prophet of Islam. Pointing at the dismay felt by many Christians at these statements, Edgar said: "Already many Southern Baptists, along with American Baptists and others, have publicly voiced their dismay at his divisive language, emphasizing that he does not speak for them. They note with sadness that Vines' remarks may well generate anger and fear among many Muslims, and move some among us to disrespect and suspicion of Muslims, if not to acts of hate against them."

With the same spirit of tolerance and Christian humaneness, the President of the Evangelical Lutheran Church in America, Bishop Mark S. Hanson, issued a letter to Christians on the third anniversary of September 11 in which he said: "We pray for those who know the isolation of being suspect simply by virtue of their ethnicity." And in opposing the bellicose fever which swept Washington after September 11, the General Assembly of the Presbyterian Church issued a "Message to the Church and the Nation" in which it stated:

> We offer this word to our church and to our government out of our own concern for peace and on behalf of our many church partners around the world who are deeply concerned about our government's new doctrine of pre-emptive military action and its possible impact on the people of Iraq.

To appreciate the influence these organizations have on mainstream Christians and the extent to which they represent, one has only to look at the churches which belong to them. Churches for Middle East Peace, for example, is a Washington-based program of the American Friends Service committee, Catholic Conference of Major Superiors of Men's Institutes, Christian Church (Disciples of Christ), Church of the Brethren, Church World Service, Episcopal Church, Evangelical Lutheran Church in America, Friends Committee on National Legislation, Maryknoll Missioners, Mennonite Central Committee, National Council of the Churches of Christ in the USA, Presbyterian Church (USA), Reformed Church in America, Unitarian Universalist Association of Congregations, United Church of Christ and the United Methodist Church.

Membership of the National Council of Churches also includes:

African Methodist Episcopal Church
African Methodist Episcopal Zion Church
Alliance of Baptists
American Baptist Churches in the USA
The Antiochian Orthodox Christian Archdiocese of North America
Diocese of the Armenian Church of America
Christian Church (Disciples of Christ)
Christian Methodist Episcopal Church
Church of the Brethren
The Coptic Orthodox Church in North America
The Episcopal Church
Evangelical Lutheran Church in America
Friends United Meeting
Greek Orthodox Archdiocese of America
Hungarian Reformed Church in America
International Council of Community Churches
Korean Presbyterian Church in America
Malankara Orthodox Syrian Church
Mar Thoma Church

Moravian Church in America Northern Province and Southern
  Province
National Baptist Convention of America
National Baptist Convention, USA, Inc.
National Missionary Baptist Convention of America
Orthodox Church in America
Patriarchal Parishes of the Russian Orthodox Church in the USA
Philadelphia Yearly Meeting of the Religious Society of Friends
Polish National Catholic Church of America
Presbyterian Church (USA)
Progressive National Baptist Convention, Inc.
Reformed Church in America
Serbian Orthodox Church in the USA and Canada
The Swedenborgian Church
Syrian Orthodox Church of Antioch
Ukrainian Orthodox Church of America
United Church of Christ
The United Methodist Church

Of the prominent individual voices opposing the post-September
11 policies, mention should be made of the Rev. Dr. Charles Kimball,
Baptist minister and Chair of the Department of Religion at Wake
Forest University, who commented on pro-Israeli statements by US
politicians and Christian leaders. It noted:

> It is my hope that Christians in the US will affirm solidarity with *both* Israelis
> and Palestinians in their quest for peace, justice and security. Jesus was a
> peacemaker. We are called to a ministry of reconciliation as peacemakers. To
> suggest that Jesus would want the expulsion of Palestinian Christians and
> Muslims from Israel and Palestine or that he would support the continued
> killing of any people in the Middle East represents Christian theology at its
> worst. (Received from Jim Wetekam, Churches for Middle East Peace,
> September 30, 2002)

Former US President Jimmy Carter, who is a prominent figure in the
Southern Baptist Convention, has spoken out many times against what
he sees as misguided religious and political policies and practices.
Carter described religious interference in politics as "brought about by
the abandonment of some of the basic principles of Christianity."
Carter also criticized the Fundamentalist self-righteous habits of
branding everyone who disagreed as wrong, inferior and subhuman
(interviewed for *Prospect* by Ayelish McGarvay, May 4, 2004).

The list of groups and individuals who oppose the extreme right-wing tendencies that have gained ground in the United States is very long. Their voices are sometimes drowned by the din of drumbeats and Christian Zionists rhetoric. They are, nonetheless, there and have made their imprint on the religious and political scene.

10

America and the Millennial Fever

> I have not sent these prophets, saith the Lord, yet thei
> ranne: I have not spoken to them, and yet thei prophesied.
>
> Jeremiah, 23:21

When Saint Augustine wrote his great book, *The City Of God* (AD 426),
he referred to a pure spiritual state into which the church community
entered. This symbolic interpretation, however, was discarded by the
majority of Christian Europe in favor of a literal interpretation. Pope
Urban II's call for a campaign to "regain" the Holy Land was supported with the claim that this was "the will of God." In fact, from
the tenth century on, literal interpretations of the prophetic sacred
texts invested the elements of historical determinism with goals
more relevant to political geography and socio-economic considerations. As early as AD 950, the French monk Adso, in his book, *Letters
on the Antichrist*, laid the groundwork for subsequent literal interpretations of the Bible, especially the prophetic texts.

And when Richard the Lionheart joined the Third Crusade, he
stopped in Messina, Italy, to consult with Joachim of Fiory who had
claimed in 1184 that he received a revelation of "God's Plan" for the
universe. Richard was told that he would play a vital role in the
"plan" by defeating Saladin, the Antichrist, and regaining Jerusalem.

At the turn of the sixteenth century, there came a second and
more intense phase in the efforts to carry out God's plan for the universe. Christopher Columbus carried this millennial discourse further by claiming that since his childhood he had been receiving
instructions and inspirations from the Holy Ghost to undertake his
"Enterprise of the Indies." As we have seen, Columbus wrote about
his role in the divine plan in many letters, journal entries, and especially in his only book, *The Book of Prophecies*. His ultimate goal, he
said, was to discover new lands, enlist new nations in the war
against the evil empire of Muhammad, and finally repossess the
Holy Land and Jerusalem in preparation for Christ's return. When

Columbus returned from his last trip, he offered to finance a fourth crusade. The Holy Ghost, he said, repeatedly touched him and told him that he would have a hand in bringing about the Millennial reign of Christ on his throne in Jerusalem.

Throughout the European presence in North America, the concept of the Coming Kingdom and a host of other prophetic events have been a basic paradigm in American culture. The preceding chapters of this work have demonstrated this aspect, and the list of selected samples of American predictions of the end of the world which is appended to this chapter shows American preoccupation with this concept. The concept remains today just as basic, indeed more potentially dangerous, in American thinking and action.

Only three days after the September 11 attacks, and in a rare joint appearance on television, Jerry Falwell and Pat Robertson discussed the significance of the event. They decided that "we made God mad" and that in these horrible deeds "God gave us what we deserve." The two old rivals who have been competing for the leadership of the religious Right in the US agreed that Americans have "just seen the antechamber of terror." Falwell elaborated on the theme: "I blame the CL groups, the feminists, the homosexuals, the abortionists, and the federal courts, because they threw God out of the public square … I put the finger in their face and say 'You helped this happen!'" Pat and Jerry did blame the "terrorists legally and morally," but in their view it was these groups that brought about God's punishment.

Both religious preachers, who enjoy phenomenal popularity among the Fundamentalists and the Christian Right constituencies, agreed that the terrorists were simply tools in the hands of an angry God, used to punish Americans for the sins of liberals, feminists, and homosexuals. That the terrorists may have had their own reasons or motives was of no consequence. Moreover, and just as importantly, both Robertson and Falwell have ardently and unconditionally supported Israel for over 40 years, and have consistently cited God's "purpose and plan" to explain every event that has taken place since the establishment of the state of Israel. The conversation between Falwell and Robertson and their espousal of the cause of Israel with reference to apocalyptic beliefs are at the heart of the American Judeo-Christian tradition and are a major factor in the culture clash with the Arab/Muslim World. This, however, is not a new development. The September 11 attacks served to intensify the millennial discourse, but it did not start it. The horrible event provided many in the Christian and political Right with the license to demonize Islam and to establish new intolerant rules of debate and encounter which would have been unacceptable before.

The association of the divine plan for the world with the conflict with Islam, however, has been a constant component in the American formula for end-of-the-world scenarios. The nineteenth-century biographer of the Prophet of Islam, George Bush, and his contemporary missionaries in the cause of Zion, Henry Jessup and John Barclay, actually discovered that the rise and fall of Islam and the entire career of Muhammad were essential parts of the divine plan. In 1847, Bush said that his "grand object in writing the biography" was "to exhibit the Arabian prophet as a signal instrument in the hands of Providence, and to put the whole system of his imposture, with its causes, accomplishments, and effects, where it properly belongs, into the great scheme of the Divine administration of the world."[1]

In the United States of America, "Providential plan" explications and "divine map-making" have been going on for centuries. During the second half of the twentieth century, and at the turn of the present century, this cultural exercise took on a more populist phase, thanks to the tremendous progress in the publishing industry, radio and television broadcasting and electronic communications.

One illustration of the use of the World Wide Web by prophecy advocates merits detailed analysis because it represents this trend in the Christian Right. In 1974 the Bible Believers' Evangelistic Association published the first of a series of pictures and posters graphically describing "God's Plan" and purpose for the universe.[2] This is representative of hundreds of electronic and hard-copy publications on millennial expectations. The "Plan" has sold millions of copies and is used as a teaching tool in religious courses and seminars and missionary schools. The picture in this publication presents the Fundamentalist artist's concept of the events which take place during the "Rapture of the saved." The figure of Christ in the clouds appears at the top center stretching His arms to "receive up to Himself" those who believed in Him. The "dead in Christ" rise from the grave, and the "living in Christ" are "caught up" or quickly removed to meet Christ in the clouds. The text explains the events of the Rapture which include the sudden and mysterious disappearance of millions of people, and the resulting "world crisis, confusion and panic." Cars, trains and other vehicles have crashed; an airplane slams into a large building complex; there are fires, looting, "rampage, lawlessness, crimes and mobs" running out of control; and "families 'Terrified and in Shock' over missing saved family members (and babies?), while the unsaved family members are still left on the earth." According to this "map," "signs of the times" which lead the Fundamentalists to believe that the Rapture and the Return of Christ are around the corner—if indeed they have not happened already— are indicated by the following events:

• June, 1967—The Israeli "Six Day War." Israel regained Jerusalem and old Temple site. This was necessary before building of the Tribulation Temple (Rev. 11:1, 2).
• The increase of demon activity, homosexuality and drugs (I Tim.4:1; II Tim. 3:1–13; Rev. 9:21).
• 1973—Energy crisis, setting the stage for global hunger and starvation of millions during the Tribulation (Rev. 6:5–8).
• 1991—Gulf War in Iran and world coalition of (*New Age terms*) the "*Global Community*" and "*New World Order*." These further set the stage for the world leader (Antichrist) to control world trade and the worship of the world during the Tribulation (Rev. 13:7, 8; 13–17).

Another publication of the Bible Believers' Evangelistic Association which came out at the same time (1974) was a poster entitled "A Tribulation Map." In the "divine plan" according to the Christian Right groups, "Rapture" precedes "Tribulation" and prepares for it. The events which take place during the Tribulation seven-year period—especially those which closely follow the Rapture—are of special significance. They include:

• The Return of Jesus Christ in glory (Rev. 19:11–16).
• Conclusion of the Battle of Armageddon (19:17–19).
• Destruction of Antichrist "world leader" (19:20).
• Destruction of the people who followed him (19:21).

THE PROVIDENTIAL PLAN

What Robertson, Falwell, the Evangelistic Association, and hundreds of preachers and religious leaders in the West have been advocating is a "divine plan" drawn up by God for the universe and for all of humanity, from Creation to Judgment Day; a plan with God's signature and seal, that cannot be disputed or altered. The "plan," furthermore, presents a number of themes, the most important of which is the central position given to the Arab region, more particularly to the Holy Land and Israel.

Indeed, it has been the singular misfortune of the Arab World to be situated in an area to which the West has laid claim by virtue of a distorted religious ideology, which has been the focus of the activities and statements of Western religious and political leaders for centuries. These activities and statements have gained momentum during the past century, especially after the creation of the state of Israel. They have increased further in intensity and volume shortly before the end of the second and the beginning of the third millennium. The events of the war against Iraq and of September 11, 2001, have given more fuel to these millennial activities.

Western religious claims to this part of the world are based on perceived divine dispensation and consequently they are not subject to negotiation. So strong is the belief in the "divine plan" that history as written and witnessed by men is faulted in favor of "history written in advance." This is how one prophecy advocate presented his concept of history as recently as April, 2002: History written by men—described in the title as "Elusive and Fickle Descriptors"[3]—is untrustworthy and subject to change with changes of alliances and allegiances. But, says the writer,

> There is, of course, a very interesting exception to that principle. While the world can only tell (albeit imperfectly) which nations are allied at the moment, the Bible reveals which nations will be allied at some point in the future, and it's the interim steps that are, perhaps, vague.
>
> Take, for instance, the battle of Ezekiel 38–39. When a great nation from the north (presumably Russia) launches its invasion of the Middle East during the Last Days, it will be accompanied by Ethiopia, Libya, Iran, Egypt and Turkey. Now, we can't say as a certainty how or when those nations will join together in a common goal. But we do know that they will. And so, whereas man writes his version of history after the fact, God wrote history in advance, in the pages of the Prophetic Word, so that we might know what lies ahead and decide how to prepare for the things which are to come.

The prophecy writer ends a seven-page explanation of this thesis with the conclusion:

> The promises and advantages of studying Bible Prophecy are valuable beyond description. Bible Prophecy is history written in advance, and therefore, it is

God who will, in the end, write the saga of human history. May we therefore challenge you to look for yourself into the golden pages of the Bible, and discover the light that our *"more sure word of prophecy"* (2 Peter 1:19) can shed on your life? I pray that you will. I promise: it will be worth it!

As will be illustrated later, this is not an isolated trend of thinking held by fringe groups. The millions of copies of books and scores of websites advocating this ideology indicate a fairly widespread popularity. Three main elements make these claims non-negotiable and impossible to reason with. First, they are based on a historical determinism of the kind that is presented by prophecy advocates, as seen in the previous example. This is, after all, history written and predetermined by the Creator and Author of history. Naturally, reading the mind of God becomes the profession and specialty of prophecy advocates. It becomes also an essential part of the millennial discourse.

Second, these prophecies are derived from "sacred texts," another factor which makes them indisputable. This element is also based on absolute faith in the veracity of the sacred texts as they have come down to us and as interpreted by those prophecy advocates. The Creator of history is also the Author of the text, either directly or through the writers of the Bible and the interpretations of these advocates.

The third element is what is perceived as sacred geography superimposed on natural and political geography. The "Kingdom of God" and the "City on a Hill" become associated with the Holy Land and Jerusalem and subsequently with Palestine.

The "Chosen People"—the tribes of Israel of old—are then identified with the Jews of today and with the political state of Israel. Thus sacred and political geography become the same, and sacred text "predictions" are applied with absolute certainty to political history and geography. More dangerously, they are applied to the future as predicted history. The pictures and posters of the "Rapture," "Tribulation," and "God's Plan for the Ages" show clearly that fusion between sacred text predictions and modern political history. In fact, the last four Ages in "God's Plan" are mainly concerned with the history and fate of the Jewish people and Israel. What happens to the rest of humanity is incidental.

First "the Promise," then the "giving of the law," then the "Dispersion of Israel," then the "Regathering of Israel" lead to where "we are now." This will inevitably be followed by the "Tribulation" which will lead to the "Kingdom and Restoration of Israel." Once the identification with politics and geography is made, the logical consequence is the great emphasis placed on the state of Israel and the Jewish people and the absolute support for Israel's goals and policies because, after all, this is "God's will." To make the association more potent, most televangelists, millennial preachers, and right-wing Christians and politicians in general, look for details in modern events and try to find suitable interpretations of the "prophecies" to fit these details.

Jerry Falwell's views on Israel are representative of those held by most Fundamentalists and Christian extremists. Asked by his biographer about the links between Christianity and a reborn Jewish State, Falwell answered:

> Anyone who truly believes in the Bible sees Christianity and the new State of Israel as inseparably connected. The reformation of the State of Israel in 1948 is, for every Bible-believing Christian, a fulfillment of Old Testament and New Testament prophecy.

Falwell explained the relationship between Christians, the Covenant, and Israel:

> When God established the boundaries of Israel in Genesis 15, He was very explicit. Because we are Bible-believing Christians, we know that no word of prophecy can ever be broken. As Christians we also believe in the Abrahamic Covenant, which in essence states that God deals with nations in relation to how nations deal with Israel. It is my feeling that every American Christian should be exerting all influence available to him in guaranteeing that his government is ever in total support of this land of Israel, this state that has miraculously evolved before our very eyes.[4]

The two Evangelist Association posters provide clear examples of this exercise: the creation of Israel, the "repossession" of Jerusalem and the Temple site, the energy crisis, the 1973 "attack on Israel" by the alliance with the "armies of the north," the seven-year peace treaty; all these and more are painstakingly made to fit prophecy. Indeed, the millennialist "Plan" pinpoints the stage where "we are now." What is left is the "Return of Christ in Glory" and the Battle of Armageddon. And these momentous events cannot be far off in the future. One has only to browse through the shelves of bookstores and libraries, and to surf the Web to see the enormous number of books, films, videotapes, posters and the like which deal with millennial applications to current events and predictions of coming events. One website, "Armageddon Books," lists in 14 pages about 600 titles of related materials. There are also scores of sites of prophecies and predictions which monitor current events in light of "prophecy." "The Gog Index," "Nearing Midnight," "The Rapture Index," and "Storm Ministries" are examples.

The kind of ideas, prophecy interpretations and predictions—and their direct association with Israel and Islam—which are fed to millions of readers and viewers can be gleaned from the following examples. On March 17, 2002, the "Gog Index" writer told his readers that:

> The Gog Index continues to remain at an all-time high level as tension in the Middle East builds to a breaking point. The War in Afghanistan has waned, but terrorist cells are regrouping. There have been numerous threats of biological, chemical, and even nuclear strikes against Israel and or the US. Further concerns include Iran's threat of eliminating Israel with one nuclear strike and Iraq's threat of striking Israel with unconventional weapons if the US attacks Iraq. This year may be far more dangerous than the last with fears of an India vs. Pakistan War, continued terror plots against the US, and the Islamic countdown to the day when they use a nuclear weapon against Israel. A regional or possibly world war is still a great possibility. As the end-times approach, there is a likelihood that the US global power diminishes considerably as the US is seldom found in the end-times prophecy unless the US is thought of as the new Babylon. In either case, America faces an extreme crisis in which all should be prepared spiritually and continue to witness in order to save as many as possible. The US has faced one severe blow so far, others have been forewarned by many in the intelligence branches. Currently, there are numerous warnings of a possible nuclear terror strike. A severe terrorist strike from biological, chemical, or nuclear weapons would likely diminish the US economy and strength. Further concern emanates from Israel as the PA looks towards an open war with Israel. Iran has decided to openly support the PA and thus, the Hezbollah are training their sights on Israel too. A war in the coming months may lead to the fulfillment of prophecy and the true opening of the end-times chapter.[5]

These are definitely real concerns and warnings that many people share, and their current nature is confirmed in the "Gog Index" by graphic pictures of the burning and collapsing twin towers of the Trade Center, pictures of American troops on the battlefield, and a modern political map of the Middle East. But the reader is also treated to "prophetic" Biblical quotations and interpretations that fuse "prophecy" with facts, and predictions with fears and concerns. It is this practice that the "prophets of doom" have employed with great success to convince unsuspecting believers of their cause.

On April 21, 2002, the "Storm Ministries" website flashed the following warnings and predictions on the opening page:

> There is a Storm Coming
> Nostradamus prophesied attacks on New York City!
> Nostradamus prophesied his third anti-Christ would rise up in the Middle East!
> Nostradamus prophesied a great Holy War in the last days!
> Nostradamus prophesied the last war known to mankind … Armageddon!
> Did God reveal these things to Nostradamus?
> Could God reveal these things to a modern day prophet?
> Could Mickey Banks be God's End-Time Prophet?

To make the subject more immediate and current, the page is also decorated with a round pocket watch whose hands indicate that the time is one minute to twelve with pictures of Saddam Hussein and Nostradamus mounted in it.

The same website posed on the same day the dire question:

> ARE YOU READY FOR THE "WAR OF WARS"… ARMAGEDDON?

The association of Armageddon with current events is made indirectly, yet very clearly. The World Wide Web has also provided religious prophecy experts with a perfect medium to continuously update their predictions of the unfolding of the sacred texts prophecies, and thus maintain the sense of urgency in the public consciousness. In a 56-page document packed with predictions, hypotheses, biblical texts and firm dates based on these texts, the "Researcher," Paul Robertson, of "Apocalypse Soon" concludes with the certainty of his absolute faith that

> the Temple will be standing no later than May of 2007. An Orthodox Jewish rabbi told me that the Jews, using modern technology, can build the third Temple in three years. Thus, Temple construction would begin no later than May of 2004. Before the Temple is standing, the Gog/Magog war will be complete. Before the Gog/Magog war happens, Damascus will be destroyed and

will no longer be a city. Therefore, the destruction of Damascus may be imminent.

More interesting is the sensational website "The Xcellent Files" flashing in color on its opening page the title:

Damascus Will No Longer Be a City

followed by the verse from Isaiah (17:1): "An oracle concerning Damascus: See, Damascus will no longer be a city but will become a heap of ruins." Although the title-page says that the original publication date of this document was October 1997 and that it was updated on November 30, 1998, the same text appeared again, rather curiously, in May 2002.

This is not a suggestion of a cause-and-effect connection. Yet, the fact is that on March 9, 2002 an official announcement was issued that the US has a contingency plan to use limited nuclear strikes against a handful of countries, including Syria. In March 2002 also, the "Gog Index" website suggested in its "Gogindex Newsletter," which is "Updated Constantly ... for the Latest Information and Commentary on ISRAEL and America," that:

> Prior to the Gog-Magog War, there likely will be a war in which Damascus is destroyed as described in Isaiah 17: "An oracle concerning Damascus: 'See, Damascus will no longer be a city but will become a heap of ruins. The cities of Aroer will be deserted ...' '... and left to flocks, which will lie down, with no one to make them afraid. The fortified city will disappear from Ephraim,' '... and royal power from Damascus; the remnant of Aram will be like the glory of the Israelites,' declares the Lord Almighty." (Isaiah 17:3 NIV)[6]

Thereafter, the story of the probable nuclear strikes gained momentum on a number of prophecy websites; in April, "the Prophetic Newsletter" gave a logical politically oriented justification of such strikes, but it couched this justification in a comforting series of Biblical quotations, with the constant reminder that "certainly, we know that the words of Bible Prophecy are true, and we know precisely what will be the outcome of the intrigue here on Planet Earth."

The "Gog Index" picked up the story again and predicted that when the war breaks out, "this will create a world coalition against Israel as Israel so strongly defeats the Palestinians and Syria. The

World is strongly against Israel as it is now with daily shootings of Israelis by terrorists. Most nations do not want Israel to strike back. So when Israel does, look out. The coalition will be built up and then Ezekiel 38 comes into play."

The frenzied interest in the Apocalyptic vision in the electronic media was preceded, and is now accompanied, by hundreds of books on the subject written during the last 50 years. The popular appeal of such publications can be measured by the millions of copies sold and the ranks these books have occupied on best-seller lists. A quick look at the titles of some of these books will show the application of sacred texts prophecies to current events on the world stage; more particularly, it illustrates the central position given to Israel, America and Islam in relation to these prophecies:

(1) *Israel, Islam and Armageddon*, Dave Hunt (2002), VHS video
(2) *Unholy War: America, Israel and Radical Islam*, Randall Price (2002)
(3) *The Last War: The Failure of the Peace Process and the Coming Battle for Jerusalem*, David Allen Lewis with Jim Fletcher (2001)
(4) *Israel: The Blessing or the Curse*, John McTernan and Bill Koenig (2001)
(5) *Storm Clouds on the Horizon; Bible Prophecy and the Current Middle East Crisis*, ed. Charles Dyer (2001)
(6) *The Battle For Jerusalem*, John Hagee (2001)
(7) *The Coming Last Days Temple*, Randall Price (1999)
(8) *25 Messianic Signs in Israel Today*, Ken Klein Productions (2001), VHS video
(9) *25 Messianic Signs in Israel Today*, Dr. Noah Hutchings with Gilla Treibich (1999)
(10) *Jerusalem in Prophecy: God's Stage for the Final Drama*, Randall Price (1998)
(11) *Saddam's Mystery Babylon*, Arno Froese (1998)
(12) *Israel, The Land and the People: An Evangelical Affirmation of God's Promises*, ed. H. Wayne House (1998)
(13) *Messiah's Coming Temple: Ezekiel's Prophetic Vision of the Future Temple*, John W. Schmitt and J. Carl Laney (1997)
(14) *The Beast of the East*, Dr. Alvin Shifflett (1992)
(15) *Petra Today*, Dr. N. W. Hutchings (1998)
(16) *Petra in History and Prophecy*, Dr. N. W. Hutchings (1991)
(17) *The Bargaining For Israel: In the Shadow of Armageddon*, Mona Johnian (1997)

(18) *The Last of the Giants: Lifting the Veil on Islam and the End Times*, George Otis, Jr. (1991)

(19) *God Intervenes in the Middle East*, Marion F. Kremers (1992)

(20) *War On Terror: Unfolding Bible Prophecy*, Grant R. Jeffrey (2002)

(21) *Prophecies of the Coming Darkness: A Documentary*, Dr. Daniel E. Bohler (2001), VHS video

(22) *Attach On America: New York, Jerusalem, and the Role of Terrorism in the Last Days*, John Hagee (2001)

(23) *Prophetic Review of 2001*, Hal Lindsey (2002), CD

(24) *Where Is America In Prophecy?* Hal Lindsey (2001), VHS video or audio cassette

(25) *America At Crossroad: Destruction or Revival*, Hal Lindsey (2001), CD or audio cassette

(26) *Terror Over America: Understanding the Tragedy*, Arno Froese (2001)

(27) *US In Prophecy*, Dr. Noah Hutchings (2000)

(28) *The Last War: The Failure of the Peace Process and the Coming Battle for Jerusalem*, David Allen Lewis with Jim Fletcher (2001)

(29) *Through the Prophet's Eye*, Marshall Best (2000)

(30) *Nostradamus: Attack on New York ... and Other Amazing Prophecies*, Ray Comfort (2001), VHS video

(31) *Why Do We Have Trials?* Hal Lindsey (2001), also available in audio cassette

(32) *God's Final Warning To America*, John McTernan (1996, 1998)

(33) *Countdown to Armageddon*, Paul McGuire (1999)

A classic example of prolific writers on end-times predictions is Hal Lindsay. Lindsay's first book, *The Late Great Planet Earth* (1970), which was on the nonfiction best-seller list, applied sacred text prophecies to events such as the Cold War and the Communist threat, but emphasized the establishment of the state of Israel and the "repossession of Jerusalem and the Temple site" as sure signs of end-times events. Lindsay went on to write twelve or more other books on the subject and to preach and write hundreds of sermons and essays which attracted popular as well as official attention. He continues to be a force to be reckoned with in the prediction business. Of his other books one should mention the following which are very relevant to the subject at hand:

The Terminal Generation (1976)
The 1980s: Countdown to Armageddon (1980)

The Final Battle (1995)
The Apocalypse Code (1997)
Planet Earth: The Final Chapter (1998)

The sensational manner of connecting prophecy with current events, especially in Israel and America, is seen in the publishers' descriptions of some of these products:

Israel, Islam and Armageddon
Jerusalem is mentioned an astonishing 80 times in the Bible, and prophesied to play a key role in world destiny. This video shows how the current peace process is fraught with peril, why it is impossible for Jerusalem to know true peace in our age, how the Antichrist will lead the world's armies to destroy Israel, the truth about the Vatican's intentions, and the Palestinian myth. It powerfully corrects much of "the misinformation and propaganda" aggressively advanced by the world media and others. Includes footage of the terrorist attack on the World Trade Center. 60 minutes. VHS video.

Israel the Blessing or the Curse
Today, the Muslim nations who have persuaded the world powers to help in the "land for peace" plan are closing in on Israel. They have brought her to the edge of war and have put her in great danger. However, the Bible says that God will be Israel's protector. The Scriptures indicate that the world will side with the Arab nations and that God will stand with Israel. The Bible (Zechariah 12:9) also says clearly that those who come against Israel will be destroyed. 199 pages paper.

The Coming Last Days Temple
Right now in Israel, plans are well underway to construct a new Temple. From drawing up the blueprints to detailing the furnishings to preparing for the new priesthood, much is being done for what could be the most significant building effort of our time. Price surveys the latest developments and offers a fascinating perspective on how they fit the Bible prophecies about the Temple. 732 pages, paper, subject index, scripture index.

Prophetic Review of 2001
Hal Lindsey takes a look back at the prophetic events of 2001 in ten messages titled:

(1) 2001: Prophecy Takes a Quantum Leap
(2) The Euro Dollar: The United States of Europe
(3) The September 11th Terrorist Attack
(4) Four Biblical Stages of a Nation's Destruction
(5) Why God Protected America in the Past
(6) Two Things That Could Happen to America Now

(7) Islamic Fundamentalism

(8) The Russia–Iran Threat

(9) Israel: The Focal Point of the Whole World

(10) How To Be Certain in Uncertain Times

Where is America in Prophecy?

Where is America in Prophecy—One of the most often-asked questions is "Where is America in Bible Prophecy?" America is without question the most powerful nation on earth—it is inconceivable that such a formidable nation plays no role in the last days. Yet she is nowhere to be found in the Scriptural record. Where is she? Will she play a role? Join Hal Lindsay as he takes on this toughest of questions about the Bible, the last days and the United States of America. Find out what role America plays in the final countdown. 55 minutes, VHS video.

Nostradamus: Attack on New York ... and Other Amazing Prophecies

Did Nostradamus predict the attack on the World Trade Center in 2001? Did he prophesy of the assassination of President Kennedy? Was he able to predict that man would land on the moon, and that someone named Hitler would lead Germany? Did he mention America by name? Is there anything in his writings about the outcome of the Third World War? Some say Nostradamus was a man who heard from God. Others say his knowledge was obtained through the occult. This fascinating video will reveal to you that there was another means by which he acquired such incredible insight. 36 minutes, VHS video.

This chorus of concordant notes is a practical example of the Millennial discourse—Northrop Frye's "order of words"—to which fundamentalist ears are attuned and which they are ready to see fulfilled. For, as the "Prophetic News Letter" explains: "Bible Prophecy is history written in advance, and therefore, it is God who will, in the end, write the saga of human history."

Although millennial predictions have appeared periodically throughout the Christian World, Americans have shown greater interest in the culture of the Jeremiad and in the literal interpretation of prophecies than people of any other nation.

To discuss America's preoccupation with millennial beliefs on the eve of the third millennium, the PBS *Frontline* program held an "Apocalyptic Roundtable" to which a group of distinguished specialists were invited. They included: Paul Boyer, Professor of History at the University of Wisconsin (Madison); Michael Barkun, Professor of Political Science at Syracuse University; Richard Lands, Professor of History at Boston University and Director of the Center for Millennial Studies; Catherine Wessinger, Professor of History at Loyola

University; Eugene Gallagher, Professor of Religious Studies at Connecticut College; Stephen O'Leary, Professor of Communications at the University of Southern California; Bernard McGinn, Professor of Historical Theology at the University of Chicago; James Tabor, Professor of Religious Studies at the University of North Carolina (Charlotte); and John Collins, Professor of the Hebrew Bible at the University of Chicago.[7]

These scholars were asked to comment on some questions including America's particular fascination with Apocalypticism, the uniqueness of the year 2000 in the millennial scheme, America's "doom industry" and the reading of prophecy into current events.

There was a general agreement among them that there has been throughout American history a public interest and belief in end-times prophecies. Boyer explained the historical depth and the reasons for these beliefs by relating them "to images of America as a specially favored nation, with a special divine destiny, that go back to the very beginning of European settlements." He also cited as one explanation the "manifestation of evangelical, traditionalist religion in general, which remains much more prevalent and vital in America." Gallagher, on the other hand, saw the reason in the role played by the Bible in the daily lives of Americans:

> I'd situate the apparent American fascination with Apocalypticism in a broader context, the role that the Bible has played in American culture from the beginning ... In a culture soaked, to varying depths, with biblical imagery, it becomes important for an Apocalyptic group or individual to address that common culture, at least tangentially, in order to elicit the attention and comprehension of possible converts. In brief, wherever the Bible is, there, potentially, is the Apocalypse.

Barkun's comment was that "awareness of the millennium has become so pervasive in the culture that it's turned everyone into some sort of millennarian, regardless of the degree or kind of religiosity." Lands summed up the American millennial situation: "From the perspective of the millennial historian, America fell in the millennial vat at birth and, despite many efforts, has yet to get out of it." Finally, Barkun put the American Apocalyptic vision in a historical context. He said:

> From Columbus, to the Puritans, to the process of westward expansion, America was often portrayed (to Native Americans' hurt) as empty, virgin,

malleable, uncorrupted—hence made available by the deity or by the forces of history for a new start. That image, present from the fifteenth century and confirmed in subsequent eras, invited an American self-understanding in millennial terms.

The dangers inherent in this "Judeo-Christian" literal interpretation of sacred text prophecies and the concept of the millennium can be clearly seen in the unconditional support given by the United States to Israeli policies and actions that violate the principles of human rights, international law, and the UN Charter. It entices persons like Michael Rohan to set fire to the Dome of the Rock to prepare for the Kingdom of the Prince of Peace in the Temple. It encourages persons like Baruch Goldstein to slaughter 29 Muslims while they were praying in a Hebron mosque, and it allows the most disgusting parades of his funeral and praise of his martyrdom.[8]

A more lasting danger is the license taken by political and religious leaders to violate basic American principles of justice, freedom and self-determination. Inherent also in this millennial zeal is what Robert Bellah described by saying: "Behind the civil religion at every point lie Biblical archetypes: Exodus, Chosen people, Promised Land, New Jerusalem."[9] "Those on our side," said Bellah, "become 'the free world.' It is then part of the role of America as the New Jerusalem and 'the last hope of earth' to defend the free world."[10]

As America's "enemies" are in turn perceived as "the empire of evil," "the axis of evil," "the enemies of freedom and democracy," America's "allies"—Israel, for one—become "freedom-loving," "civilized," "democratic" and "men of peace." Thus, as Bellah put it, "With respect to America's role in the world, the dangers of distortion are greater and the built-in safeguards of the tradition weaker. The theme of the American Israel was used, almost from the beginning, as a justification for the shameful treatment of the others."[11]

More closely tied to the dangerous application of millennial expectations to the Arab–Israeli conflict is the total oblivion to the suffering of the Palestinian people and the encouragement of violent action against them and their land. Catherine Wessinger, Professor of the History of Religion at Loyola University, warned of the dangers of making Jerusalem the focal point of millennial expectations, adding that "the desire of the Jewish right to destroy the Dome of the Rock and build the Temple in its place is supported by the literal millennial interpretations in the West because this confirms their expectations of Armageddon and the Kingdom."[12]

Wessinger warned that the political consequences of destroying the Dome are much more serious than anyone can imagine.

Recently Jimmy Carter, the first Evangelical Baptist US President, criticized literal interpretations of the sacred text. In a May 4, 2004 interview for *Prospect*, Carter told Ayelish McGarvey that the

> strong support for Israel, based on the New Testament prophecy that the reconstruction of the ancient kingdom of David will usher in the "end times" and the Second Coming of Christ, is a completely foolish and erroneous interpretation of the Scriptures. And it has resulted in these last few years with a terrible, very costly, and bloody deterioration in the relationship between Israel and its neighbors. Every president except for George W. Bush has taken a relatively balanced position between the Israelis and their enemies, always strongly supporting Israel but recognizing that you have to negotiate and work between Israel and her neighbors in order to bring about a peaceful resolution.
>
> It's nearly the 25th anniversary of my consummation of a treaty between Israel and Egypt—not a word of which has ever been violated. But this administration, maybe strongly influenced by ill-advised theologians of the extreme religious right, has pretty well abandoned any real effort that could lead to a resolution of the problems between Israel and the Palestinians. And no one can challenge me on my commitment to Israel and its right to live in peace with all its neighbors. But at the same time, there has to be a negotiated settlement; you can't just ordain the destruction of the Palestinian people, and their community and their political entity, in favor of the Israelis.
>
> And that's what some of the extreme fundamentalist Christians have done, both to the detriment of the Israelis and the Palestinians. (www.prospect.org)

This danger is felt by many other intellectuals and scholars of Biblical studies. The historian Timothy Webber predicted that "this tendency in the West will lead to major catastrophes, because it leads the West to try to fulfill these prophecies one way or another."[13]

The great danger of millennial ideology, according to these objective views, "is the excessive emphasis on the establishment of the state of Israel as a sign of the fulfillment of God's Plan. This is connected to a greater danger which is the attempt to prove that by the use of force."[14]

The logical (if "logical" is the right word) consequence of this millennial tendency is the belief that, for the fulfillment of prophecy, Damascus has to become a heap of ruins; ethnic cleansing is desirable; the Dome of the Rock should be destroyed; war—the final battle—is inevitable; and that it is America's "Manifest Destiny" to see to it that these events take place, regardless of the suffering and tragedies they entail. In fact, everything else becomes irrelevant, "collateral."

Early in the last century, Richard Niebuhr, in his *The Kingdom of God in America*, said that for many generations, Americans believed that it was their sacred mission to spread the light of the Gospel and of freedom and education throughout the world with "lamps manufactured in America." Today, we witness another "sacred mission"—more immediate and dangerous—undertaken in the context of this millennial discourse.

The September 11 attacks have fed into this righteous self-image and the evil image of the "others," in this case Islamic terrorism and the parties which "harbor," "support," "incite," or do not condemn it. It is as though these terms are designed to set up as many enemies as are needed in any given situation. These parties become the "evil-doers"; they hate freedom and "our way of life." All of this creates a fuzzy set of images in the public perception; they can apply to anybody and to nobody in particular. It also makes it easy, if not totally legitimate, to demonize these "others" at will; it allows certain circles to condemn such general entities and ideologies as Communism, Islam, Iraq, Iran, and, by implication, all adherents to these entities. Consequently, we hear statements and opinions of condemnation from religious, political and public figures.

Furthermore, this environment of danger and fear and of demonization of others has given license to new sets of rules of encounter and measures that would normally be considered "un-American." The principles of humanity, equal justice, right to privacy and presumption of innocence go by the wayside in the effort to protect these same principles. What we see is a tolerant attitude to—indeed a legitimization of—the presumption of guilt by association or belonging; what we see is an easy acceptance of "collateral" damage in the process of going after the evil ones. The death of close to half a million Iraqi children during the embargo becomes an "acceptable price," according to an American Secretary of State. Although these policies were applied to Germans and Japanese in the US during the World Wars, today the suffering inflicted on whole populations because of the behavior of a regime, a head of state or a group of terrorists defies description. By contrast, those who are with us, no matter how oppressive, brutal and unjust, are allies against terrorism and are peace-loving. The dangers of this trend of thought cannot be measured now; the hope is that prudence and common sense will temper anger and fear before it is too late.

APPENDIX: SAMPLE AMERICAN END-TIMES PREDICTIONS

Cotton Mather predicted that the end of the world would come in 1916; then he changed that date to 1736.

The Methodist minister George Bell predicted that the end of the world would come on February 28, 1763.

On May 19, 1780 the skies over New England turned dark as a result of forest fires. This led some people to believe that it was the end of the world.

The Shakers announced that the end of the world would be in 1792, then in 1794.

Charles Wesley, brother of John Wesley and one of the founders of the Methodist church, predicted that 1794 would see the end of the world.

Joanna Southcott, the self-styled "virgin prophetess," claimed that she was pregnant (at 64) with the Christ child. She said that Christ would be reborn on December 25, 1814. She died on that day, and the pregnancy proved to be a hoax.

John Turner, follower of Southcott, said that the end would be on October 14, 1820.

The Baptist minister Benjamin Keach said that the end would come in 1689.

The founder of the Methodist Church, John Wesley, predicted that the Millennium would begin in 1836.

The self-styled prophetess Margaret McDonald predicted in 1830 that Robert Owen, who founded New Harmony in New York, was the Antichrist.

The Crimean War (1855–56) sparked a series of predictions, some of which described it as the Battle of Armageddon.

Harriet Livermore Parousia said that the end of the world would be in 1843.

In 1832, Joseph Smith, the founder of the Church of Jesus Christ of Latter-day Saints (the Mormon Church), had a dream which he interpreted as telling him that the end would come in 1890.

William Miller's followers predicted that April 28, 1843 would usher in the end of the world.

William Miller announced that Jesus Christ would return on March 21, 1843, and when this did not happen he set the date at October 22, 1844. These failed predictions resulted in "The Great Disappointment."

The Second Adventists, extremist followers of Miller, predicted the Coming would happen in 1845, then in 1846, 1849 and 1851.

Joseph Smith called a church meeting on February 14, 1835 because "God had commanded it" and announced that Jesus would return in 1891.

Pastor Robert Reid of Eric, Pennsylvania, predicted that the end of the world would come in 1895.

Jehovah's Witnesses predicted that the War of Armageddon would begin in 1914. The Watchtower Bible and Tract Society (organized by Jehovah's Witnesses) went on to set dates: 1918, 1920, 1925, 1941, 1975, 1994 and other years.

Henry Adams predicted that the end of the world would be in 1950.

Billy Graham, the famous Baptist minister, predicted in 1950 that "we may have another year, maybe two; then, I believe it is going to be over."

Herbert W. Armstrong, founder of the Worldwide Church of God, said that the Lord would return in 1936; then he set the dates at 1972 and 1975.

A California pastor, Mihran Ask, said the Battle of Armageddon would destroy the world between April 16 and 23, 1957.

The State of Israel was established in 1948, which set off scores of end-times predictions.

The Cult followers of the Branch Davidians of Waco, Texas, predicted that they would be killed and go to heaven before April 22, 1959.

In 1967, Israel occupied all of Arab Jerusalem in the Six Day War. This sparked a new wave of predictions of the end of the world.

Jim Jones, leader of the People's Temple cult, predicted that the end would be brought about in a nuclear war in 1967.

George Williams, leader of a Mormon group, said that the end would be on August 9, 1969.

Hal Lindsay's *The Late Great Planet Earth* came out in 1970, which predicted that in 1988, 40 years after the establishment of Israel (one generation of Scripture), the Rapture would begin.

Moses David, the founder of the Children of God, predicted that a comet would destroy the United States in 1973.

Pastor Church Smith of Cost Mesa, California, predicted that the Rapture would begin in 1981.

Pat Robertson predicted that the end would come in 1982.

Lester Sumrall published his *I Predict 2000 AD* in 1987, in which he predicted a series of events ending in the Coming Kingdom in AD 2000.

Edgar Whisenant, a NASA scientist, wrote a book *88 Reasons Why the Rapture Will Occur in 1988*.

Peter Ruckman's study of the Bible led him to predict that the end would come in the early 1990s.

Moses David predicted that 1986 would witness the Battle of Armageddon and that the Second Coming would happen in 1993.

Notes

INTRODUCTORY ESSAY

1. Lanigan probably knew Edward Lear's the "Akoond of Swat," printed in his *Laughable Lyrics* (1877). Actually, the long obituary in *London Times*, January 22, 1878, p. 4, gave much political and historical detail. The bare announcement ran on January 18.
2. See the entry under "Lanigan" in Alan Gribben, *Mark Twain's Library: A Reconstruction*, Vol. 1 (Boston: G. K. Hall, 1980), pp. 396–7.
3. Petroleum Vesuvius Nasby, *The Morals of Abou Ben Adhem* (Boston, MA: Lee and Shepard, 1875), p. 14.
4. Horace Perry Jones, "Southern Editorial Humor and the Crimean War," *Studies in American Humor*, NS 2 (Winter 1983–84), pp. 171–84.
5. For a definitive survey, see Waldemar Zacharasiewicz, "National Stereotypes in Literature in the English Language," *Yearbook of Research in English and American Literature*, Vol. 1 (1982), pp. 75–120. Mahadev L. Apte, *Humor and Laughter: An Anthropological Approach* (Ithaca, NY: Cornell University Press, 1984), pp. 113–14, sums up the cross-cultural research into the humorous, denigrating use of ethnic stereotypes.
6. George William Curtis, *Nile Notes of a Howadji* (New York: Harper, 1851), pp. 43–4.
7. Page Smith, *The Rise of Industrial America* (New York: McGraw-Hill, 1984), p. 554.
8. See Richard D. Mosier, *Making the American Mind: Social and Moral Ideas in the McGuffey Readers* (New York: King's Crown Press, 1947), pp. 164–5. The Readers invariably glorified missionaries (pp. 90–1).
9. C. Eric Lincoln, *Race, Religion, and the Continuing American Dilemma* (New York: Hill and Wang, 1984), pp. 131–2.
10. *Mark Twain's Travels with Mr. Brown*, ed. Franklin Walker and G. Ezra Dane (New York: Russell and Russell, 1971), pp. 85–6.
11. *The Innocents Abroad* was based upon newspaper letters now collected in *Traveling With the Innocents Abroad*, ed. Daniel M. McKeithan (Norman, OK: University of Oklahoma Press, 1958). Though significant, the revisions are not crucial here. Dewey Ganzel, *Mark Twain Abroad: The Cruise of the "Quaker City"* (Chicago: University of Chicago Press, 1968), is helpful. More generally, see Franklin Walker, *Irreverent Pilgrims: Melville, Browne, and Mark Twain in the Holy Land* (Seattle, WA: University of Washington Press, 1974).
12. The letters, which ran in the *New York Herald* on July 1, 4, 9, 11 and 19, 1873, were reprinted in *Europe and Elsewhere*, ed. Albert Bigelow Paine (New York: Harper, 1923). For Twain's later comment, see Everett Emerson, *The Authentic Mark Twain: A Literary Biography of Samuel L. Clemens* (Philadelphia, PA: University of Pennsylvania Press, 1984), p. 76.

13. Now available in *Mark Twain's Satires and Burlesques*, ed. Franklin R. Rogers (Berkeley, CA: University of California Press, 1967). Incidentally, Huck Finn, on Tom Sawyer's advice, tries to summon up "genies" by rubbing an "old tin lamp". Of course, the harem and its rumored customs lurked behind "1,002d Arabian Night." In "Autobiography of a Damned Fool" (1877), the American speaker, having converted to the "religion of Mahomet," saw a "plain religious duty, now, that I should have a harem" and issued invitations to several spinsters—*Twain's Satire and Burlesques*, pp. 145–6.

14. For identification of the five tales, see "Explanatory Notes" in *The Adventures of Tom Sawyer; Tom Sawyer Abroad; Tom Sawyer, Detective*, ed. John C. Gerber, Paul Baender, and Terry Firkins (Berkeley, CA: University of California Press, 1980).

15. *Mark Twain's Rubaiyat*, Introduction by Alan Gribben (Austin, TX; Santa Barbara, CA: Jenkins Publishing Co., 1983).

16. *Christian Science* (New York: Harper, 1907), p. 96.

INTRODUCTION

1. T.S. Eliot, "Notes Toward the Definition of Culture" (London: Faber & Faber 1953), p. 304.

2. Ibid.

3. Northrop Frye, *The Great Code: The Bible in Literature* (New York: Harcourt Brace Jovanovich, 1982), p. 325.

4. Willa Cather, *Not Under Forty* (New York: Alford A. Knopf, 1936), p. 102.

5. "Orientalism," *Knickerbocker*, 41 (June 1853), p. 479.

6. Ibid.

CHRISTOPHER COLUMBUS AND THE QUEST FOR ZION

1. Kevin A. Miller, "Why Did Columbus Sail?," *Christian History*, issue 35, vol. XI, no. 3 (1992), p. 3.

2. David Burner, Eugene D. Genovese and Forrest McDonald, *The American People* (St. James, N.Y: Revisionary Press, 1980), p. 23.

3. J. Brian Harley, *Maps of the Columbian Encounter* (Milwaukee, WI: University of Wisconsin Press, 1990), p. 5.

4. Robert Clouse, Robert Hosack and Richard Pierard, *The New Millennial Manual* (Grand Rapids, MI: Baker Books, 1999), p. 87; see also Pauline Moffitt Watts, "Science, Religion, and Columbus's Enterprise of the Indies," *OAH Magazine of History*, vol. 5, no. 4 (Spring 1991), p. 102.

5. Harley (1990), p. 29.

6. Quoted by Watts, "Science, Religion, and Columbus's Enterprise of the Indies," p. 6.

7. See Delno C. West, "Columbus and His World," in *The Proceedings of the First San Salvador Conference, February 1986*, p. 1.

8. Miller, "Why Did Columbus Sail?," p. 3.

9. Quoted by West, "Columbus and His World," p. 6.

10. Samuel Eliot Morrison, *Admiral of the Ocean Sea: A Life of Christopher Columbus* (Boston, MA: Little, Brown, 1942), p. 28.
11. Quoted by Miller, "Why Did Columbus Sail?," p. 12.
12. See Watts, "Science, Religion, and Columbus's Enterprise of the Indies," p. 6.
13. Quoted by West, "Columbus and His World," p. 6.
14. J.S. Cummins, "Christopher Columbus: Crusader Visionary and Servus Dei," *Medieval Hispanic Studies* (London: Tamsis, 1976), p. 45.
15. Quoted by Miller, "Why Did Columbus Sail?," p. 12.
16. Delno C. West, "Medieval Ideas of Apocalyptic Mission and the Early Franciscans in Mexico," *The Americas*, vol. 45, no. 3 (January 1989), p. 293.
17. Ibid., p. 303.

A PLACE FOR MY PEOPLE: THE PILGRIMS IN THE NEW WORLD

1. Sydney E. Ahlstrom, "Theology in America," in James Ward Smith and Jamison A. Leland (eds), *Religion in American Life* (Princeton, NJ: Princeton University Press, 1961), Vol. I, p. 236.
2. For further information on the subject, see the works by Vernon Lewis Parrington, Charles Feidelson, Jr. H. Richard Niebuhr and Perry Miller.
3. The concepts of manifest divine favor and "Manifest Destiny" are important factors which often influenced American political and diplomatic thought, dealings with Indians, and relations with other nations.
4. John Cotton, "God's Promise to His Plantation," *Old South Leaflets*, vol. III, no. 53 (Boston, MA: Old South Association, n.d.), title page.
5. Ibid., p. 5.
6. Cotton Mather, *Magnalia Christi Americana* (Hartford, CT: S. Andrews & Son, 1855), Vol. I, p. 69.
7. John Winthrop, "Winthrop's for the Plantation in New England Conclusions," *Old South Leaflets*, Vol. II, No. 50, p. 10.
8. Roger Williams, "Letters of Roger Williams to Winthrop," *Old South Leaflets*, vol. III, no. 54 (Boston, MA: Old South Association, n.d.), p. 4.
9. Increase Mather, "Prevalency of Prayer," *Early History of New England* (Albany, NY: J. Munsell, 1864), p. 255.
10. Mather, *Magnalia Christi Americana*, Vol. I, p. 131.
11. George Washington, "Washington's Addresses to the Churches," *Old South Leaflets*, vol. III, no. 56 (Boston, MA: Old South Association, n.d.), p. 15.
12. Perry Miller, "From the Covenant to the Revival" in Smith and Jamison (1961) Vol. I, p. 325.
13. Ahlstrom in Smith and Jamison, ibid., pp. 240–1.
14. Ibid., p. 241.
15. Mather, *Magnalia Christi Americana*, Vol. I, p. 71.
16. Ibid., pp. 71–3.
17. Ibid., pp. 10–12, 28.
18. Samuel Worcester, *Two Discourses* (Salem, MA: Haron Pool, 1805), pp. 5–6.
19. Ibid., p. 8.

20. Ibid., p. 40.
21. See also the theme of life as a spiritual journey from captivity in sin to freedom in faith, as in Thomas Carleton's *The Captives' Complaint* (1668) and Thomas Bayle's *A Relation of a Mans Return and His Travails Out of a Long and Sore Captivitie* ... [London? 1677]; *Zyons Travellers* (1677). Here again freedom and true belief are represented by the symbolic Holy Land. For these and other references on this theme, see Marcia J. Pankake, *Americans Abroad* (Unpublished Ph.D. dissertation, University of Minnesota, 1975), pp. 9–12.
22. As quoted by Vernon L. Parrington, "The Puritan Divines, 1620–1720," in *Cambridge History of American Literature*, Vol. I (New York, G.P. Putnam, 1917–21), p. 41.
23. William Bradford, "History of Plymouth Plantation," *Old South Leaflets*, vol. 7, no. 153 (Boston: n.d.), pp. 12–13.
24. Ibid., pp. 13–14.
25. Mather, *Magnalia Christi Americana*, Vol. I, p. 60.
26. Parrington, "The Puritan Divines," p. 32.
27. As quoted by Niebuhr, *The Kingdom of God in America*, p. 48.
28. Ibid., p. xii.
29. Ibid., p. 48.
30. Stephen Olin, *The Works of Stephen Olin*, Vol. I (New York: Harper, 1852), p. 61.
31. Ibid., p. 62.
32. Winthrop, "Conclusions," p. 4.
33. Olin, *The Works*, Vol. I, pp. 114–15.
34. Winthrop, "Conclusions," p. 1.
35. Olin, *The Works*, Vol. I, p. 62.
36. Frederick Merk, *Manifest Destiny and Mission in American History* (New York: Alfred A. Knopf, 1963), p. 3.
37. "The United States: A Commissioned Missionary Nation," *The American Theological Review*, vol. I (January 1859), pp. 166–7.

THE STAR IN THE WEST: THE UNITED STATES AS THE LIGHT OF THE WORLD

1. Joel Barlow, *The Works of Joel Barlow* (Gainesville, FL: Scholars' Facsimiles & Reprints, 1970), Vol. I, p. 527.
2. William Ray, *Poems on Various Subjects* (Auburn, N.Y: U.F. Doubleday, 1821), p. 56.
3. Timothy, Dwight, *The Major Poems of Timothy Dwight* (Gainesville, FL: Scholar's Facsimiles & Reprints, 1969), p. 511.
4. Ezra Stiles, *The United States Elevated to Glory and Honor* (1783), in John Wingate Thornton, *The Pulpit of the American Revolution* (Boston: Gould & Lincoln, 1860), p. 440. Stiles, President of Yale College, stated that he chose this text from Deuteronomy "as introductory to a discourse upon the political welfare of God's American Israel, and as allusively prophetic of the future prosperity and splendor of the United States" (ibid., p. 473).

5. David Humphreys, quoted by James A. Field, *America and the Mediterranean World 1776–1882* (Princeton, NJ: Princeton University Press, 1969), p. 14. That the establishment of the new state was part of the Providential plan can be seen in many sermons and political speeches, as in George Duffield's *"Sermon Preached in the Third Presbyterian Church of Philadelphia," December 11, 1783 (Philadelphia, PA, 1784).* The day of Independence, for Duffield, was "a day whose evening shall not terminate in night; but introduce that joyful period, when the outcasts of Israel, and the dispersed of Judah, shall be restored; and, with them, the fulness of the Gentile world shall flow to the standard of redeeming love," pp. 16–18.

6. Barlow, *Works*, Vol. 1, pp. 4–9.

7. Ibid., p. 9.

8. Ray, *Poems*, pp. 20–1.

9. Thus when he spoke of the Constitution of the new nation, John Adams said that Americans "have now the best opportunity and the greatest trust in their hands that Providence ever committed to so small a number since the transgression of the first pair." *A Defence of the Constitutions of Government of the United States of America* (London: C. Dilly, in the Poutry, 1787).

10. Barlow, *Works*, Vol. 1, p. 527.

11. Miller, "From Covenant to Revival," in Smith and Jamison (1961), Vol. I, p. 332.

12. Quoted by Edward M. Burns, *The American Idea of Mission* (New Brunswick, NJ: Rutgers University Press, 1947), p. 141.

13. *New York Times*, March 29, 1955. In the second half of the twentieth century, the concept of God's favoring the American political system and the divine mission to spread American ideals became part of what came to be known as "civil religion." This important modern development will be dealt with in some detail in this work.

14. *The Constitution of the American Bible Society* (New York, 1816), p. 13. The same tendency to see the hand of Providence in the political events and in Independence led Samuel West to say in 1776 "that Providence has designed this continent to be the asylum of liberty and true religion; for can we suppose that the god who created us free agents, and designed that we should glorify and serve him in this world that we might enjoy him forever hereafter, will suffer liberty and true religion to be banished from off the face of the earth?" (Thornton (1860), p. 311). See also American Board of Commissioners for Foreign Missions (ABCFM), 7th *Annual Report*, pp. 8–9, 13; and Stuart Moses, *A Sermon Preached in the Tabernacle Church, Salem, November 5, 1818* (Andover, AH: Flagg and Gould, 1819), pp. 26–7.

15. Enoch Lincoln, *An Oration, Pronounced at Worcester in Commemoration of American Independence, July 4th, 1812* (Worcester, MA: printed by Henry Rogers, 1812), p. 14.

16. Ahlstrom, "Theology in America," I, p. 241.

17. Quoted by Alice Felt Tyler, *Freedom's Ferment* (New York: Harper & Row 1944), p. 1.

18. "The United States: A Commissioned Missionary Nation," pp. 153–4.

19. Ibid., p. 154.
20. Gouverneur Morris, as quoted by George Burns, *The Life of Mohammad, Founder of the Religion of Islam, and of the Empire of the Saracens* (New York: Harper, 1947), pp. 61–2.
21. Alexander Hamilton, *The Works* (New York: J.F. Trow, 1850–51), Vol. VII, pp. 152–3.
22. "The United States: A Commissioned Missionary Nation," p. 154.
23. Ibid.
24. Ibid., p. 155.
25. Barlow, *Works*, Vol. I, pp. 526–7.
26. Ibid., Vol. 1, p. 12.
27. Dwight, "Greenfield Hill," in *The Major Poems*, p. 516.
28. Niebuhr, *The Kingdom of God in America*, pp. 178–9.
29. "The United States: A Commissioned Missionary Nation," p. 153.
30. Ibid., 156.
31. Ibid., pp. 156–7.
32. William Swain, *Philadelphia Public Ledger* (October 25, 1847).
33. Stiles, *The United States Elevated*, p. 18.
34. Barlow, *Works*, Vol. II, p. 348.
35. See Niebuhr, *The Kingdom of God in America*, pp. 123 ff.
36. Ray, *Poems*, pp. 54, 57.
37. Ahlstrom, "Theology in America", p. 332.
38. David F. Dorr, *A Colored Man Round the World By a Quadron* (Cleveland, OH: printed for the author, 1858), p. 12.
39. William F. Lynch, *Narrative of the United States' Expedition to the River Jordan and the Dead Sea*, 9th rev. ed. (Philadelphia, PA: Blanchard and Lex, 1853) p. 126.
40. Ibid., p. 119.
41. Barlow, *Works*, Vol. 1, p. 527.
42. Thomas Paine, *Common Sense*, as quoted by Burner et al., *The American People*, p. 72.
43. Barlow, *Works*, Vol. I, p. 4. See also p. 532.
44. Dwight, *The Major Poems*, p. 500.
45. Ibid., p. 511.

THE GREAT SEAL OF THE UNITED STATES OF AMERICA

1. An official website: <www.greatseal.com>, accessed May 22, 2003.
2. Samuel Sherwood, *The Church's Flight Into the Wilderness* (New York: published not mentioned, 1776), p. 24.
3. Ibid., p. 25.

THE VISION OF ZION: THE AMERICAN MYTH OF THE CITY ON A HILL

1. John Pierpont, *Airs of Palestine: A Poem* (Baltimore, MD: B. Edes, 1816), pp. 5–6.
2. "The American Adam" (R.W.B. Lewis's phrase), as it will be clearly seen was not, after all, so "emancipated from history and undefiled by the

usual inheritances of family and race." (R.W.B. Lewis, *The American Adam*, 3rd ed. Chicago: University of Chicago Press, 1961, p. 5.) The American Adam was indeed deeply immersed in the religious past of his race, carrying the burden of the original sin and the responsibility of preparing for the Second Kingdom.

3. Lewis, *The American Adam*, p. 2.
4. Ralph Waldo Emerson, "American Civilization," in *The Collected Works of Ralph Waldo Emerson*, Vol. XI (Cambridge, MA: Belknap Press of Harvard University Press, 1971–), p. 299.
5. Herman Melville, *White Jacket or the World in a Man-of-War* (London: Harper Brothers, 1850), p. 217.
6. Parrington, *Main Currents in American Thought*, p. 23.
7. Quoted by Mather, *Magnalia Christi Americana*, p. 265.
8. See for an example of this thought, an article entitled "The Flight of Imagination," *Graham Magazine (The Casket)* (1826), vol. I, pp. 105–7, where Milford Bard extolls the power of the imagination which, with "invincible, and irresistible power" leaves "its natal age and shore, and travels back to the remotest periods of antiquity."
9. Parrington, "The American Divines," p. 40.
10. Ibid.
11. Quoted by Parrington, ibid.
12. Winthrop, *Papers*, Vol. II, p. 117.
13. Ibid., Vol. II, p. 295.
14. Feidelson, *Symbolism and American Literature*, p. 78.
15. Ibid., pp. 78–9.
16. Ibid., p. 79.
17. Similarly, funeral sermons had such titles as "A Great Man Fallen in Israel" (Nathaneal Appleton, Boston, 1724). Samuel Willard referred to John Hull's death as "a public loss, and deserves *the tears* of Israel." (*New England Funeral Sermons*, p. xvii.)
18. There were many references to "God's people" and the "chosen" and "Israel" in the arguments for and against the war with Britain.
19. Timothy Dwight, "The Conquest of Canaan," *The Major Poems*, p. 21.
20. Ibid.
21. Ibid.
22. Ibid., p. 20. According to Kenneth Silverman, *Timothy Dwight* (New York: Twayne, 1969), Dwight's readers were used to comparing Washington to Joshua, pp. 31–2.
23. Barlow, *Works*, Vol. II, pp. 29–30.
24. Charles Burr Todd, *Life and Letters of Joel Barlow, LL.D.* (New York: G. P. Putnam's Sons, 1886), p. 8.
25. Ibid., pp. 48–9.
26. Ibid., p. 49.
27. Quoted by Silverman, *Timothy Dwight* "Preface."
28. David Osgood, *A Solemn Protest Against the Late Declaration of War, a Sermon* (Cambridge, MA: Hilliard & Metcalf, 1812), p. 3.
29. The Mormons' belief in the descent of the Indians from the Israelites is another example which will be dealt with later.
30. *The Great Commission* (Hartford, CT: Silas Andrus, 1856), pp. 388–9.

31. Ellen Clare Miller, *Eastern Sketches* (New York: Arno Press, 1977), pp. 209–10.
32. Ibid., pp. 205–6.
33. Mather, "Prevalency of Prayer," *Early History of New England*, p. 253.
34. *The Illustrated Hand-Book to All Religions: From the Earliest Ages to the Present Time* (Chicago: W.H. Harrison, 1877).
35. Niebuhr, *The Kingdom of God America*, p. 141.
36. Ibid.
37. Ibid., pp. 141–2.
38. *The Illustrated Hand-Book to All Religions*, p. 17.
39. Buck, Charles, *A Theological Dictionary* (Philadelphia, PA: Crissy & Markley, 1854), p. 478. See also pp. 282–3 on the "Millennium."
40. Ibid.
41. *The Illustrated Hand-Book to All Religions*, p. 19.
42. Buck, *A Theological Dictionary*, p. 479.
43. Ibid.
44. *The Constitution of the American Bible Society*, p. 14.
45. Ibid., p. 15.
46. Buck, *A Theological Dictionary*, p. 479. There were frequent references to the connection between the fall of Islam and the Millennium, especially by Henry Jessup, Barclay, Harland and Haight.
47. Henry Harris Jessup, *Foreign Missions: Sermon Delivered at the Opening of the General Assembly of the Presbyterian Church America at Saratoga, May 15th, 1884* (Saratoga, NY: Friends of Foreign Missions, 1884), p. 22.
48. Ibid., p. 21.
49. Henry Harris Jessup, *The Mohammedan Missionary Problem* (Philadelphia, PA: Presbyterian Board of Publications, 1879), p. 13.
50. Ibid.
51. Ibid., p. 17.
52. Ibid., p. 23. See also J.T. Barclay, *The City of the Great King* (Philadelphia, PA: James Challen, 1858), pp. xiv–xx.
53. Jessup, *Sermon Delivered*, p. 25. See also Henry Harris Jessup, *Fifty-Three Years in Syria*, 2 vols (New York: Fleming H. Revell, 1910), pp. 790 ff. for a detailed survey of the method of reaching this goal in the Orient.
54. *The Illustrated Hand-Book to All Religions*, p. 340.
55. Ibid., p. 339. On the building of New Jerusalem in America, there is no better illustration than Chapter 13 of *The Book of Mormon*.
56. Examples of these periodicals are *The Signs of the Times* (Boston), *Midnight Cry* (New York), and *The Millennial Star* (Salt Lake City). One of the best expressions of the millennial tendency is the *Millennial Harp*, 1843, a hymn book for the millenarians. (See Buck, *A Theological Dictionary*, pp. 479 ff.)
57. Buck, *A Theological Dictionary*, p. 479.
58. Heyman Humphrey, *The Promised Land: A Sermon* (Boston, MA: Samuel T. Armstrong, 1819), pp. 3–6.
59. Ibid., p. 19.
60. Ibid.
61. Ibid.
62. Barclay, *The City of the Great King*, p. 580.
63. Ibid., pp. 580–1.

64. Worcester, *Two Discourses*, title-page.
65. Stuart was a member of the American Oriental Society and a noted Hebraist at Andover Seminary.
66. Stuart, *A Sermon*, p. 44.
67. Travelers speak of these colonies in accounts of their visits to Palestine. See, for example, Marion Harland, *Under the Flag of the Orient* (Philadelphia, PA: Historical Pub. Co., 1897), Chapter 32, "The Box Colony," pp. 288–93.
68. Robert Barr, *The Unchanging East* (Boston, MA: L.C. Page, 1900), p. 207.
69. Ibid., p. 208.
70. Ibid., pp. 208–9.
71. Ibid., p. 209.
72. Annie DeWitt Shaw, *Will, Annie, and I: Travellers in Many Lands* (New York: L.A. Skinner, 1898), p. 115.
73. Ibid., p. 117.
74. Ibid.
75. Barclay, *The City of the Great King*, p. xiii.
76. Lydia Shuler, "A Letter from the Holy Land," *The Monthly Gospel-Visitor*, vol. V, no. 12 (December, 1855), p. 286.
77. Lydia Shuler, "A Letter from Jerusalem," *The Monthly Gospel-Visitor*, vol. IX, no. 7 (July, 1859), pp. 210–11. Barclay, *The City of the Great King*, pp. xiii and 590, gives an account of the work done by the Dicksons for the sake of the Jews in Palestine.
78. See the list of travel books in the forthcoming bibliography of American travel literature by the present writer.
79. Barclay, *The City of the Great King*, p. 3.
80. For this aspect of American journeys in the Holy Land, see Part III of this volume.
81. Olin, *Trends in Egypt*, pp. 348–9.
82. Buck, *A Theological Dictionary*, p. 213.
83. Ibid.
84. *The Illustrated Hand-Book to All Religion*, pp. 240–1.
85. Brewer, however, found more Jews in Turkey and proposed that effort should be directed there rather than to the Holy Land. See Josiah Brewer, *A Residence of Constantinople, in the Year 1827*, 2nd ed. (New Haven, CT: Durrie & Peck, 1830), pp. 67 ff.
86. Buck, *A Theological Dictionary*, p. 213.
87. Charles Wesley Andrews, "Letter from Jerusalem," in *Private Correspondence* (Duke University Manuscript Department), February 25, 1842.
88. Frederick Jones Bliss, *The Development of Palestine Exploration Being the Ely Lectures for 1903* (New York: Arno Press, 1977), p. xiv.
89. Lee S. Smith, *Through Egypt to Palestine* (Chicago: Fleming H. Revell, 1896), p. 114.
90. Ibid.
91. Ibid.
92. Ibid., p. 117.
93. See also Shaw, *Will, Annie and I*, p. 141. Shaw vividly remembered her visit to the Wailing Wall on Friday when Jews prayed and wept, "others were reading from the Psalms and chanting the Lamentations of Jeremiah."

94. Barclay, *The City of the Great King*, p. 582.
95. Harland, *Under the Flag of the Orient*, p. 281.
96. Ibid., p. 286.
97. Ibid.
98. Ibid.
99. Ibid., pp. 286–7.
100. Barclay, *The City of the Great King*, p. 619.
101. Ibid., p. xii.
102. George Jones, *Excursions to Cairo, Jerusalem, Damascus and Balbec* (New York: Van Nostrand & Wright, 1836), title-page.
103. Ibid., p. 161.
104. Ibid., pp. 263–4.
105. Ibid., p. 264.
106. Bliss is awed by visiting places where holy men of the past had trod and had "held converse with the Most High," "Key-Note" to *Development of Palestine Exploration*.
107. Andrews, "On the Bosom of the Nile," letter to his wife, *Private Correspondence*, November 18, 1941.
108. Sarah Rogers Haight, *Letters from the Old World by a Lady of New York*, 2 vols (New York: Harper, 1840), Vol. I, p. 115.
109. Barclay, *The City of the Great King*, pp. 598–601.
110. Ibid., p. 599.
111. Ibid.
112. Ibid., p. 601.
113. J.V.C. Smith, *A Pilgrimage to Palestine* (Boston, MA: David Clapp, 1853), p. 118.
114. Ibid., pp. 118–19.
115. Ibid. As far as it is possible to tell from internal evidence, there is no indication that either of the two American travelers knew of the other's work.
116. Ibid., pp. 328–9.
117. Barclay, *The City of the Great King*, pp. 601–2. See also Barclay's quotation from a Dr. Tyng, p. 603.
118. Haight, Vol. I, p. 255.
119. *Journal of the American Oriental Society*, Vol. I, p. xi (1849): "List of members." Haight presented some books to the collection of the Society.
120. Haight, *Letters from the Old world*, Vol. I, p. 256.
121. Ibid., p. 257.
122. Ibid., pp. 259–60.
123. Ibid., p. 260.
124. Ibid.
125. Ibid., p. 263.
126. Ibid., p. 261.
127. Ibid.
128. Ibid., p. 262.
129. Ibid., pp. 261–3.
130. Ibid., pp. 263–4.
131. Ibid., pp. 266–7.
132. Mentioned by Field, *America and Mediterranean World*, p. 284.

133. Barclay, *The City of the Great King*, p. xii.
134. Ibid., pp. xii–xiii.
135. Ibid., p. 614.
136. Ibid.
137. Ibid., p. 615.
138. Ibid., p. 616.
139. Ibid., p. 617.
140. Ibid.
141. Ibid., pp. 618–19.
142. Ibid., pp. 619–21.

ZION AND THE AFRICAN-AMERICAN EXPERIENCE

1. As quoted by John Greenleaf Whittier, "Man's Property in Man," *The Annals of America*, vol. 6, 1976, p. 8.
2. Ibid., p. 2.
3. John L. Sullivan, "Our Manifest Destiny," *The Annals of America*, vol. 7, 1976, p. 290.
4. Texts of the argument for and against slavery are printed in *Annals of America*, vol. 7, 1976.
5. Henry Wadsworth Longfellow, "The Republic," *Annals of America*, vol. 7, 1976, p. 563.
6. Richard Barksdale and Kenneth Kinnamon. *Black Writers of America*, (New York: Macmillan, 1972), p. 2.
7. Michael Kammen, *People of Paradox* (New York: Oxford University Press, 1980), p. 192.
8. Barksdale and Kinnamon, *Black Writers of America*, p. 30.
9. Ibid., p. 41.
10. Ibid.
11. Ibid., p. 47–8.
12. Ibid., p. 26.
13. Ibid., p. 862.
14. Ibid., p. 720.
15. All texts of Negro spirituals have been derived from sources on the Internet.
16. Barksdale and Kinnamon, *Black Writers of America*, p. 447.
17. *Annals of America*, vol. 15, p. 159.
18. Ibid., p. 149.
19. See for this topic Eliot, "Notes on the Definition of Culture," and Frye, *The Great Code*.
20. See the same two references as in the previous note.

AMERICAN TRAVELERS IN THE ORIENT: THE QUEST FOR ZION

1. *New York Herald*, May 4, 1840.
2. John Lloyd Stephens, *Incidents of Travel in Greece, Turkey, Russia, and Poland In Remarkable Voyages and Travels* (reprinted Norman, OK: University of Oklahoma Press, 1970), p. 175.

3. Charles Edwin Bergh, *Private Correspondence* (Duke University Manuscript Department). Letter to his father from London, August 25, 1841.

4. Ibid., September 20, 1841.

5. Some lists are to be found in contemporary accounts such as those kept by the Gliddens in Egypt; Jessup, *Fifty-Three Years in Syria*; Edwin Munsell Bliss (ed.), *Encyclopaedia of Missions* (New York: Harper & Brothers, 1889–91). Of the modern works which deal with the subject of travel, I have made use of the lists provided by David H. Finnie, *The American Experience in the Middle East* (Cambridge, MA: Harvard University Press, 1967); Ahmed Mohammed Metwalli, *The Lure of the Levant* (unpublished Ph.D. dissertation, State University of New York); Harold F. Smith, *American Travellers Abroad: a Bibliography of Accounts Published Before 1900* (Carbondale, Il: Southern Illinois University Press, 1969).

6. John Lloyd Stephens, *Incidents of Travel in Egypt, Arabia Petraea, and the Holy Land* (Norman, OK: University of Oklahoma Press, 1970), Vol. I, p. v.

7. Lynch, *Narrative*, p. vi. The demand for Oriental travel accounts can be seen also in a notice by the publishers of one of the earliest missionary travel works written by Josiah Brewer. The notice says that the second edition of Brewer's A *Residence at Constantinople* had to be printed even before the distribution of the first edition because it was discovered that there were not enough copies for the actual subscribers in the immediate vicinity. Brewer, "Note by the Publishers," p. 4.

8. Stephens, *Incidents of Travel in Egypt*, p. xxxix.

9. Ibid., p. xl. See also Jones, *Excursions to Cairo, Jerusalem, Damascus and Balbec*, p. i.

10. Metwalli, *The Lure of the Levant*, p. 6.

11. Haight, *Letter*, Vol. I, p. iv.

12. Ibid., Vol. I, p. v.

13. Lynch, *Narrative*, p. v.

14. Curtis, *George William. The Howadji in Syria* (New York: Harper & Brothers, 1856), p. iii.

15. Haight, *Letters*, Vol. I, p. 91.

16. Andrews, *Private Correspondence* Bergh, Private Correspondence.

17. Metwalli, *The Lure of the Levant*, p. 8. Taylor also edited collections of travel literature which were very popular.

18. See for this aspect of American involvement in the Orient, William B. Hasseltine and Hazel C. Wolf's *The Blue and the Gray on the Nile*, (Chicago: University of Chicago Press, 1961); and William M. Thayer's *From Tannery to the White House: The Life of Ulysses S. Grant* (Boston, MA: James H. Earle, 1885).

19. David Porter, *Constantinople and Its Environs*, 2 vols. (New York: Harper & Brothers, 1835), Vol. II, pp. 7–8.

20. Haight, *Letters*, Vol. I, p. 33.

21. Ibid., Vol. I, p. 42.

22. Lynch, *Narrative* (Monday, February 21, 1848) p. 64.

23. Ibid.

24. Porter, *Constantinople*, Vol. II, pp. 311–12.

25. Haight, *Letters*, Vol. I, pp. 45–6. See also Harland, *Under the Flag of the Orient*, pp. 289–90 on the work of two American missionaries in Jerusalem.

26. Haight, *Letters*, Vol. II, p. 72.
27. Ibid., Vol. I, p. 298.
28. Lynch, *Narrative*, p. 489.
29. Ibid., p. 504.
30. Ibid., pp. 506–7.
31. Haight, *Letters*, Vol. 1, pp. 120–1.
32. Bergh, *Private Correspondence*, letter to his mother, Jerusalem, February 13, 1842.
33. Andrews, *Private Correspondence*, "Grand Cairo," November 20, 1841.
34. *New York Morning Herald*, May 4, 1840.
35. Andrews, *Private Correspondence*, letter to his wife, Paris, September 6, 1841. See also David Millard, *A Journal of Travels in Egypt, Arabia Petrea, and the Holy Land* (New York: Lamport Blakemann & Law, 1853), pp. 11–12.
36. Herman Melville, *A Journal of a Visit to Europe and the Levant* (Princeton, NJ: Princeton University Press, 1955), p. 4.
37. Ibid., p. 6.
38. Ibid., p. 4.
39. See James Eliot Cabbot, *A Memoir of Ralph Waldo Emerson* (Boston, MA: Houghton Mifflin, 1887), p. 659.
40. Melville, *Journal*, pp. 4–5.
41. Haight, *Letters*, Vol. I, p. 13.
42. Ibid., Vol. I, pp. 27–8.
43. Bergh, *Private Correspondence*, letter to his father, Berlin, September 28, 1842.
44. Robinson, *Biblical Researches*, Vol. I, p. 1.
45. Lynch, *Narrative*, p. 18.
46. Edward Robinson, *Biblical Researches in Palestive and the Adjacent Regions*, Vol. I (London: John Murray, 1867), p. 46.
47. Lynch, *Narrative*, p. v.
48. Millard, *Journal*, pp. 11–12.
49. Andrews, *Private Correspondence*, letter to his wife, Paris, September 6–7, 1841.
50. Jones, *Excursions*, pp. 29–30.
51. Brewer, *Residence*, p. 13.
52. W. M. Thomson, *The Land and the Book* (London: Harper & Brothers, 1905), p. 46.
53. Ibid., p. xx.
54. Ibid., January 19, 24, 1857 [Gen. xiii. 17].
55. Andrews, *Private Correspondence*, September 24, 1841.
56. Bergh, *Private Correspondence*, letter to his father, Beirut, March 6, 1842.
57. A good example of this feeling of belonging to the Orient is Bayard Taylor's Poem "The Poet in the East."
58. Stephen Olin, *The Life and Letters of Stephen Olin* (New York: Harper, 1853), Vol. II, p. 112.
59. Ibid., p. 329. See also Millard, *Journal*, p. 249, for similar emotional expressions.
60. Robertson [McI.], *Journal of Travel* "handwritten document at Duke University Library, Manuscript Department," p. 30.

61. Haight, *Letters*, Vol. II, p. 34.
62. Brewer, *Residence*, p. 77.
63. Thomson, *The Land and the Book*, p. xi.
64. Ibid., p. xii.
65. Ibid., p. xiii.
66. Haight, *Letters*, Vol. I, p. 245.
67. Ibid., p. 246.
68. Ibid., p. 307.
69. Stephens, *Incidents of Travel in Egypt*, p. 138.
70. Edgar Allan Poe, *New York Review* (October 1837) p. 18.
71. *Graham's Magazine* (August 1841).
72. Ibid.
73. Haight, *Letters*, Vol. II, pp. 97–8.
74. Stephen Olin, *Travels in Egypt, Arabia Petrae and the Holy Land*, 2 vols., 4th ed. (New York: Harper, 1884), Vol. II, p. 117.
75. Bergh, *Private Correspondence*, letter dated March 6, 1842.
76. Lynch, *Narrative*, p. 153.
77. Brewer, *Private Correspondence*, p. 94.
78. Ibid., p. 65.
79. Haight, *Letters*, Vol. I, p. 43.
80. Ibid., p. 26.
81. Ibid., p. 80.
82. Ibid., p. 31.
83. Ibid.
84. Ibid., pp. 31–2.
85. Ibid., pp. 39–40.
86. Dorr, *A Colored Man Round the World*, p. 180.
87. Ibid., p. 184.
88. Robertson, *Journal*, p. 110.
89. Ibid.
90. Ibid., Jerusalem, Wed., April 29, 1854, p. 110.
91. Smith, *A Pilgrimage to Palestine* p. 120.
92. Ibid., p. 123.
93. Millard, *Journal*, p. 267.
94. Bergh, *Private Correspondence*, letter to his mother, Jerusalem, February 13, 1842.
95. Andrews, *Private Correspondence*, December 8, 1841.
96. Bergh, *Private Correspondence*, letter to his mother, Jerusalem, February 13, 1842. See also Olin, *Life and Letters*, Vol. II, pp. 52–3.
97. Bergh, *Private Correspondence*, letter to his father, Beirut, March 6, 1842.
98. Millard, *Journal*, p. 97.
99. Ibid., p. 98.
100. Ibid., p. 107.
101. Ibid., pp. 107–8.
102. Ibid., p. 109.
103. Ibid., p. 186.
104. Ibid., p. 191.
105. Ibid., pp. 191–2. See also Stephens, *Incidents of Travel in Egypt*, p. 187.
106. Stephens, *Incidents of Travel in Egypt*, pp. 234–60.

107. Ibid., pp. 234–5.
108. Ibid., p. 235.
109. Ibid., pp. 235–6.
110. Ibid., p. 237.
111. Ibid., p. 259.
112. Ibid., pp. 258–9.
113. Ibid., pp. 259–60.

THE JUDEO-CHRISTIAN TRADITION: PRELUDE

1. Merrill Simon, *Jerry Falwell and the Jews* (New York: Jonathan David, 1984), p. vii. (Subsequent references to this title are indicated by page numbers in the text.)

THE ROLE OF RELIGION IN AMERICAN LIFE

1. Winthrop W. Hudson, *Religion in America*, 3rd ed. (New York: Charles Scribner's Sons, 1981), p. 20.
2. Philip M. Hosay, *America: A Model for the World* (Electronic Video Conference, USIS, Amman: 6 March 2002).
3. Quoted by Hudson, *Religion in America*, p. 18.
4. Parrington, *Main Currents in American Thought*, p. 30.
5. Hudson, *Religion in America*, p. 19.
6. Andre Siegfried, *America Comes of Age* (New York: Harcourt Brace, 1927), p. 33.
7. Philip Schaff, *The Principles of Protestantism* (Chambersburg, PA: Publication Office of the German Reformed Church, 1845), p. 114.
8. Alexis de Tocqueville, *Democracy in America* (Chicago: University of Chicago Press, 1954), p. 310.
9. Ibid., p. 436.
10. Beecher Lyman, *A Plea for the West* (Cincinatti, OH: Truman & Smith, 1835), p. 35.
11. For American "civil religion," see Robert N. Bellah, "Civil Religion in America," *Daedalus*, vol. 96 (1967), pp. 1–21; Nathan O. Hatch, "The Origins of Civil Millenialism in America: New England Clergymen, War with France, and the Revolution," *William & Mary Quarterly*, Third Series, vol. 31 (1974), pp. 407–30; Seymour Lipset, *The First New Nation* (New York: Doubleday, 1963); J. F. Maclear, "The Republic and the Millennium," in Elwyn A. Smith (ed.), *The Religion of the Republic* (Philadelphia, PA: Fortress, 1971); Ernest Lee Tuveson, *Redeemer Nation: The Idea of America's Millennial Role* (Chicago: University of Chicago Press, 1968); Timothy Webber, "How Evangelicals Became Israel's Best Friends," *Christianity Today* (October 5, 1998).
12. Bellah, "Civil Religion in America," p. 15.
13. Ibid., p. 1.
14. Ibid., p. 13.
15. Sherwood, *The Church's Flight*, p. 46.
16. George Duffield, *A Sermon Preached in the Third Presbyterian Church* (Phildelphia, PA, publisher not mentioned, 1784), p. 17.

17. Abiel Abbot, *Traits of Resemblance* (Haverville, MA: Moore & Stebbins, 1799), p. 6.
18. Hudson, *Religion in America*, pp. 114–15.
19. *The Inaugural Addresses of the Presidents of the United States From George Washington 1789 to John F. Kennedy 1961* (Washington, DC: United States Government Printing Office, 1961), p. 21.
20. Hatch, "The Origins," p. 408.
21. Commencement speech at Bob Jones University, 1999, reported in *Newsweek* (January 11, 2001), p. 15.
22. *Inaugural Addresses*, p. 4.
23. Ibid., p. 11.
24. Ibid., p. 223.
25. See Robert Boston, *The Most Dangerous Man in America: Pat Robertson and the Rise of the Christian Coalition* (New York: Prometheus, 2003), pp. 9–14. See also Sonia Barisic, "Pat Robertson: God Told Him It's Bush in a 'Blowout,'" <www.amazon.com/erec.obidos>, accessed March 14, 2003.
26. Bellah, "Civil Religion," pp. 14–15.
27. Ibid., p. 17.
28. Ibid.
29. *Newsweek*, September 17, 1984, p. 34.
30. *Time*, September 2, 1985, p. 31.
31. *Newsweek*, September 17, 1984, p. 26.
32. Ibid., p. 25.
33. *Time*, September 10, 1984.
34. *National Journal*, March 3, 1984.
35. *Newsweek*, September 17, 1984, p. 26.
36. Ibid., p. 28.
37. Ibid.
38. Michael Ortiz Hill, "Mine Eyes Have Seen the Glory: Bush's Armageddon Obsession," *Counter Punch* (January 4, 2003), p. 5.
39. William O. Douglas, *Strange Lands and Friendly People* (New York: Harper & Brothers, 1955), p. 250.
40. Ibid., pp. 247–8.
41. Ibid., p. 264.
42. Ibid., p. 265.
43. Ibid., p. 267.
44. Ibid., pp. 268–9.
45. Ibid., p. 291.
46. *New York Times*, February 2, 2001.
47. Alfred Lilienthal, *The Zionist Connection: What Price Peace?* (New York: Middle East Perspective, Inc., 1979), p. 488.

AMERICA AND THE MILLENNIAL FEVER

1. Bush, *The Life of Mohammad*, p. 12.
2. The Association's website: <www.bbea.org/biblemap.htm>, accessed February 12, 2001. The documents described here can be seen on this site. They can also be bought from Christian bookshops.

3. Website: <www.thekingiscoming.com>, accessed October 16, 2001.

4. Simon, *Jerry Falwell.*

5. Website: <www.raptureme.com>, accessed February 12, 2001.

6. Website: <www.stormministries.com>, accessed 12 February 2001.

7. Website: <www.pbs.org/FrontlineRoundtable>, accessed January 11, 2001.

8. On this subject, see Israel Shahak and Norton Mezvinsky, *Jewish Fundamentalism in Israel* (London: Pluto Press, 1999).

9. Bellah, "Civil Religion in America," p. 18.

10. Ibid., p. 15.

11. Ibid., p. 14.

12. Website: <www.pbs.org/FrontlineRoundtable>, accessed January 11, 2001.

13. Ibid.

14. Ibid.

Bibliography

Abbot, Abiel. *Traits of Resemblance* (Haverville, MA: Moore & Stebbins, 1799).

Adams, John. *A Defence of the Constitutions of Government of the United States of America* (London: C. Dilly, in the Poultry, 1787).

Ahlstrom, Sydney E. "Theology in America: A Historical Survey." in Smith, James W. and Jamison, A. Leland (eds), *Religion in American Life* (Princeton, NJ: Princeton University Press, 1961).

Andrews, Charles Wesley. *Private Correspondence* (Duke University Manuscript Department).

Annals of America, 21 vols (Chicago: Encyclopedia Britannica, Inc., 1976).

Barclay, J. T. *The City of the Great King; or Jerusalem as It Was, as It Is, and as It Is to Be* (Philadelphia, PA: James Challen, 1858).

Barksdale, Richard and Kinnamon, Keneth. *Black Writers of America* (New York: Macmillan, 1972).

Barlow, Joel. *The Works of Joel Barlow*. With an Introduction by William K. Bottorff and Arthur L. Ford, 2 vols (Gainesville, FL: Scholars' Facsimiles & Reprints, 1970).

Barr, Robert. *The Unchanging East* (Boston, MA: L.C. Page, 1900).

Beecher, Lyman. *A Plea for the West* (Cincinatti, OH: Truman & Smith, 1835).

Bellah, Robert N. "Civil Religion in America," *Daedalus*, 96 (1967), pp. 1–21.

Bergh, Charles Edwin. *Private Correspondence* (Duke University Manuscript Department).

Bliss, Edwin Mumsell (ed.). *Encyclopedia of Missions* (New York: Harper Brothers, 1889–91).

Bliss, Frederick Jones. *The Development of Palestine Exploration Being the Ely Lectures for 1903* (New York: Arno Press, 1977).

Boston, Robert. *The Most Dangerous Man in America: Pat Robertson and the Rise of the Christian Coalition* (New York: Prometheus, 2003).

Bradford, William. "History of Plymouth Plantation." *Old South Leaflets*, vol. 7 (no. 153) (Boston, MA, n.d).

Bradford, William, *The History of Plymouth Plantation, 1606–1646*, ed. William T. Davis (New York: Charles Scribner's Sons, 1908).

Brewer, Josiah. *A Residence at Constantinople, in the Year 1827*, 2nd ed. (New Haven, CT: Durrie & Peck, 1830).

Buck, Charles. *A Theological Dictionary*, New American Edition, revised and improved by George Burns and Will D. Howe (Philadelphia, PA: Crissy & Markley, 1854).

Burner, David, Genovese, Eugene D. and McDonald, Forrest, *The American People*. (New York: Revisionary Press, 1980).

Burns, Edward M. *The American Idea of Mission* (New Brunswick, NJ: Rutgars University Press, 1947).

Bush, George. *The Life of Mohammad, Founder of the Religion of Islam, and of the Empire of the Saracens* (New York: Harper, 1947).

Cabbot, James Eliot. *A Memoir of Ralph Waldo Emerson* (Boston, MA: Houghton Mifflin, 1887).

Carpenter, Frederic Ives. *Emerson and Asia* (Cambridge, MA: 1930).

Casas, Bartolomé de las. *History of the Indies*, trans. A. Collard (New York, 1971).

Cather, Willa. *Not Under Forty* (New York: Alfred A. Knopf, 1936).

Clouse, Robert, Hosack, Robert, and Pierard, Richard, *The New Millennial Manual* (Grand Rapids, MI: Baker Books, 1999).

The Constitution of the American Bible Society (New York, 1816).

Cotton, John. "God's Promise to his Plantation." *Old South Leaflets* III (51–57) (Boston, MA: n.d).

Cummins, J. S. "Christopher Columbus: Crusader, Visionary and Servus Dei," *Medieval Hispanic Studies* (London: Tamesis, 1976).

Curtis, George William. *The Howadji in Syria* (New York: Harper Brothers, 1856).

Dorr, David F. *A Colored Man Round the World, By a Quadroon* (Cleveland, OH: printed for the author, 1858).

Douglas, William O. *Strange Lands and Friendly People* (New York: Harper & Brothers, 1955).

Duffield, George. *A Sermon Preached in the Third Presbyterian Church* (Philadelphia, PA: publisher not mentioned, 1784).

Dwight, Timothy. *The Major Poems of Timothy Dwight (1752–1817)*, with an Introduction by William J. McTaggart and William K. Bottorff (Gainesville, FL: Scholar's Facsimile & Reprints, 1969).

Eliot, T. S. "Notes Toward the Definition of Culture" (London: Faber & Faber, 1953).

Emerson, Ralph Waldo. "American Civilization," *The Collected Works of Ralph Waldo Emerson*, vol. XI, text established by Alfred R. Ferguson (Cambridge, MA: Belknap Press of Harvard University Press, 1971–2004).

Feidelson, Charles, Jr. *Symbolism and American Literature* (Chicago: University of Chicago Press, 1953).

Field, James A. *America and the Mediterranean World: 1776–1882* (Princeton, NJ: Princeton University Press, 1969).

Finnie, David H. *The American Experience in the Middle East* (Cambridge, MA: Harvard University Press, 1967).

"Frontline Roundtable," website: www.pbs.org/Frontline

Frye, Northrop. *The Great Code: The Bible in Literature* (New York: Harcourt Brace Jovanovich, 1982).

Graham's Magazine (August, 1841).

The Great Commission (Hartford, CT: Silas Andrus, 1856).

Haight, Sarah Rogers. *Letters from the Old World by a Lady of New York*, 2 vols (New York: Harper, 1840).

Hamilton, Alexander. *The Works*, Vol. VII (New York: J.F. Trow, 1850–51).

Harland, Marion. *Under the Flag of the Orient* (Philadelphia, PA: Historical Pub. Co., 1897).

Harley, J. Brian. *Maps of the Columbian Encounter* (Milwaukee, WI: 1990).

Hasseltine William B. and Wolf, Hazel C. *The Blue and the Gray on the Nile* (Chicago: University of Chicago Press, 1961).

Hatch, Nathan O. "The Origins of Civil Millenialism in America: New England Clergymen, War with France, and the Revolution," *William & Mary Quarterly*, Third Series, 31 (1974), pp. 407–30.

Hill, Michael Ortiz. "Mine Eyes Have Seen the Glory: Bush's Armageddon Obsession," *Counter Punch* (January 4, 2003).

Hosay, Philip M. *America: A Model for the World* (Electronic Video Conference, USIS, Amman: March 6, 2002).

Hudson, Winthrop S. *Religion in America*, 3rd ed. (New York: Charles Scribner's Sons, 1981).

Humphrey, Heyman. *The Promised Land: A Sermon, delivered at Godhen, (Conn.) at the ordination of the Rev. Messrs. Hiram Bingham & Asa Thurston, as missionaries to the Sandwich Island, Sept. 29, 1819* (Boston, MA: Samuel T. Armstrong, 1819).

The Illustrated Hand-Book to All Religions: From the Earliest Ages to the Present Time (Chicago: W.H. Harrison, 1877).

The Inaugural Addresses of the Presidents of the United States From George Washington 1789 to John F. Kennedy 1961 (Washington, DC: United States Government Printing Office, 1961).

Irving, Washington. *Mahomet and His Successors* (New York: The Co-operative Publication Society, 1849).

Jessup, Henry Harris. *Fifty-Three Years in Syria*, 2 vols (New York: Fleming H. Revell, 1910).

—— *The Mohammedan Missionary Problem* (Philadelphia: Presbyterian Board of Publications, 1879).

—— *Foreign Missions: Sermon Delivered at the Opening of the General Assembly of the Presbyterian Church America at Saratoga, May 15th, 1884* (Saratoga, NY: Friends of Foreign Missions, 1884).

Jones, George. *Excursions to Cairo, Jerusalem, Damascus and Balbec* (New York: Van Nostrand & Wright, 1836).

Kammen, Michael. *People of Paradox* (New York: Oxford University Press, 1980).

Lewis, R.W.B. *The American Adam*, 3rd ed. (Chicago: University of Chicago Press, 1961).

Lilienthal, Alfred. *The Zionist Connection: What Price Peace?* (New York: Middle East Perspective, Inc., 1979).

Lincoln, Enoch. *An Oration, Pronounced at Worcester in Commemoration of American Independence; July 4th, 1812* (Worcester, MA: printed by Henry Rogers, 1812).

Lipset, Seymour. *The First New Nation* (New York: Doubleday, 1963).

Longfellow, Henry Wadsworth. "The Republic," *Annals of America*, vol. 7 (1976).

Lynch, William F. *Narrative of the United States' Expedition to the River Jordan and the Dead Sea*, 9th ed., rev. (Philadelphia, PA: Blanchard and Lea, 1853).

Maclear, J. F. "The Republic and the Millenium." In Smith, Elwyn A. (ed.), *The Religion of the Republic* (Philadelphia, PA: Fortress, 1971).

—— Mather, Cotton. *Magnalia Christi Americana; or, The Ecclesiastical History of New-England, From its First Planting, in the Year 1620, unto the year of Our Lord 1698*. 2 vols (Hartford CT: S. Andrews & Son, 1853–55 [v. 1, 1855]).

Mather, Increase. *Early History of New England* (Albany, NY: J. Munsell, 1864).

Melville, Herman. *A Journal of a Visit to Europe and the Levant* (Princeton: 1955).

—— *Redburn* (London: Harper Brothers, 1850).

Merk, Frederick. *Manifest Destiny and Mission in American History* (New York: Alfred A. Knopf, 1963).

Metwalli, Ahmed Mohamed. *The Lure of the Levant* (Albany, NY: unpublished Ph.D. dissertation, State University of New York, 1971).

Millard, David. *A Journal of Travels in Egypt, Arabia Petrae, and the Holy Land* (New York: Lamport, Blakemann & Law, 1853).

Miller, Ellen Clare. *Eastern Sketches* (New York: Arno Press, 1977).

Miller, Kevin A. "Why Did Columbus Sail?" *Christian History*, issue 35, vol. XI, no. 3 (1992).

Miller, Perry. *Errand into the Wilderness* (Cambridge, MA: Belknap Press of Harvard University Press, 1956).

——. *The New England Mind: From Colony to Province* (Cambridge, MA: Harvard University Press, 1953).

—— *The New England Mind: The Seventeenth Century* (Cambridge, MA: Harvard University Press, 1954).

Morison, Samuel Eliot. *Admiral of the Ocean Sea: A Life of Christopher Columbus* (Boston, MA: Little, Brown, 1942).

Niebuhr, H. Richard. *The Kingdom of God in America* (Chicago, New York: Willett, Clark, 1937).

Olin, Stephen. *Travels in Egypt, Arabia Petrae and the Holy Land*, 2 vols, 4th ed. (New York: Harper, 1844).

—— *The Works of Stephen Olin*, 2 vols (New York: Harper, 1852).

—— *The Life and Letters of Stephen Olin*, Late President of the Wesleyan University. 2 vols (New York: Harper, 1853).

—— "Orientalism" *Knickerbocker*, 41 (June, 1853).

Osgood, David. *A Solemn Protest Against the Late Declaration of War, a Sermon* (Cambridge, MA: Hilliard & Metcalf, 1812).

O'Sullivan, John L. *The Democratic Review*, July and August, 1845.

"Our Manifest Destiny," *Annals of America*, vol. 7 (1976).

Parrington, Vernon Lewis. *Main Currents in American Thought* (New York: Harcourt, Brace, 1927–30).

Parrington, Vernon Lewis. "The Puritan Divines, 1620–1720," in *Cambridge History of American Literature*, Vol. I (New York: G.P. Putnam, 1917–21).

Pierpont, John. *Airs of Palestine: A Poem* (Baltimore, MD: B. Edes, 1816).

Poe, Edgar Allan. *New York Review* (October 1837).

Porter, David. *Constantinople and Its Environs*, 2 vols (New York: Harper Brothers, 1835).

Ray, William. *Poems on Various Subjects* (Auburn, NY: U.F. Doubleday, 1821).

Robertson, [McI.] *Journal of Travel* (handwritten document at Duke University Library, Manuscript Department).

Robinson, Edward. *Biblical Researches in Palestine and the Adjacent Regions*, Vol. I (London: John Murray, 1867).

Schaff, Philip. *The Principles of Protestantism as related to the Present State of the Church* (Chambersburg, PA: Publication Office of the German Reformed Church, 1845).

Schuler, Lydia, "A Letter from the Holy Land," *The Monthly Gospel-Visitor*, vol. V, no. 12 (December, 1855).

——. "A Letter from Jerusalem," *The Monthly Gospel-Visitor*, vol. IX, no. 7 (July, 1859).

Sha'ban, Fuad. *Islam and Arabs in Early American Thought: The Roots of Orientalism in America* (Durham, NC: Acorn Press, 1991).

Shahak, Israel and Mezvinsky, Norton. *Jewish Fundamentalism in Israel* (London: Pluto Press, 1999).

Shaw, Annie DeWitt. *Will, Annie, and I: Travellers in Many Lands* (New York: L.A. Skinner, 1898).

Sherwood, Samuel. *The Church's Flight into the Wilderness* (New York: publisher not mentioned, 1776).

Siegfried, Andre. *America Comes of Age* (New York: Harcourt Brace, 1927).

Silverman, Kenneth. *Timothy Dwight* (New York: Twayne, 1969).

Simon, Merrill. *Jerry Falwell and the Jews* (New York: Jonathan David, 1984).

Smith, Harold F. *American Travellers Abroad: Bibliography of Accounts Published Before 1900* (Carbondale, IL: Southern Illinois University Press, 1969).

Smith, James Ward and Jamison A. Leland (eds). *Religion in American Life*, 2 vols (Princeton, NJ: Princeton University Press, 1961).

Smith, J.V.C. *A Pilgrimage to Palestine* (Boston; MA: David Clapp, 1853).

Smith, Lee S. *Through Egypt to Palestine* (Chicago: Fleming H. Revell, 1896).

Stephens, John Lloyd. *Incidents of Travel in Egypt, Arabia Petraea, and the Holy Land*, ed. by Victor Wolfgang von Hagen (Norman, OK: University of Oklahoma Press, 1970). First published 1837.

——. *Incidents of Travel in Greece, Turkey, Russia, and Poland In Remarkable Voyages and Travels* (London, n.d.).

Stiles, Ezra. *The United States Elevated to Glory and Honor* (1783), in Thornton (1860).

Stuart, Moses. *A Sermon Preached in the Tabernacle Church, Salem, Nov. 5, 1818* (Andover, NH: Flagg and Gould, 1819).

Swain, William. *Philadelphia Public Ledger* (October 25, 1847).

Thomson, W.M. *The Land and the Book* (London: Harper Brothers, 1905).

Thayer, William M. *From Tannery to the White House: The Life of Ulysses S. Grant* (Boston, MA: James H. Earle, 1885).

Thornton, John William. *The Pulpit of the American Revolution* (Boston, MA: Gould & Lincoln, 1860).

Tocqueville, Alexis de. *Democracy in America* (Chicago: University of Chicago Press, 1954).

Todd, Charles Burr. *Life and Letters of Joel Barlow, LL.D* (New York: G.P. Putnam's Sons, 1886).

Tuveson, Ernest Lee. *Redeemer Nation: The Idea of America's Millennial Role* (Chicago, 1968).

Tyler, Alice Felt. *Freedom's Ferment* (New York: Harper & Row, 1944).

"The United States: A Commissioned Missionary Nation," *American Theological Review*, vol. I (January, 1859).

Washington, George. "Washington's Addresses to the Churches," *Old South Leaflets*, III (65) (Boston, MA: Old South Association, n.d.).

Watts, Pauline Moffitt. "Science, Religion, and Columbus's Enterprise of the Indies," *OAH Magazine of History*, vol. 5, no. 4 (Spring, 1991).

Webber, Timothy. "How Evangelicals Became Israel's Best Friends," *Christianity Today* (October 5, 1998).

West, Delno C. "Medieval Ideas of Apocalyptic Mission and the Early Franciscans in Mexico," *The Americans*, vol. 45, no. 3 (January, 1989).

—— "Columbus and His World." In *The Proceedings of the First San Salvador Conference, Nov. 1986*.

Whittier, John Greenleaf. "Man's Property in Man," *Annals of America*, vol. 6 (1976).

Williams, Roger. "Letters of Roger Williams to Winthrop," *Old South Leaflets*, III (53) (Boston, MA: Old South Association, n.d.).

Winthrop, John, *Papers*. ed. by A. B. Forbes, Vol. II (Boston, MA: 1929–47).

—— "Winthrop's Conclusions for the Plantation in New England," *Old South Leaflets*, II (50) (Boston, MA: n.d.).

Worcester, Samuel. *Two Discourses, on the Perpetuity and Provision of God's Gracious Covenant with Abraham and His Seed* (Salem, MA: Haven Pool, 1805).

Index